Building Comprehension
in Adolescents

Building Comprehension in Adolescents

Powerful Strategies for Improving Reading and Writing in Content Areas

by

Linda H. Mason, Ph.D.
The Pennsylvania State University

Robert Reid, Ph.D.
University of Nebraska, Lincoln

and

Jessica L. Hagaman, Ph.D.
University of Wisconsin–Whitewater

·P·A·U·L·H·
BROOKES
PUBLISHING Co.®

Baltimore • London • Sydney

Paul H. Brookes Publishing Co., Inc.
Post Office Box 10624
Baltimore, Maryland 21285-0624
USA

www.brookespublishing.com

Typeset by BLPS Content Connections, Chilton, Wisconsin.
Manufactured in the United States of America by
Versa Press, Inc., East Peoria, Illinois.

Library of Congress Cataloging-in-Publication Data

Building comprehension in adolescents : powerful strategies for improving reading and writing in content areas / edited by Linda H. Mason, Robert Reid, and Jessica L. Hagaman.
p.   cm.
Includes index.
ISBN-13: 978-1-59857-210-0 (layflat)
ISBN-10: 1-59857-210-5 (layflat)
1. Language arts (Secondary) 2. Language arts–Correlation with content subjects. 3. Self-monitoring.
I. Mason, Linda H. II. Reid, Robert, Ph.D. III. Hagaman, Jessica L. (Jessica Laurel)

LB1631.B772 2012
428.0071'2–dc23

                    2012004784

British Library Cataloguing in Publication data are available from the British Library.

2016   2015   2014   2013   2012

10   9   8   7   6   5   4   3   2   1

Contents

About the Authors

Linda H. Mason, Ph.D., The Pennsylvania State University, 213 CEDAR Building, University Park, PA 16802

Dr. Linda H. Mason has a joint appointment in the Department of Educational Psychology, Counseling, and Special Education and the Children, Youth, and Families Consortium at The Pennsylvania State University. Prior to completing her Ph.D., Dr. Mason taught special education in an inclusive public elementary school for six years. She has been awarded two U.S. Department of Education grants focusing on reading comprehension and writing intervention for low-achieving students. Dr. Mason serves on six editorial boards, including journals focused on research-to-practice. At Penn State, she teaches courses in literacy for students with special needs, curriculum development, reading and writing methods, assessment, and effective instruction. Dr. Mason was awarded the Council for Exceptional Children, Division of Research Distinguished Early Career Award in 2011 and a Fulbright Scholarship to teach in Hungary in Fall 2011.

Robert Reid, Ph.D., University of Nebraska, Lincoln, 202L Barkley Center, Lincoln, NE 68583-0732

Dr. Reid specializes in the education and treatment of children with learning disabilities and attention-deficit/hyperactivity disorder. He teaches courses on mainstreaming, cognitive strategy instruction, and special education methods. His current interests include functional assessment, treatment of attention-deficit disorder, and strategy instruction. He has done extensive work in the area of attention-deficit/hyperactivity disorder in the schools. Dr. Reid received the Jeannie Balilies Award for contributions to child mental health research. Dr. Reid also serves as a consulting editor and field reviewer for a number of special education journals.

Jessica L. Hagaman, Ph.D., University of Wisconsin–Whitewater, Department of Special Education, 4045 Winther Hall, Whitewater, WI 53190

Dr. Hagaman received her Ph.D. in educational studies from the University of Nebraska, Lincoln. She specializes in the education of students with learning disabilities and at-risk students. Prior to completing her Ph.D., Dr. Hagaman taught at the early childhood and elementary levels. Her research interests include early intervention for at-risk students, reading instruction and interventions, strategy instruction, and academic interventions.

Acknowledgments

We would like to gratefully acknowledge the contributions of Dr. Karen R. Harris and Dr. Steve Graham to the creation of this book. Without their ongoing mentorship, encouragement, and support this book would not have been possible.

We would also like to gratefully extend our thanks to our respective spouses—Dr. Paul Haspel, Dr. Melody Hertzog, and Luke Polipnick—for their forbearance with obsessed spouses and for their support in keeping us self-regulated throughout the writing process. Thank you to all!

Section I

Developing Strategy Acquisition and Self-Regulation

Chapter 1

Introduction

Mr. Foster has been teaching ninth-grade science for 5 years in a low socioeconomic urban setting. He has just learned that next year the school's model of providing instruction to struggling learners will change; he has been assigned to teach two biology classes for the lowest achieving students. He has been told that in the past teachers have not used biology text material, writing assignments, or given homework for this group of students. However, Mr. Foster is aware that the school's science assessment scores need improvement. It is critical that he include both reading to learn and writing to learn activities in his classes and that he provide students homework for practicing science objectives. Mr. Foster hopes that by teaching his students to self-regulate use of evidence-based strategies, students will demonstrate improved performance in learning biology concepts.

Given the complexity of content (e.g., science, social studies, health) text-based material, many teachers avoid reading and writing to learn text-based activities in content classes (Mason, Hickey Snyder, Suhkram, & Kedem, 2006). This lack of explicit instruction with authentic content text for reading comprehension and written expression is especially problematic for low-achieving adolescents. For low-achieving students, difficulties in self-regulating learning and motivation further impact comprehending content text and developing written text about concepts learned (Boscolo & Gelati, 2007).

In this book, we provide validated lesson plans designed to help teachers integrate reading and writing to learn in their classroom. We have included suggestions for how to effectively embed reading and writing strategies, separately or in combination, into content curriculum. Vignettes illustrating these applications in content-specific classes (e.g., middle and high school science, and social studies classes) are included. Detailed lesson plans and instructional support materials for students are provided for a number of selected evidence-based interventions. The content literacy strategies are described and introduced in four sections: 1) developing strategy acquisition and self-regulation, 2) reading to learn, 3) writing to learn, and 4) homework. References for research that supports evidence-based interventions for instructional approaches are listed at the end of each chapter.

CHAPTER REVIEWS

The next two chapters provide background information critical for understanding subsequent chapters and for effective strategy instruction, and steps of instruction for teaching self-regulation. Strategy acquisition as highlighted in Self-Regulated Strategy Development (SRSD) instruction (Harris, Graham, Mason, & Friedlander, 2008), an evidence-based instructional approach, is described in Chapter 2. Six critical stages (establish background knowledge, discuss the strategy, model the strategy, memorize the strategy, support strategy use, independent practice) for effective strategy acquisition within the context of the secondary classroom are presented. The role of the struggling adolescent learner is highlighted throughout instructional delivery. Teacher-directed and peer-assisted approaches for supporting student learning throughout strategy development are provided.

Four self-regulation strategies—goal setting, self-monitoring, self-instruction, and self-reinforcement—for supporting students' strategy use over time and across settings and content are described in Chapter 3. Each of the four self-regulation strategies is described with guidelines for teaching within the context of the content classroom. Suggestions for supporting self-regulation across tasks (e.g., self-monitoring for attention and performance) are provided. We include vignettes for implementing self-regulation interventions for a whole class and for an individual student.

Reading to Learn

Mr. Foster knows that the passages in the biology textbook are going to be too difficult for most of the students in his two lower level classes. However, he does want to use the text as the charts, diagrams, and illustrations are excellent and will support student learning. Understanding the difficult concepts, vocabulary, and structure of the text, however, will be important as Mr. Foster develops lessons. Mr. Foster plans to support his reading-to-learn activities with strategies that help students activate prior knowledge, stimulate vocabulary development, and promote reading comprehension.

In content classes, reading becomes the means by which information is obtained from text. Prior to introducing specific comprehension strategies for reading to learn, it is critical that teachers understand the difficulty of content text for many adolescent readers. Chapter 4 begins with a review of strategies for addressing prior knowledge, vocabulary acquisition, conceptual density, and text structure for the struggling reader. The rationale and theoretical frameworks for using strategies for a variety of reading purposes is noted. Vignette examples of content text are used to illustrate instruction. Methods for scaling students' reading from accessible text to complex text are illustrated.

Reading to learn chapters include a preinstruction overview, lesson plans, and instructional materials. Example scripts are provided for many lessons to illustrate procedures. Strategy instruction, however, is not intended to be scripted. These are only examples. The teacher's instructional delivery should match his or her personal style, the needs of the students, and the curriculum objectives. In the reading-to-learn section, we have included an appendix of text passages and scoring sheets for assessing students' comprehension of passages. The following three strategies are introduced:

- TRAP (**T**hink before you read, **R**ead the passage, **A**sk yourself—what is the main idea, **P**araphrase) for reading comprehension, presented in Chapter 5, helps students identify the main idea and details of a paragraph or passage.

- TRAP IDEAS (**I**dentify important details to support the main idea, **D**elete trivial details, **E**liminate redundant details, **A**dd a term for a list of words or concepts, **S**ummarize) for reading comprehension, presented in Chapter 6, assists students in developing summaries for content reading.

- TWA (**T**hink before reading, think **W**hile reading, think **A**fter reading) for reading comprehension, presented in Chapter 7, is a nine-step strategy for supporting student reading throughout all reading phases. TWA embeds TRAP IDEAS within the after-reading strategy framework. Minilessons for vocabulary development are embedded throughout the lessons. TWA provides a framework for dissecting information from a text that can support essay writing.

Writing to Learn

> Mr. Foster knows that it is important to include writing in his biology classes. In fact, the school district has adopted a policy of writing across the curriculum. For his two low-achieving classes, Mr. Foster will include short writing assignments such as Quick Writes to build students' confidence in writing to learn about biology. Mr. Foster looks forward to working with students as they develop skills to write effective biographies about scientists, to write informational passages about material read, and to write to persuade him to their point of view.

In Chapter 8, the difficulty that many students have in expressing knowledge through writing is reviewed. The problems that many students have for writing across text structure and genre is noted. Selection and timing for writing complete essays and/or short written responses, such as in quick writing, to support student learning in content classes are discussed. Specific tips for integrating writing strategies within the reading to learn strategies are noted. The theoretical frameworks for each strategy to be presented in Chapters 9–12 are briefly reviewed including reference for each strategy. Vignettes for using the four strategies in the content classroom are included.

As in the reading-to-learn chapters, we include preinstruction overview, lesson plans with example scripts, and instructional materials for each writing intervention. Four strategies for developing written expression are described:

- Story writing, personal narrative writing, and biography writing are supported by the C-SPACE (**C**haracters—**S**etting, **P**urpose, **A**ction, **C**onclusion, and **E**motion) strategy, which is highlighted in Chapter 9.

- STOP (**S**uspend judgment, **T**ake a side, **O**rganize ideas, **P**lan more as you write) and DARE (**D**evelop a topic sentence, **A**dd supporting ideas, **R**eject an argument, **E**nd with a conclusion), presented in Chapter 10, are strategies that help students develop effective arguments for writing a persuasive essay.

- TWA is combined with PLANS (**P**ick goals, **L**ist ways to meet goals, **A**nd make **N**otes, **S**equence notes) in Chapter 11. TWA + PLANS assist students in setting goals for developing effective informative essays. Minilessons are embedded for combining sentences to improve the quality of essays.

- Quick Writes are short student written responses used to support or assess student learning before, during, or after content instruction. The POW (**P**ick an idea, **O**rganize notes, **W**rite and say more) strategy in combination with strategies for writing a narrative, persuasive, or informative response is presented in Chapter 12.

Homework

> Mr. Foster wants to include appropriate biology homework for all his students. He notes that many of his struggling learners have the skills to do his assigned homework, but lack the organizational skills to complete work in a timely manner and often simply do not turn in assignments.

Homework completion can be a chronic problem for some students. Chapter 13 presents self-regulation procedures to enhance classroom preparation skills (e.g., seated when bell rings, eye contact with teacher when instruction begins, pen or pencil on desk, relevant instructional materials open when the lesson begins), and homework completion. We focus on strategies for how teachers can more effectively use homework, and how students can self-regulate homework performance. Five lesson plans are provided for the A-WATCH homework strategy: (**A**ssignment notebook—get it out; **W**rite down the assignment and due date; **A**sk for clarification on the assignment if needed; **T**ask-analyze the assignment; **C**heck all work for completeness, accuracy, and neatness; **H**and it in).

REFERENCES

Boscolo, P., & Gelati, C. (2007). Best practices for promoting motivation in writing. In S. Graham, C.A. MacArthur, & J. Fitzgerald (Eds.), *Best practices in writing instruction* (pp. 202–221). New York, NY: The Guilford Press.

Harris, K.R., Graham, S., Mason, L.H., & Friedlander, B. (2008). *Powerful writing strategies for all students.* Baltimore, MD: Paul H. Brookes Publishing Co., Inc.

Mason, L.H., Hickey Snyder, K., Sukhram, D.P., & Kedem, Y. (2006). Self-regulated strategy development for expository reading comprehension and informative writing: Effects for nine 4th-grade students who struggle with learning. *Exceptional Children, 73,* 69–89.

Chapter 2

Effective Strategy Instruction

Adolescents are required to have proficient skills in reading and writing to be successful in school. For example, as students progress through middle and high school, reading comprehension becomes increasingly important across subject areas, with information derived from text becoming a primary source of knowledge (Smagorinsky, 2001). In addition, adolescents require proficient writing skills to demonstrate their knowledge (e.g., state exit exams) and communicate with others (e.g., letters, e-mails). However, data suggest that adolescents are experiencing difficulty mastering literacy skills. For example, in the area of reading, 27% of eighth graders scored at the *below basic* level of proficiency (Perie, Grigg, & Donahue, 2005). With regards to writing, the National Assessment of Educational Progress (NAEP; Salahu-Din, Persky, & Miller, 2008) reports that few high school students are meeting expected achievement levels in writing, with nearly 75% of students unable to meet the requirements for the *proficient* standard. If adolescents are unable to acquire the necessary literacy skills, successful employment, and positive life outcomes may be limited.

One approach that educators can use to improve the literacy skills of adolescents is Self-Regulated Strategy Development (SRSD). SRSD is an instructional approach that combines explicit instruction in self-regulation with strategy instruction (Harris, Graham, Mason, & Saddler, 2002). The model is well validated, based on sound instructional theory, and a powerful instructional tool (Graham & Harris, 2003). Recent empirical studies investigating SRSD-taught literacy strategies have seen positive effects. For example, in the area of reading, multiple studies have reported marked improvements in reading comprehension when struggling readers were taught strategies within the SRSD framework (e.g., Hagaman & Reid, 2008; Mason, 2004; Mason, Hickey Snyder, Sukhram, & Kedem, 2006). In the area of writing, students have shown longer, higher-quality essays and narratives when taught strategies using SRSD (e.g., De La Paz, 2005; Reid & Lienemann, 2006b; Thompson Jacobson & Reid, 2010). These studies, among others, suggest that strategy instruction is an appropriate, research-based approach to improving the literacy skills of adolescents.

It is important to note that SRSD is not a strategy, but a model for teaching a chosen strategy. Put simply, it helps a teacher teach a strategy. Using a model insures that teachers will follow all the steps needed for students to successfully master a strategy, and thus derive maximum benefit from the strategy (Reid & Lienemann, 2006a). SRSD consists of six stages. In the following section we will present how a strategy might be taught using SRSD. We will present the stages of strategy instruction in the order that is most commonly used; however, these stages can be reordered, combined, or even skipped based on the needs of the students. Table 2.1 shows the stages and examples of activities for each stage.

Table 2.1. Self-regulated Strategy Development (SRSD) Stages

SRSD stage	Description	Writing examples
Stage 1: Develop and activate background knowledge	• Make sure students possess the skills necessary to use the strategy • Task Analysis	• Determine if students have skills necessary to perform C-SPACE • Do the students know story elements (e.g. character, setting) • Discuss what makes a good story/narrative (e.g., makes sense, fun to read)
Stage 2: Discuss the Strategy	• Discuss present performance • Present the strategy • Model and discuss self-instructions • Describe goal-setting and self-monitoring procedures	• Present C-SPACE, discuss what happens at each step • Students analyze one of their own stories to identify story parts present in story • Graph number of story parts • Set a goal to write a story with all six parts
Stage 3: Model the Strategy	• Teacher models strategy • Think-Aloud using self-instructions, goal setting, and self-monitoring	• Teacher models strategy using a Think-Aloud • Students identify self-statements to use when writing • Teacher and students collaboratively write a narrative and make sure all six story parts are present
Stage 4: Memorize the strategy	• Students commit to memory the strategy's steps • Memorize self-instructions • Students do not necessarily need to achieve automaticity before moving to the next step • Provide students with a prompt or cue card	• Quick "quizzes" to test for memorization of mnemonic/strategy steps • Students practice steps of C-SPACE • Cue cards are used to facilitate memorization • Individual or peer memorization activities and games are used
Stage 5: Support the strategy	• Collaborative practice: Teacher models the strategy and works together with students • Scaffolding: Teacher provides more support initially, less support as students are ready to use the strategy independently	• Collaborative writing between teacher/peer and student • Teacher/peer provides support as needed • Students graph the number of story parts • Scaffolding continues until mastery (a story with all six parts)
Stage 6: Independent performance	• Students perform the strategy without support or feedback and with goal-setting and self-monitored procedures • Reteaching the strategy may be in order	• Students are able to write a story independently • Teacher monitors to ensure proper strategy use and determine whether performance improved

Stage 1: Develop and Activate Background Knowledge

During this stage, the teacher will determine whether students have the necessary skills to perform a chosen strategy. In some cases the teacher will already know this information. If not, a task analysis can be performed. This is done by identifying and defining the skills necessary to complete the strategy and then assessing the students to ensure they have the necessary skills. The assessment can be done through direct observation of the students, or through assessments such as curriculum-based measures.

Once it is determined that students have the necessary skills to perform the strategy, the strategy should be introduced to them. Often, the teacher will present the strategy and a corresponding mnemonic as a "trick" to help remember the important parts of a story. The teacher should explain what each step of the strategy stands for (e.g., POW stands for "**P**ick my ideas, **O**rganize my notes, **W**rite and say more"). At this time, the students may be given a graphic organizer or other support to help them remember the steps of the strategy.

Stage 2: Discuss the Strategy

In the second stage of SRSD, students will continue to focus on the uses for the strategy. An important component of this stage is obtaining students' "buy in." This can be done by discussing the usefulness of the strategy with students and encouraging them to be willing to learn and use the strategy. In some cases, it would be appropriate for the teacher to help students brainstorm where the strategy could be used and how the strategy might help them become a better reader or writer. Getting students to "buy in" to using the strategy is extremely important. Unless students commit to learning and using the strategy they are unlikely to use it independently. One of the goals of SRSD instruction is for the students to use the strategy independently. The teacher also discusses present levels of performance by reviewing past work.

Another important component to Stage 2 is goal setting. Setting a goal helps to motivate students. For example, the teacher could discuss that the goal in writing a good personal narrative is to include all six parts (e.g., C-SPACE; see Chapter 9). The use of graphing at this stage is a powerful way to show students' progress towards their identified goals. For example, the teacher may have the students graph the number of parts present in their first narrative. Students can compare this baseline with their subsequent narratives. The graphing and goal setting also serve as self-regulation strategies. Students will frequently monitor progress towards the goal of six story parts in their personal narratives. In practice, goal setting and progress monitoring often prove to be highly motivating to students and help them to maintain effort.

Stage 3: Model the Strategy

For strategy instruction to be successful students must have an understanding of why they are using a strategy, how the strategy helps them, and the reason behind the steps of the strategy (i.e., the "hows" and "whys" of the strategy). This is vital information if the students are to derive maximum benefit from the strategy. To provide this information, the teacher should model how the strategy is used. Effective modeling is a critical component of strategy instruction. It is much more than simply going through the steps of a strategy. Good modeling allows the students to see the thought processes of an "expert" learner as she or he uses the strategy, and provides critical information on how to use the strategy. Through exposure to modeling, students learn why steps are performed and how the steps can help them to write better narratives or become better readers. This is important because it helps students understand that using a strategy is not a passive process; it requires effort. The procedure used in modeling is often referred to as a "Think-Aloud." In this procedure the teacher demonstrates the use of the strategy while verbalizing his or her thought processes.

When teaching a strategy, it is important to explicitly teach and model both the strategy *and* the self-regulation components of the strategy (e.g., goal-setting, self-monitoring). SRSD is designed to include self-regulation strategies (discussed in further detail in Chapter 3). In the Think-Aloud, self-instructions model for students how to literally talk themselves through the strategy. Self-instructions are a good way to help students who have motivational problems or experience anxiety. As part of the strategy process, students should be taught and shown that specific self-statements and self-instruction can help them cope with negative thoughts. For example, statements such as, "I know I have my strategy to help me write a good narrative," or "It's okay. I can do this. Take a deep breath" should be included in the Think-Aloud.

Stage 4: Memorize the Strategy

Memorization of the strategy is crucial in order for students to focus on the task at hand (e.g., reading, writing a narrative) rather than on the steps of the strategy. It is important that students are able to do more than simply recite the steps of the strategy; they should also be able to describe what is involved at each step of the strategy. If students have developed self-statements, these should be memorized as well. It is important to note that some students may be unable to memorize either the strategy or the self-statements. In this case, use of cue cards or other materials would be appropriate. Memorization of the strategy can occur at any stage and should be incorporated throughout strategy instruction. Example memorization activities can be found in Table 2.1.

Stage 5: Support the Strategy

Teacher-Directed Support

The support stage is a collaborative process between teacher and students. By now, the students should be well acquainted with the steps of the strategy; however, the students will still require practice in using the strategy before it is mastered. This stage uses scaffolded instruction to help the students learn to use the strategy independently. During this stage the teacher and students will practice using the strategy until the students are able to use the strategy independently. At first, the teacher will support the students through all the steps of the strategy. As the students become more proficient with the strategy, teacher support is systematically decreased. Progress through this stage of SRSD is dependent upon the students. The teacher will decrease support and give the students more responsibility for the strategy as they are ready. The end result of this stage should be the students' independent use of the strategy.

Scaffolding can occur at any stage during the SRSD process. For example, in Stage 1 the students may be provided with a strategy mnemonic chart to help remember the steps of the strategy. Other scaffolding activities occur during instruction and practice activities. For example, the teacher could begin scaffolding instruction by writing a narrative with the students. If the students are able to perform any steps of the strategy on their own, they should be allowed to do so. Once the narrative is written, the students could be asked to identify each strategy element (e.g., character, setting) present by underlining or highlighting them. The teacher should encourage students to determine whether their goal (set in Stage 2) was met, and results should be graphed. The teacher should also encourage students to identify how the strategy improved their narrative writing. At this stage, supports such as graphic organizers and checklists could be used to help the student remember the steps of the strategy, and to guide planning. However, these prompts should be faded as students become proficient with the strategy. For further examples of scaffolding, see Table 2.2.

Peer-Directed Support

It is important to note that peers can play an important role in the strategy instruction process. Scaffolding can also be done through peer support. For example, students may work together to plan collaboratively prior to writing essays or narratives, or to identify main ideas in content area reading. Peers can also play an important role in the editing of written work. For example, you may have students pair up and give each other feedback on essays or personal narratives (see Chapters 9 and 10).

Stage 6: Independent Performance

In this stage, students should be ready to use the strategy independently. During this stage, there are two main tasks. First, the students' performance should be monitored to ensure proper and consistent strategy use. Monitoring academic performance is critical because the goal of strategy instruction is to increase academic performance; the students' work should show improvement. Second, teachers should watch to see if students alter the strategy or skip steps when using it on their own. Note that if a student modifies a strategy, but performance

Table 2.2. Examples of Scaffolding

Types of scaffolding	Explanation	Writing example
Content scaffolding	• Teacher uses material that is at an easy level (e.g., text below the students' grade level). • Teacher uses content the students are interested in to teach the strategy. • Teacher teaches the easier steps of the strategy first, then more difficult steps. In initial practice sessions the students would perform the easy steps while the teacher models the more difficult steps.	• The students are allowed to write a shorter story that still contains all six story parts. • The students write stories on topic(s) that they have knowledge of/interest in. • The teacher teaches the students the "Character" and "Setting" steps of C-SPACE first, and more difficult steps of the strategy later.
Task scaffolding	• Ownership of the strategy is gradually transferred by letting the student perform more and more of the strategy during practice sessions.	• Step 1: The teacher asks the students to name the strategy step that should be performed; the teacher describes the step and models it. • Step 2: The teacher asks the students to name the step and describe the step; the teacher models them. • Step 3: The students name, describe, and model the step.
Material Scaffolding	• Prompts and cues are used to help the students use the strategy. Typically, these are faded over time.	• The students are given a graphic organizer or cue card. As the students gain mastery of the strategy, the prompts are faded.

remains high, there is no cause for concern. It is common for students to adapt the strategy to meet their needs. Changes are acceptable as long as student performance remains high. However, if a student is performing the strategy correctly but is not attaining (or maintaining) a high level of performance, then reteaching the strategy or considering a different strategy may be in order.

FINAL THOUGHTS

In this chapter we have presented the SRSD model for strategy instruction. It is important to remember that strategy instruction is a *process*. Strategy instruction is a powerful tool that takes time and effort. Teachers should also remember that strategy instruction should be customized to the students. That is, instruction should continue until students have mastered the use of the strategy (i.e., using the strategy correctly and consistently). The number of lessons required will depend on the strategy being taught and how quickly the students are able to master the strategy.

REFERENCES

De La Paz, S. (2005). Effects of historical reasoning instruction and writing strategy mastery in culturally and academically diverse middle school classrooms. *Journal of Educational Psychology, 97,* 139–156. Doi :10.1037/0022-0663.97.2.139.

Graham, S., & Harris, K.R. (2003). Students with learning disabilities and the process of writing: A meta-analysis of SRSD studies. In H.L. Swanson, K.R. Harris, & S. Graham (Eds.), *Handbook of learning disabilities* (pp. 323–344). New York, NY: Guilford Press.

Hagaman, J.L., & Reid, R. (2008). The effects of the paraphrasing strategy on the reading comprehension of middle school students at risk for failure in reading. *Remedial and Special Education, 29,* 222–234. Doi 10.1177/0741932507311638

Harris, K.R., Graham, S., Mason, L.H., & Saddler, B. (2002). Developing self-regulated writers. *Theory into Practice, 41,* 110–115.

Mason, L. H. (2004). Explicit self-regulated strategy development versus reciprocal questioning: Effects on expository reading comprehension among struggling readers. *Journal of Educational Psychology, 96*, 283–296.

Mason, L.H., Hickey Snyder, K., Sukhram, D.P., & Kedem, Y. (2006). Self-regulated strategy development for expository reading comprehension and informative writing: Effects for nine 4th-grade students who struggle with learning. *Exceptional Children, 73*, 69–89.

Reid, R., & Lienemann, T.O. (2006a). Self-Regulated Strategy Development for written expression with students with attention deficit/hyperactivity disorder. *Exceptional Children, 73*, 53–68.

Reid, R., & Lienemann, T.O. (2006b). *Strategy instruction for children with learning disabilities.* New York, NY: Guilford.

Salahu-Din, D., Persky, H., & Miller, J. (2008). *The nation's report card: Writing 2007* (NCES 2008-468). National Center for Education Statistics, Institute of Education Sciences, U.S. Department of Education, Washington, DC.

Smagorinsky, P. (2001). If meaning is constructed what's it made from? Toward a cultural theory of reading. *Review of Educational Research, 71*, 133–169.

Thompson Jacobson, L., & Reid, R. (2010). Improving the persuasive essay writing of high school students with ADHD. *Exceptional Children, 76*, 157–174.

Chapter 3

Teaching Self-Regulation

Self-regulation is highly valued by teachers (Harris, Reid, & Graham, 2004). Any teacher would love to have a class full of students who can perform independently and who do not need to be constantly monitored or prompted to remain on task. When students can self-regulate teachers have much more flexibility. They can work with one group while others are productively engaged or set up class-wide independent activities. Unfortunately, in most classrooms, there may be several students who experience difficulty with self-regulation. These students will have many problems such as maintaining effort, focusing on a task, blocking out distractions, or persisting in the face of difficulty. These students have not developed the capacity to self-regulate their behavior. Luckily there are techniques that can be used to help students self-regulate their behavior. There are four major techniques (Graham, Harris, & Reid, 1992): self-monitoring, goal setting, self-instructions, and self-reinforcement. Each of these techniques can help students to self-regulate their behavior. Each may be used alone or in combination with other techniques (e.g., self-monitoring combined with goal setting, or self-instructions combined with self-reinforcement). They are also commonly used with content area strategies and are included in each of the strategies included in the book. More important, all of the techniques are highly effective for students who struggle with self-regulation (e.g., Reid, Trout, & Schwartz, 2005). In this chapter we will discuss each of the self-regulation strategies and provide a vignette to illustrate how self-regulation might be used in the classroom.

SELF-MONITORING

Have you ever asked a student "What are you doing?" and gotten a blank stare? One problem that many students have is that they are literally not aware of what they are doing. For example, they are not aware that they are often off task, that they frequently talk with their neighbor, or that they are not completing their work in a timely manner. This type of self-awareness is critical if self-regulation is to occur. Self-monitoring techniques can help to provide students with feedback on their performance. This feedback enables them to be aware of their behavior and can help them to self-regulate their behavior.

There are two steps in self-monitoring. First, students self-assess whether or not a target behavior has occurred. Then the students self-record the target behavior. Self-monitoring usually does not involve the use of external reinforcers as the act of self-recording is known to act as a reinforcer. Note, however, that self-monitoring can effectively be combined with external reinforcers, and that for some students adding external reinforcers may be helpful.

Self-monitoring is extremely flexible and can be used for a variety of behaviors. In this chapter we will focus on the two most commonly used types of self-monitoring interventions: self-monitoring of attention (SMA) and self-monitoring of performance (SMP). Both of these have been used successfully with a wide range of students who experience difficulties self-regulating their behavior (Reid, 1996). In SMA, students are taught to self-assess whether or not they are paying attention. This is typically done by cuing students to self-assess through the use of an auditory cue (e.g., taped tones presented at random intervals). After the students self-assess, they self-record the results on a tally sheet. Figure 3.1 shows an example of a SMA tally sheet. In SMP students monitor some aspect of their academic performance. In SMP students typically complete an academic task, self-assess their performance, and then self-record the results. SMP can be used in many situations. Students may self-assess their productivity (e.g., the number of math problems they attempted), accuracy (e.g., the number of math problems they completed correctly), or strategy use (e.g., whether or not they performed the steps in a math strategy). Graphing is often used for self-recording. In practice, graphing can be very motivating for many students. Figure 3.2 shows an example of an SMP graph.

Steps in Implementing Self-Monitoring

The steps in implementing self-monitoring are well established (Reid & Lienemann, 2006). Note that the time needed for some steps may vary dramatically depending on what type of self-monitoring is used.

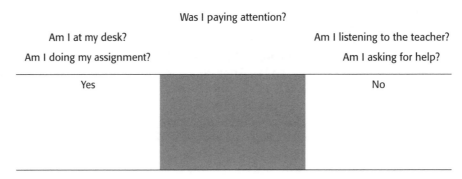

Figure 3.1. Example self-monitoring of attention tally sheet.

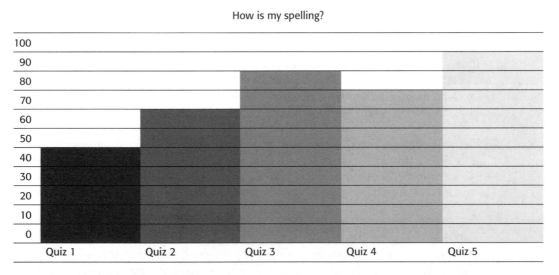

Figure 3.2. Example self-monitoring of performance graph.

STEP 1: Select a target behavior

The first step is to decide what behavior the students will self-monitor. It's important that the behavior be well specified. For example "doing your best work" is much too vague; "percent correct on my math work" is much better. For self-monitoring to work, the students must understand exactly what they will self-assess and self-record. Make sure that the behavior is one that the students are already able to perform. Self-monitoring will not create new knowledge or behavior; it will, however, change the frequency, intensity, of duration of behaviors that students are *already able to perform*. It is also critical that the behavior be under the students' control.

STEP 2: Collect baseline data

Before starting self-monitoring, it is necessary to collect baseline data on the students' behavior. This will allow the teacher to assess accurately whether self-monitoring was effective. Collecting baseline data can be very straightforward; for example, if the teacher planned to use SMP to increase the number of math problems students completed on their daily math seat work, collecting baseline data might be as easy as compiling and graphing worksheets over three or four days.

STEP 3: Obtain students' cooperation

For self-monitoring to be effective, the students must be active and willing participants. Remember that the students will actually perform the self-monitoring. Teachers should meet with the students and talk about the problem frankly by discussing the benefits of improving the behavior, (e.g., staying in your seat means you don't lose recess; doing all your arithmetic problems means you'll do better on the test). The discussion should be positive; the teacher should stress, without making exaggerated claims, that self-monitoring has helped many students. In practice, the great majority of students will immediately buy in to trying self-monitoring. If any student is unsure, try using a contingency contract. In this case, the student agrees to try self-monitoring for a set period of time and will receive a reinforcer simply for trying it. After you have enlisted cooperation, explain when and where self-monitoring will be used (e.g., during second period math class seat work time).

STEP 4: Teach the self-monitoring procedures

In this stage the students are taught how to self-monitor. Note that although the time needed to teach procedures can vary widely (depending on the type of self-monitoring used) this process is not time consuming; instruction time is typically well under one hour. There are three critical tasks at this step. First, the teacher needs to define the target behavior for the students. The teacher simply explains to the students exactly what constitutes the target behavior. This typically is quite simple. For example in SMP this may entail little more than telling the students to count the number of correctly worked math problems. For other types of self-monitoring, defining the target variable may be more complex. In SMA this may mean teaching the students what it means to "pay attention." Here the teacher and the students can develop a list of specific behaviors that constitute "paying attention" such as looking at the teacher or your work, writing answers, listening to the teacher, or asking a question. Remember that students must understand the target behavior to be able to self-assess whether the behavior has occurred.

Next the teacher needs to be sure that the students can discriminate the target behavior from other behaviors, (e.g., the students can tell whether they were paying attention or not paying attention). This is rarely an issue in SMP, but sometimes can be a problem with SMA.

If there is any doubt whether the students can accurately discriminate the target behavior, the teacher should model examples and nonexamples of the target behavior and assess whether the students can tell which is which. For example, if the target behavior was paying attention, the teacher might leave her seat and walk around the room (nonexample) or raise her hand to ask a question (example). This provides reinforcement of the knowledge of the target variable gained in the previous stage and also provides evaluative feedback for the teacher.

The last step in this stage is to explain the procedures involved in self-assessing and self-recording the target behavior. First, the teacher models the self-monitoring procedures while verbalizing the steps. The students are then asked to verbalize the steps as the teacher performs them. Following this, the students are asked to both model and verbalize the procedures. The students must be able to perform the self-monitoring procedures effortlessly. Self-monitoring procedures should not be a distraction for the students. If the procedures are difficult for the students to remember or if the students have trouble performing the procedures, they are probably inappropriate for the students. After the students can demonstrate the procedures correctly, the teacher should provide a brief period of guided practice where the teacher and students collaboratively practice the procedures. This provides structured experience for the students and also allows the teacher to assess mastery. Again, in practice this entire procedure can be done very quickly.

STEP 5: Implement self-monitoring

The first time the students are to use the self-monitoring procedures it is a good idea to prompt the students, (e.g., remember to listen for the beep and then mark down whether you were paying attention or not). During the first few sessions, the teacher should monitor the students to ensure that the self-monitoring procedures are used consistently and correctly. This is critical for self-monitoring effectiveness. If any students appear to be having difficulty using the procedures, reteaching may be needed. Sometimes simply providing students with prompts, such as reminders of what constitutes the target behavior or cues to self-assess or self-record may be all that is required. Be sure to note that if a student consistently has difficulty, self-monitoring may not be appropriate. The teacher should continue to collect data on the target behavior in order to determine the effectiveness of the intervention. With self-monitoring, improvement usually is rapid (in a matter of days) and pronounced. The teacher should also make periodic checks to assess whether improvements are maintaining. In practice, students can maintain increased performance levels for considerable periods of time in the classroom. However, if the students' performance begins to deteriorate, the teacher should schedule "booster sessions" in self-monitoring procedures. The following vignette illustrates self-monitoring in practice:

> Ms. Casey teaches eighth grade earth science. She recently adopted a new approach to teaching the content that is more hands on. Much of her class now requires students to work in groups on projects. Ms. Casey works with each group for a few minutes to ensure that they are on the right track before moving to another group. This group work is then followed by independent follow up assignments. It is a large class with 35 students, and it is very difficult her to monitor that many students all doing different tasks. She realizes that students are failing to complete group projects in the allotted time, and that some students are not finishing their independent follow-up work. It does not seem to be a problem with grasping the content; the work that is completed is acceptable. It's not a discipline problem either; the students are not breaking rules or being disruptive. Rather, it looks as if the students are simply wasting a lot of time during group projects with horseplay or gossip, and failing to focus on their independent assignments. It's getting to the point where it's affecting students' grades. Ms. Casey knows she needs to do something quickly. She decides that she will try self-monitoring to see if it can keep the students on task.

She decides that she will use completing assignments as a target behavior. This is easy to define and students should have not problem understanding what it means to complete an assignment. Because her group projects have a consistent format with six activities, she uses percent of activities completed as a target behavior. To be counted as complete, an activity must be completed with at least 80% accuracy. Since she is worried about both the group and individual portions of assignments, Ms. Casey decides to use self-monitoring in both settings. She does not want to introduce too much too quickly, so she decides to start with group-work assignments. Then, if she is successful, she can move to individual work. Next, Ms. Casey collects baseline data. This is simple All she needs to do is go back through the group assignments for the last week. She takes the last three assignments for each of her groups and computes the percent of completion for each group for each assignment. She then graphs the results for each group individually (see Figure 3.3). Collecting this data shows her that there is indeed a serious problem.

The next class period, Ms. Casey talks to the class about the problem. She gives each of the groups the graph she created and has the students look at the percent of assignments that the group has completed. She notes that this is starting to be a serious problem for some students, and that almost all the groups have room for improvement. She stresses that the assignments are a major part of each student's grade and that she does not want anyone to get a bad grade for this reason. She also reminds the students that exams will cover work they should have completed on assignments. Many students are shocked; they had not realized that they were doing so poorly at completing assignments. Ms Casey then tells the class that she believes that the problem is that groups are getting distracted, and that she has a way to help them stay focused on their work. She asks the students to agree to try something new that she believes will really help them. The students agree.

Next, Ms. Casey shows the students how they will self-monitor. During group activities, each group will have its completed assignment graph. Ms. Casey reviews what it means to complete an activity with the students, stressing to the students that to complete an assignment all parts must be completed correctly. Next, Ms. Casey establishes how the students will self-assess and self-record. Ms. Casey tells the students that the time scheduled for assignments will be divided into six equal segments. At the end of each segment she will cue the groups to self-assess how many parts of their assignment they have completed. They then will mark their graphs with the amount of work they have completed. She tells the students that they will practice the procedures today on a short assignment. She uses an egg timer to track the time. Each time it rings, the students self-assess and self-record. Ms. Casey monitors the students during the practice session and answers any questions. She tells the students that tomorrow they will be using the graphs and self-monitoring during their regular class.

Group members: Elwood, Dixie, Steve, Fred

Step	66%	33%	50%							
6										
5										
4	▒									
3	▒		▒							
2	▒	▒	▒							
1	▒	▒	▒							
	Asmt.	Asmt.	Asmt.	Asmt.	Asmt.	Asmt.	Asmt.	Asmt.	Asmt.	Asmt.
	___	___	___	___	___	___	___	___	___	___

Figure 3.3. Ms. Casey's self-monitoring graph.

The next day, when it is time for group work, Ms. Casey passes out the assignment graphs. She reminds the students of their purpose and briefly reviews the self-monitoring procedures. She then tells the students to begin their work and starts the timer. The first two times the egg timer goes off she prompts the students to self-assess and self-record. After this the students are sensitive to the procedures, and Ms. Casey does not think additional prompts are needed. Ms. Casey uses the procedures for the rest of the week. She tracks assignment completion for each group. She notes that after one week of using self-monitoring, the students almost always complete the entire group assignment.

GOAL SETTING

Helping students to set goals can be very useful (Schunk, 2001). First, goals serve to focus effort by providing a target (e.g., I want to get at least a B in math). This in turn provides information on how to accomplish the goal, (e.g., I need to practice my math facts). Second, goals provide information on progress. For example, I would monitor my scores on math quizzes to see if I am making progress meeting the goal. Finally, goals can motivate performance (e.g., My average is now above 80%). Progress toward a goal and achieving that goal is highly motivational. Everyone enjoys reaching a goal.

Unfortunately some students do not set goals, or even worse, may set maladaptive goals that can serve to inhibit performance. For example, some students set performance-avoidance goals; they are not concerned with accomplishing tasks, but instead seek to avoid being seen as lacking ability. Note that for goal setting to be effective goals *must be valued*. If a goal has no value for students, then it is unlikely to improve performance or maintain motivation or effort. Thus teachers may need to point out the benefits of accomplishing a goal (e.g., getting better grades can mean a discount on auto insurance). Choosing appropriate goals is important. Good goals have three properties (Schunk, 2001):

- Specific. A good goal is well defined. Goals that are nebulous (e.g., do your best) are not as effective as those that are well specified (e.g., get a B on the math test).

- Proximal. The best goals are ones that can be reached fairly quickly (e.g., get all my spelling words correct on the test on Friday). Students with academic difficulties need more frequent reinforcement for their efforts. The time taken to accomplish the goal may reduce or eliminate reinforcement or motivation. However, it is possible to use a series of proximal goals to accomplish a long-term goal.

- Moderately difficult. The best goals are those that are moderately difficult. They are neither too easy nor too difficult. Goals that are easily attained do not serve to enhance or maintain effort (Johnson & Graham, 1990).

Because the actual goal or goals selected are so important, it is best for the teacher to help with setting goals to ensure that goals are realistic and attainable. Otherwise students may set goals that are either much too high or much too easy.

Teaching goal setting is a straightforward process. First, the teacher and students meet and discuss performance in an area (e.g., spelling test results). Together the teacher and students decide on an appropriate goal, determine a time line for meeting the goal, and establish how progress toward the goal can be monitored. Teachers should also ensure that students are aware of progress toward their goals. This provides students with self-evaluative feedback that increases motivation. One good way to help students see progress toward goals is to combine goal setting and self-monitoring where students self-record and graph their performance. Graphing provides powerful feedback and in practice is highly motivating to many students. Teachers should emphasize to students that progress toward a goal is the result of their efforts rather than simply luck or external factors. Also teachers need to establish procedures to help the students attain the goal. For example, the teacher might suggest daily 10-minute practice sessions on multiplication facts and have the students self-monitor the number of facts completed correctly. The following illustrates goal setting with a student who is struggling with spelling vocabulary words:

Mr. Graham teaches ninth grade language arts. Vocabulary development is very important to him. Every week students are given 20 new vocabulary words. They are responsible for learning the definitions and the spelling of each word. Every Friday there is a quiz over the words. Students are required to spell 10 words from the list and to take a multiple-choice quiz over the definitions. Students are given the word list on Monday. On Tuesday, Wednesday, and Thursday they practice the spelling and learning the definitions to prepare for the test on Friday. One student, Rochelle, seems to be having some problems with the spelling portion of the quizzes. She does well on the multiple-choice portion, but her grades on the spelling are in the D to F range because she misspells about half the words. This is hurting her class grade. Rochelle is concerned that she might not be academically eligible for the field hockey team and this is upsetting her. Mr. Graham suspects that the problem is that Rochelle is not practicing spelling the words. He decides to use goal setting and self-monitoring with Rochelle.

Mr. Graham sets up a meeting with Rochelle to talk about the problem with her spelling quizzes. He brings her last three quizzes. Her scores on the quizzes were 50%, 60%, and 30%. Her average was 46%. They both agree that this is a problem. Mr. Graham asks Rochelle to think about a goal for her spelling quizzes. Rochelle immediately says, "100%!" Mr. Graham tells her that this is a great long-range goal, but it might be a little high for now. They decide to set a 70% goal for the next week. Next Mr. Graham asks Rochelle about how she studies for the spelling quizzes. Rochelle is a little embarrassed. She admits that she really hasn't been practicing her spelling words because "it's dumb." Mr. Graham reminds her that "practice makes perfect," and that to raise her grade she really will need to practice the spelling words.

Together, they discuss when and where Rochelle can practice spelling. They decide that she can allot 15 minutes during her study hall to practice spelling. Then they discuss how she should practice her spelling. Mr. Graham shows her a simple method of practice: "Look at the word. Say the word. Cover the word. Write the word three times. Check to see if it is correct." Rochelle agrees to practice the words three times a week during study hall. Mr. Graham creates a goal sheet to help her track her progress (Figure 3.4). She will use this procedure for the entire list. If she finishes the list before the 15 minutes are up, she will start over. Rochelle decides that she will come by at the end of the day to show Mr. Graham her practice sheet. Knowing that she must show the goal sheet to Mr. Graham will motivate her to do her practice sessions.

Circle the goal for each week, then, check the box for each practice.

Thur Y/N	100	Thur Y/N	100	Thur Y/N	100	Thur Y/N	100
	90		90		90		90
	80		80		80		80
Wed Y/N	70	Wed Y/N	70	Wed Y/N	70	Wed Y/N	70
	60		60		60		60
	50		50		50		50
Tues Y/N	40	Tues Y/N	40	Tues Y/N	40	Tues Y/N	40
	30		30		30		30
	20		20		20		20
	10		10		10		10
Practice	Test	Practice	Test	Practice	Test	Practice	Test

Figure 3.4. Example goal setting sheet.

Subsequently, each day after her study hall Rochelle stopped by Mr. Graham's room with her practice sheet. On the first week's spelling test she scored 80%. She was ecstatic. She saw that the practice had paid off. Mr. Graham and Rochelle decided to set a new goal of 90%; Rochelle decided to do extra practice. She would do the practice routine twice for each word in the list. Soon, Rochelle's spelling scores were averaging above 90%.

SELF-INSTRUCTIONS

Most people use language to mediate their behavior. We all have that "little voice" in our head that helps to guide behavior. Self-instruction interventions involve the use of induced self-statements to direct or self-regulate behavior affect, or cognitions (Harris, 1990). Self-instruction strategies quite literally help students to talk themselves through a task or activity. Self-instructions can be used for many different purposes. Table 3.1 shows some common functions of self-instructions.

Teaching students to use self-instructions involves four steps. First, the teacher and student discuss why what we say to ourselves is important, and how what we say to ourselves can help or hurt us. This is very important because many students who struggle academically also have high rates of negative self-statement (e.g., "I'm dumb," "I can't do this"). The teacher stresses that students can learn to use words to help themselves complete tasks. Second, the teacher and students collaborate to develop meaningful, individualized, task appropriate self-instructions together. Note that self-instructions are not simply repeating the statements created by the teacher. For self-instruction to be successful self-statements must be meaningful to the student—often the most meaningful self-statements are those that the student develops. Next, the teacher models the use of self-statements and discusses situations where the self-statements could be used. Finally, the teacher creates collaborative practice activities to allow the student to practice using self-instructions to perform a task. During these activities the teacher and students model the use of the self-statements and discuss how and when to use the self-statements. The goal is for students to progress from the use of overt self-statements (i.e., talking aloud to oneself) to covert, internalized speech. The following illustrates self-instruction in practice:

Mrs. Hallahan, a 10th grade American history teacher, is beginning to be concerned about Jaron. Jaron is a bright student. He contributes in class and his homework is always done well and handed in on time. His comments in class suggest that he really has a grasp of the topics covered. However, his test

Table 3.1. Examples of self-statements.

Type of self-instruction	Example
Problem definition: defining the nature and demands of a task	• Okay. What do I have to do? • What's my first step?
Focusing attention/planning: attending to task and generating plans	• I need to read very carefully. • I need to lay out a plan for this job.
Strategy related: engaging and using a strategy	• I need to remember to use my strategy. • What's the first step in my strategy
Self-evaluation: error detection and correction	• How am I doing? Am I on track? • Does this answer look reasonable? • This answer looks way off. I need to fix it.
Coping: dealing with difficulties/failures	• If I keep at it I can do it. • I know I can do this if I try my hardest. • Stay cool, fool.
Self-reinforcement: rewarding oneself	• Super job! • I tried my best and I got it right!

scores are very poor. On one test he failed to answer almost half the questions. Many of the questions were ones that Mrs. Hallahan considered fairly easy. On another test, a number of answers appeared to be written hastily, and Jaron lost points because he failed to include relevant information. Mrs. Hallahan can't understand why there is such a disparity between homework and classwork and test performance.

Mrs. Hallahan schedules a meeting with Jaron to talk about the problem. When Jaron comes to the meeting she can tell that he is aware of the problem and is upset by it. She reassures him that his homework and class participation are excellent and she knows he is a conscientious student. Jaron tells her that he is uncomfortable taking essay tests. His other classes have used multiple-choice or fill-in-the-blank type items. Jaron tells her that he has a lot of problems with completing the tests. On his first test, for example, he got overly focused on the first few questions and wrote long, detailed responses. As a result, he used up so much time for these questions that time was up before he could get to the rest of the test; half the questions were left blank. On the second test, Jaron noted that he was determined to make sure that he completed the entire test. He sped through the test and made sure he had something written down for every question. Unfortunately, because his answers were so hastily written, he did poorly. Jaron noted that he has lost confidence. He says that he is so worried about doing poorly that he literally feels nauseated when the test is passed out. If he sees a question he is unsure about he freezes and wastes time fretting about the question. Mrs. Hallahan can see the problem now—although Jaron realized that he needed to change his study habits for the essay tests, he didn't realize that he needed to develop new test-taking strategies.

Mrs. Hallahan decides to use a self-instruction strategy to help Jaron improve his test scores. She will teach Jaron to use self-instructions to help him take the tests more strategically. Jaron is eager to improve his test scores and wants to try the new approach. First Mrs. Hallahan works with Jaron to define his major problems. There seem to be two major problems: poor time management and freezing when he sees a question about which he is unsure. First, they work together to develop some effective time-management techniques. They decide that when Jaron receives his test, he will first scan the test and mark the questions he can answer easily; those are the questions he will answer first. Next he will answer the tougher questions. Jaron will also keep a close watch on the time. He will glance at the clock between questions and during his responses to closely monitor the time remaining. This will help him allot time more evenly to questions.

Next, Mrs. Hallahan talks with Jaron about the importance of self-speech and how what we say to ourselves can influence what we do. Jaron notes that he has been making a lot of very negative self-statements to himself during examinations. Mrs. Hallahan and Jaron work together to develop self-statements that Jaron can use to help him remember to use the test-taking strategies that they have developed. To help remind himself to look for the easy questions, Jaron will tell himself to "Look for the freebies (i.e., easy to answer questions)." To remind himself to monitor time, Jaron will tell himself, "Tick Tock o'clock." Jaron isn't sure he will remember to do this one. Mrs. Hallahan suggests that he write "TT" for Tick Tock on the top of each page of the test. Jaron thinks this will help. Jaron also works on giving himself a pep talk before he receives his copy of the test, and when he sees himself beginning to fret over a question.

Jaron loves to play basketball and is very talented at it. Mrs. Hallahan asks him what he says to himself when he shoots a basketball. Jaron says he tells himself "Nothing but net." He likes this idea. Next they talk about what he can do when he starts to get nervous about a question and feels himself beginning to freeze. Jaron says it's like a big black rain cloud covers him. Mrs. Hallahan asks what he could do to get rid of the cloud. Jaron says that sun can burn away the clouds. They decide that he will tell himself to "Think sun." To remind him to use the self-statements he will use a mnemonic "Next Free Throw Shot." The first letter stands for each of the self-statements: "**N**othing but net," "Look for the **F**reebie," "**T**ick Tock O'clock," and "Think **S**un."

Now that the self-statements are developed, and Jaron knows when he should use them, Mrs. Hallahan schedules a practice session. She uses one of Jaron's old tests. First, she asks Jaron what he will say to himself before getting the test. He remembers the "Next Free Throw Shot" mnemonic. She models using the mnemonic. She tells herself "Nothing but net," and mimes shooting a basketball.

Jaron thinks her form is hilarious, but it gets the point across. Next she says "Look for the Freebies," and pages through the test making an X by easy questions. On each page she writes TT at the top to remind herself to monitor the time. She writes out answers to a few questions and asks Jaron what she should be doing. Jaron tells her Tick Tock o'clock, which means to check the time. Finally Mrs. Hallahan, looks at the test, drops her pencils and says, "Oh man, I can't get this question. I'm never going to get this done." She asks Jaron what she should do next. Jaron smiles and tells her to, "Think Sun 'cause it will burn the clouds away." After she has modeled using the self-instructions, Jaron works through the test and practices using the self-instructions. At each step, she asks probing questions to see if Jaron understands and remembers the purpose of the self-statements, for example: why say, "Next Free Throw Shot"? Because it reminds him to say his self-statements.

Jaron is now ready to try using the strategy with a real test. The day before the test, Mrs. Hallahan and Jaron discuss how he will use the strategy. As an additional prompt, Mrs. Hallahan writes the mnemonic "Next Free Throw Shot" on the top of the first page of Jaron's test. When Jaron gets his test, she sees him mime shooting a basket (the first self-statement). She is hopeful. Jaron finishes his test on time and passes with flying colors!

SELF-REINFORCEMENT

Self-reinforcement occurs when students select a reinforcer and self-award when a predetermined criterion is reached or exceeded (e.g., when I work 10 math problems, I get a break; Graham et al., 1992). This process is akin to the natural developmental process where a child learns that meeting expectations often results in positive reinforcement, and that failing to reach expectations results in no reinforcement or a negative response (Barkley, 2006). As a result, many students have already learned to self-reinforce their own behavior. Learning to self-reinforce appropriately may be important for many struggling learners. These students may require frequent reinforcement to maintain or change behavior, and self-reinforcement can be an efficient and effective means of providing needed reinforcement.

Self-reinforcement is taught using a four-step process. First, the teacher sets the standard for receiving a reward. If at all possible this should be done collaboratively with the students. The standard for receiving a reward should be clear and objective. For example, "getting better at spelling" would not be a good standard; getting 80% correct on weekly spelling tests would be more appropriate. The initial standard should be set low enough that the students can receive at least some reinforcement relatively quickly. If the students do not receive reinforcement there will be no behavior change. Next, the teacher and students together select a reinforcer. Students should be involved in this process for practical reasons—they know what is rewarding to them. Third, teacher and students establish how students will determine whether or not they have met the standard for reinforcement. For example, the students may self-correct, or bring the work to the teacher to check. At least initially, it is often a good idea for the teacher to work with the students to determine if the standard was met. Finally, if students meet or exceed the standard they may award themselves the reinforcer. Awarding reinforcements does not need to be totally independent. For example, the students might be required to check with the teacher before self-awarding reinforcement. Self-reinforcement can easily be combined with goal setting since they have so much in common (e.g., setting standards for performance, reinforcement based on meeting standards). The following illustrates self-reinforcement in practice:

Mr. Epstein is a ninth grade social studies teacher. Each Friday his students are required to write a brief essay about the topic of the week. Mr. Epstein gives them a prompt and the students have 20 minutes to write their response. He is beginning to have serious concerns about Emma. Mr. Epstein is confident that the problem is not with her lack of skills or an inability to write an essay. Some of Emma's essays are top notch and rival the best in the class. The problem is that her essays vary dramatically in quality. Many are little more than a series of disconnected sentences. These essays count for 20% of her grade in the class and Mr. Epstein is afraid that her inconsistent performance is going to hurt her grade. He decides to talk with Emma about the problem. As it turns out, Emma is quite aware that some of her in-class essays are poor. She knows she didn't do a good job or try her best on these essays. She says that some of the topics are "lame," and she just can't get motivated. She begins to daydream or just wishes she was done and soon her writing time is nearly gone. Then she has to hastily scribble down anything she can think of.

Mr. Epstein decides that a combination of self-reinforcement and goal setting might help Emma to write more high-quality essays on a consistent basis. He tells Emma that he might have a way to help her stay motivated. First, Mr. Epstein wants to make sure that Emma understands what is expected of her. He shows her three of her earlier essays. Two of them are very poor; one is very well done. He asks her if she can see the differences. Emma readily points out the aspects of the papers that are different (e.g., topic sentences, reasons for her opinion, supporting detail, conclusions). Mr. Epstein and Emma agree that this is the level of quality that she should strive to attain on future papers.

Next, Mr. Epstein tells Emma that if she is willing to commit to improving the quality of her essays that he will reward her efforts. Emma likes this idea. Together they discuss possible reinforcers. Emma suggests being allowed to skip homework assignments. Mr. Epstein vetoes that idea. After more discussion they come up with a list of possible rewards. Emma really likes listening to music, so she decides that she would like that for a reward. Mr. Epstein tells Emma that each time she writes a quality essay, he will arrange for her to listen to music for 20 minutes in the computer lab during her last period study hall. Mr. Epstein also wants to set a goal with Emma that will help her be more consistent. He asks Emma how many good essays she could write if she really gave it her best. Emma says that she probably could do well on all essays if she gave it her best. Mr. Epstein asks Emma how many consecutive good essays she could write. Emma says she could do easily write 10 or 15. Mr. Epstein thinks that might be a bit high and suggests a goal of five to start with. He tells Emma that if she can get five in a row he will allow her to listen to music for 20 minutes on his iPod. Emma loves that idea.

Mr. Epstein creates a goal sheet for Emma. She will keep the goal sheet on her desk when she writes her Friday essay to remind her of the reward she can receive. When she finishes her essay, she will bring it to Mr. Epstein. He will check to see if it meets criteria. If it does, he will sign off in a box and give Emma a pass for the computer lab last period. Emma can then listen to music. Before the next Friday essay, Mr. Epstein reminds Emma of the reward, and the procedures. The self-reinforcement seems to be working. Emma does a great job on her next two essays and is excited at the prospect of getting to listen to the iPod.

Final Thoughts

In this chapter we presented an overview of self-regulation strategies that can be used in the classroom. These strategies are simple to implement and can be extremely effective. Moreover, after implementation, the teacher's time involvement is minimal. Thus, there is much to recommend. However we would stress that there are limitations.

Students must be able to perform the behavior

Self-regulation strategies *do not* create new behaviors. They help to enable students to use behaviors that they can already perform. Self-regulation strategies can increase the frequency of behaviors (e.g., persisting on a task), or help students talk themselves through a task. For example, teaching students to self-monitor the number of steps completed in their group assignment would be appropriate if and only if the students had the necessary skills to complete the assignments. Self-monitoring alone would not teach the students new skills. It can only help them to utilize skills that they already possess.

Extreme behavior problems

Self-regulation strategies are not appropriate for students who exhibit serious behavior problems (e.g., physical violence) on a frequent basis or are out of control. Behavioral interventions are more appropriate for these types of problems.

Generalization

Even if students shows major improvements in one setting it is not likely that the improvements will generalize to other settings or behaviors. For example, Jaron learned to use self-instructions to talk himself through examinations and his performance improved dramatically, but it is unlikely that he would spontaneously use the self-instructions for other stressful situations or for examinations in other classrooms. Remember that in practice, the most effective self-regulation interventions are those that are targeted at a specific behavior in a specific setting. A teacher can, however, work with students to help them use the technique in a different setting or for a new task. Thus, for example, the teacher could work with Jaron to help him use or develop new self-instructions for exams in another class. Students frequently find self-regulation strategies helpful and even enjoyable. They are generally agreeable to using them for other purposes or in other settings; it is just that students are unlikely to do it on their own.

Classroom environment

Self-regulation does not occur in a vacuum. The classroom environment can make or break self-regulation interventions (Mace, Belfiore, & Hutchinson, 2001). In a disorderly, chaotic classroom, it's highly unlikely that any self-regulation intervention will be effective. A structured classroom environment with a predictable, stable routine greatly increases the likelihood of effective self-regulation. Students also may self-regulate their environment to help themselves complete tasks (e.g., finding a place to study that is quiet and free of outside distractions). Remember that even in the best possible environment some students will have some problem with self-regulation.

REFERENCES

Barkley, R. A. (2006). *Attention-deficit hyperactivity disorder: A handbook for diagnosis and treatment* (3rd ed.). New York, NY: Guilford Press.

Graham, S., Harris, K.R., & Reid, R. (1992). Developing self-regulated learners. *Focus on Exceptional Children, 24*, 1–16.

Harris, K.R. (1990). Developing self-regulated learners: The role of private speech and self-instructions. *Educational Psychologist, 25*, 35–49.

Harris, K.R., Reid, R., & Graham, S. (2004). Self-regulation among children with LD and ADHD. In B. Wong (Ed.), *Learning about learning disabilities* (pp. 167–195). San Diego, CA: Elsevier.

Johnson, L., & Graham, S. (1990). Goal setting and its application with exceptional learners. *Preventing School Failure, 34*, 4–8.

Mace, F.C., Belfiore, P J., & Hutchinson, J.M. (2001). Operant theory and research on self-regulation. In B. Zimmerman & D. Schunk (Eds.), *Self-regulated learning and academic achievement* (pp. 39–65). Mahwah, NJ: Lawrence Erlbaum.

Reid, R. (1996). Self-monitoring for students with learning disabilities: The present, the prospects, the pitfalls. *Journal of Learning Disabilities, 29*, 317–331.

Reid, R., & Lienemann, T. O. (2006). *Strategy instruction for students with learning disabilities*. New York, NY: Guilford Press.

Reid, R., Trout, A.L., & Schartz, M. (2005). Self-regulation interventions for children with attention-deficit/hyperactivity disorder. *Exceptional Children, 71*, 361–377.

Schunk, D. (2001). Social cognitive theory and self-regulated learning. In B. Zimmerman & D. Schunk (Eds.), *Self-regulated learning and academic achievement* (pp. 125–151). Mahwah, NJ: Lawrence Erlbaum.

Section II

Reading to Learn

Chapter 4

Reading to Learn in Content Text

Once students have achieved learning to read objectives for decoding and fluency, reading becomes the means in which information is obtained from text—reading to learn. Prior to introducing comprehension strategies to support reading to learn, it is critical that teachers understand the difficulty of content text for many adolescent readers and the various structures that can be found in content text books.

Content text, generally, fits in the classification of informational text, written to explain and describe new content supported by empirical evidence (Graesser, Leon, & Otero, 2002). Informational text can have either a narrative structure, such as found in biographical text, or an expository structure for communicating new or unfamiliar facts, theories, and dates. Four characteristics of informational text make it challenging for many students—expectations of prior knowledge, vocabulary, conceptual density, and unfamiliar expository text structures (Mason & Hedin, 2011; Saenz & Fuchs, 2002). Expository structures can be especially problematic for students who have learning difficulties. We will use the following passage, an excerpt from an address Elizabeth Cady Stanton delivered after the conventions of 1848, to illustrate the four characteristics of challenging text as is often found in Social Studies text. We will provide a vignette for science text later in this chapter.

Woman's Rights • Among the many important questions which have been brought before the public, there is none that more vitally affects the whole human family than that which is technically termed Woman's Rights. Every allusion to the degraded and inferior position occupied by woman all over the world has ever been met by scorn and abuse. From the man of highest mental cultivation, to the most degraded wretch who staggers in the streets do we hear ridicule and coarse jests, freely bestowed upon those who dare assert that woman stands by the side of man—his equal, placed here by her God to enjoy with him the beautiful earth, which is her home as it is his—having the same sense of right and wrong and looking to the same Being for guidance and support. So long has man exercised a tyranny over her injurious to himself and benumbing to her faculties, that but few can nerve themselves against the storm, and so long has the chain been about her that however galling it may be she knows not there is a remedy.

PRIOR KNOWLEDGE

Reading informational text requires world knowledge and concept knowledge. It also requires students to make inferences. Making inferences from reading is most difficult for students with weak prior knowledge and for those who struggle with comprehension and only read at a literal level. After reading the *Woman's Rights* illustration, it is clear that this text, taken out of context and without establishing prior knowledge, would be difficult for many students. First, students would have to understand that at the time the text was written, women did not benefit from laws to protect their rights as equal members of society. The inference to be made is that by joining the cause of Women's Rights in 1848, one could expect to be made fun of and that courage would be needed.

Prior to reading the text, the teacher should help students access the knowledge they do have about the topic. Group brainstorming, for example, listing all that is known about the Women's Rights movement, is one effective method for stimulating prior knowledge and assessing students' correct assumptions and misconceptions about the topic. In addition, scanning the text for titles and headings is an excellent way to focus students' attention on the material that is to be read. Using techniques such as quick writing (see Chapter 12) to assess what individual students know about the topic can also be beneficial. For example, the teacher could ask the students to write all they know about the Women's Rights movement in 10 minutes.

Brainstorming, text preview, and prewriting activities are excellent methods for connecting information to be learned with students' prior knowledge. The teacher can also help the students make associations with current events, other civil rights movements, or ongoing issues for women's rights through teacher-screened newspaper articles or websites to help students make the connection with their current world knowledge. For those students with limited knowledge, providing an alternative source text, one that outlines the Women's Rights movement, to read prior to reading the original source document will often facilitate understanding. Of course, the Woman's Rights text has other characteristics which should be addressed prior to student reading.

VOCABULARY

Vocabulary knowledge is a strong predictor of student achievement in content areas such as science, social studies, and health (Borsuk, 2010; Espin & Foegen, 1996). For many students gaps in vocabulary knowledge begin early and continue to increase over time. Unfortunately, these struggling learners also have difficulty using the words they do know to help them understand the new words they encounter during reading. Given this fact, it is critical that teachers first identify problematic vocabulary. Once this vocabulary has been identified, teachers need to select key, generalizable vocabulary words for vocabulary instruction.

The *Woman's Rights* paragraph is loaded with difficult vocabulary! Students may be unfamiliar with the following words, within and/or out of the context of the passage: among, public, vitally, human family, technically, termed, allusion, degraded, inferior, occupied, scorn, abuse, mental cultivation, degraded, wretch, staggers, ridicule, coarse, jests, bestowed, assert, guidance, tyranny, injurious, benumbing, faculties, nerve, galling, and remedy. Note that this is 32 words out of a 181-word paragraph. The teacher may decide to select 10–15 focus words for the majority of students. For struggling learners it is best practice to select approximately five highly generalizable words at a time. For example, words such as inferior, scorn, assert, guidance, and remedy have important relevance to the topic and can be generalized across topics and content.

Vocabulary should be taught through a variety of indirect instructional methods (e.g., noting words in text and discussing meanings) and direct methods (e.g., individual word knowledge, morphological analysis and use of contextual cues; National Reading Panel, 2000). When teaching individual words selected from texts, a vocabulary study journal can be used to present definitions along with several sentences that contain the targeted words (see Chapter 7). Discussions of related synonyms and antonyms can further support vocabulary acquisition. Word knowledge can also be expanded through categorization activities, construction of semantic maps, and comparisons of targeted words to similar words (Stahl & Nagy, 2006).

CONCEPTUAL DENSITY

The methods in which concepts, logical–causal relationships, and vocabulary are introduced in informational text result in conceptually dense reading (Dreher & Singer, 1989). Informational text often contains little explanation, elaboration, or illustration of concepts through use of examples and non-examples (Dornish, Sperling, & Zeruth, 2011). For students with limited prior knowledge and vocabulary knowledge, conceptual density intensifies difficulties with understanding what is read.

Without a doubt the *Woman's Rights* paragraph is dense (Kincaid, Fishburne, Rogers, & Chissom, 1975). The concepts and logical–causal relationships get lost in complex and outdated syntax. The rate that unfamiliar vocabulary is introduced also contributes to the paragraph's density. The Flesch Kincaid grade level is 19.40! Is it bad practice to expose students to conceptually dense text? We would not dispute the benefits of exposing students to a variety of speaking and writing styles. To support comprehension, however, we would assert that some text, for many students, simply needs to be rewritten or paraphrased. For example:

Women's Rights • Among the many important questions which have been brought before the community, there is one question that affects all people—women's rights. In all countries when women's inferior position is mentioned, scorn and abuse follows. This occurs in the most educated people as well as those living on the street. The idea that women are equal to men and were placed on earth by God to enjoy earth, and to share a home with men and have a sense of right and wrong as men do seems ridiculous to some people. Because of the years of tyranny that women have faced, many women cannot get the nerve to fight for women's rights. These women, without guidance to help them see that they can have rights, do not know that there is a remedy to their inferior position. • Flesch Kincaid grade level: 10.00

TEXT STRUCTURE

Informational text contains few of the simple text structures (e.g., story structures or simple description) found in passages used in primary grade level and remedial reading text (Saenz & Fuchs, 2002). Informational texts are often written using more complex structures such as lists, compare–contrast, time–sequence, procedural, problem–solution, classification, concept, and cause–effect. In addition, informational text is often written with a number of text structures imbedded in a hybrid, mixed-text style. These structures can occur at sentence, paragraph, and passage levels. Given the text structure complexity often found in content text, it is critical that the teacher identify the structures key for supporting curriculum objectives.

Women's Rights, for example, has an embedded cause–effect structure (e.g., alluding that women's rights results in scorn) and a concept structure (e.g., women, by being placed on earth, are created equal and deserve equal rights) which serve to persuade the reader to be brave for the fight ahead. For many students, the gist of the passage (the persuasive element) could be missed! Some students may simply rely on the easier cause–effect structure and miss the concepts. How does a teacher assist students in breaking down the structure and meaning of structurally difficult text? Research-based evidence has clearly established that reading comprehension strategy instruction is most effective in addressing the difficulties many students have in understanding informational text (Jitendra, Burgess, & Gajria, 2011).

READING COMPREHENSION STRATEGIES

Researchers have clearly established that reading comprehension strategies taught in combination with procedures for self-regulating learning (e.g., self-monitoring) have the greatest effects in improving students' understanding of text (NRP, 2000; Jitendra, Burgess, & Gajria 2011). Evidence-based practices include interventions for text structure, main idea identification, summarization, and multicomponent instruction. How do these strategies work when teaching students to read content text? To start, cueing the students to a passage's text structure provides students with a strategic way to access information, discriminate between main and incidental details, and retrieve information systematically. For example, prior to teaching the original *Women's Rights*, or the rewritten *Women's Rights*, the teacher should note that the paragraph has a persuasive message based on the causes and effects of woman achieving equality. With a dense text, the teacher will need to take the lead. Students can also be taught to look for the structure. We will illustrate this in Chapter 7, Thinking About Reading with TWA.

Strategies to support main idea identification and summarization have demonstrated a positive impact on reading comprehension for students who are struggling to learn from text. These evidence-based interventions assist students in using strategies such as self-questioning in order to find the main idea and in paraphrasing the main idea (see Chapter 5, TRAP for Reading Comprehension), and summarizing by locating important supporting details or ideas, and deleting or ignoring incidental information (see Chapter 6, TRAP IDEAS for Summarizing). Multicomponent reading strategy interventions combine several evidence-based practices into one instructional package targeting reading comprehension. These approaches present strategies for prior knowledge acquisition, text structure, comprehension monitoring, and summarization of information throughout reading. One approach, TWA (see Chapter 7), also includes embedded vocabulary instruction. All of these strategies approaches can be applied to difficult text such as found in the *Woman's Rights* paragraph.

SCIENCE TEXT VIGNETTE

Mr. Hepburn has decided to enhance his school's science text chapter on genetics by using the development of dog traits for illustrating how traits can be modified or changed naturally and artificially (i.e., initiated by people). The science text briefly alludes to dog trait genetics, but the text passage is conceptually dense, uses non-generalizable vocabulary, and lacks clear examples. Mr. Hepburn knows that many of his students are going to need enhanced and modified instruction as well as self-regulated strategy instruction.

The first thing Mr. Hepburn does in planning the lesson is complete an Internet search for articles that may be of high interest to the students. He locates a few resources in scientific-based websites such as sciencedaily.com and news.sciencmag.org. Although both sources provide clear examples of naturally and artificially developed traits, the passages have more information than is needed to provide a clear illustration. He knows that his more advanced students will be able to sort through some of the information on these websites. However, to ensure that all students acquire the critical concepts, he plans to scaffold instruction from an easier text to those he located on the web and in the text book. To do this, Mr. Hepburn, using the information from the science text book and the Internet resources, writes a brief informative passage to be used for initial instruction. By rewriting the text, Mr. Hepburn has reduced its *conceptual density*.

Dog Breeds • Dogs have helped people do work for thousands of years. In earlier times, people needed dogs to help them hunt and to give them protection. So the dogs they kept around their homes or camps were hunters and watchdogs. In later times, people needed dogs that could act as shepherds to watch their sheep. So breeds, or kinds, of dogs that would protect other animals were developed. Today, dogs are used in the ways mentioned and in other ways as well. Dogs guide the blind, pull sleds through the snow, rescue people who are lost, and often provide friendship.

Scientists think that a long time ago all dog breeds looked very much such as wolves. Some modern dog breeds look more such as their wild ancestors than other breeds do. Some breeds of dogs have developed naturally. For example, dogs whose ancestors lived in cold climates for many years grow thick coats of fur. The dingo, whose ancestors hunted the speedy kangaroo, has long legs for running. But most breeds of dogs have been developed by people.

Developing new breeds or making changes in a breed of dogs takes a long time. Many generations of puppies must be born and bred before the traits of the new breed are established. When people needed a fast, fearless hunter, they chose dogs with those traits. Only the fastest and bravest dogs were bred. The best puppies were then raised and mated, and so on. When people needed dogs with short legs to hunt animals that live in holes in the ground, the dogs with the shortest legs were raised and mated. • Flesch Kincaid grade level: 6.16. *Source:* Mason, L.H. (2002).

Prior to reading the passage, Mr. Hepburn establishes *prior knowledge* in two ways. First, he shows the students pictures of and writes the names of four dog breeds (e.g., chihuahua, beagle, German shepherd, greyhound) on the chalkboard and asks the students to brainstorm what they know about each breed. Mr. Hepburn facilitates the discussion on the similarities and differences in traits. He then asks the students to briefly complete a Quick Write to one of two prompts, "Which dog would you want as a pet? Explain why using some of the traits listed on the board," and, "Which dog would you not want as a pet? Explain why using some of the traits listed on the board." To stimulate interest and support conversation on the topic, Mr. Hepburn allows students to share their selection with a peer.

Each student in Mr. Hepburn's class maintains a *vocabulary* study journal. In these journals, students list key vocabulary words and their definition, and then write sentences using the vocabulary words to practice application. Mr. Hepburn selected the following words, to teach in the context of the topic of genetic traits, for the dog breed passage: breed, ancestors, traits, generation. He lists these words, and helps students define and apply the words in their journals prior to reading. Students are then told to look for the words when reading the passage and to refer to their journals if needed. Mr. Hepburn knows that this is only a start to developing vocabulary for this topic; when he returns to the science textbook passage and/or the Internet readings he will need to revisit and add to vocabulary specific to genetics.

The students are now prepared to read the text. Mr. Hepburn has the students look at the passage and solicits students understanding of the *text structure* to be read. He notes that they have been comparing dog breeds; however, the passage is about how breed traits are developed, and this is the concept in the text and the one to be learned. Mr. Hepburn tells the students to look for information that supports the concept when they are reading. To help students identify important details and ideas about the concept, Mr. Hepburn will select a previously taught reading comprehension strategy. The students have learned to apply three reading strategies—TRAP, TRAP IDEAS, and TWA—to reading text in

Mr. Hepburn's class. Which strategy should Mr. Hepburn select for this lesson? Mr. Hepburn, correctly, will make his decision based on his objectives, the texts (created and others selected) to be read, and the needs of his students.

REFERENCES

Borsuk, E. (2010). Examination of an administrator-read vocabulary-matching measure as an indicator of science achievement. *Assessment for Effective Intervention, 35,* 168–177. doi:10.1177/1534508410372081

Dornish, M., Sperling, R.A., & Zeruth, J.A. (2011). The effects of levels of elaboration on learners' strategic processing of text. *Instructional Science, 39,* 1–26. doi:10.1007/s11251-009-9111-z

Dreher, M.J., & Singer, H. (1986). Friendly text and text-friendly teachers. *Theory into Practice, 28,* 98–104.

Espin, C.A., & Foegen, A. (1996). Validity of general outcome measures for predicting students' performance on content-area tasks. *Exceptional Children, 62,* 497–514.

Gordon, A., Gaskill Miller, T., Kriv, A., Kinlock Sewell, S., Pfau, A. (Eds.). (1997). In the school of anti-slavery, 1840 to 1866. *The selected papers of Elizabeth Cady Stanton and Susan B. Anthony* (Vol. 1). New Brunswick, NJ: Rutgers University Press.

Graesser, A.C., Leon, J.A., & Otero, J. (2002). Introduction to the psychology of science text comprehension. In J. Otero, J.A. Leon, & A.C. Graesser (Eds.), *The psychology of science text comprehension* (pp. 1–18). Mahwah, NJ: Erlbaum.

Kincaid, J.P.; Fishburne, R.P., Jr.; Rogers, R.L.; and Chissom, B.S. (1975); *Derivation of new readability formulas (Automated Readability Index, Fog Count and Flesch Reading Ease Formula) for Navy enlisted personnel,* Research Branch Report 8-75, Millington, TN: Naval Technical Training, U. S. Naval Air Station, Memphis, TN.

Mason, L.H. (2002). *Explicit self-regulated strategy development versus reciprocal questioning: Effects on expository reading comprehension among struggling readers.* Unpublished Dissertation. College Park, MD: University of Maryland.

Mason, L.H., & Hedin, L. (2011). Reading science text: Challenges for students with learning disabilities and considerations for teachers. *Learning Disabilities Research and Practice, 26,* 214–222.

National Reading Panel (2000). *Teaching children to read: An evidence-based assessment of the scientific research literature on reading and its implication for reading instruction.* Washington, DC: National Institute of Child Health and Human Development.

Jitendra, A. K., Burgess, C., & Gajria, M. (2011). Cognitive strategy instruction for improving expository text comprehension of students with learning disabilities: The quality of evidence. *Exceptional Children, 77,* 135–160.

Saenz, L.M., & Fuchs, L.S. (2002). Examining the reading difficulty of secondary students with learning disabilities: Expository versus narrative text. *Remedial and Special Education, 23,* 31–41. doi:10.1177/074193250202300105

Stahl, S. & Nagy, W. (2006). *Teaching word meanings.* Mahwah, NJ: Lawrence Erlbaum.

Chapter 5

TRAP for Reading Comprehension

TRAP

Think before your read

Read a paragraph

Ask "What is the paragraph mostly about? What is the most important information?"

Paraphrase the important information

MATERIALS

TRAP mnemonic chart

Goal chart

Reading passages for Lesson 2

TRAP checklist

TRAP worksheet

For students to remember information such as the main idea and important details from text they have read, they must first be able to locate this information. They must realize that passages have a main idea, and they must have a strategy for finding the main idea. They must also know that some details are more important than others. Next they must process the information they have gained from the text in some way to enable the information to be stored in long-term memory. Information that is not processed in some way is unlikely to be remembered. One very effective means of processing information is to use paraphrasing, that is, putting the information in "your own words." Doing this increases the likelihood that students will remember the important information in what they have read. In the following lessons we introduce the TRAP reading comprehension strategy. TRAP helps students to find and remember the main idea of expository text that they have read. TRAP is an acronym for: **T**hink before your read (what is the purpose for reading the passage), **R**ead a paragraph (carefully read the text), **A**sk "What is the paragraph mostly about? What is the most important information?" (find the main idea of the paragraph and important details), **P**araphrase the important information (put the main idea and two important details into your own words). The TRAP strategy was based on the RAP strategy of Schumaker, Denton, and Deschler (1984).

Prior to Instruction

Before beginning instruction, the instructor should gather information on the students' current level of comprehension. This information will be used as a baseline to help assess the effectiveness of the strategy. It will also be used in lesson one to establish that there is a problem and that the TRAP strategy can help the student to remember more information. There are a number of possible sources for this information. For example, if the student has regular quizzes in a class these might serve as material for a baseline. Alternatively the teacher might wish to use structured oral retells to help assess comprehension. The Reading to Learn Appendix shows how to create and score oral retells. The teacher will also need to locate a series of passages that the student can use to practice using the TRAP strategy. We recommend that reading level be at or slightly below the student's current independent reading level for introducing and guided TRAP practice. Remember, reading fluency and comprehension are highly correlated. If a student struggles with decoding text she or he will have few cognitive resources available to help with comprehension. It's critical that the student be able to decode text reasonably fluently for the strategy to be effective.

Introduce TRAP

LESSON OVERVIEW

The purpose of the first TRAP lesson is to introduce and describe the strategy, discuss current performance, obtain student(s) commitment to learn and use the strategy, and set an initial performance goal.

STUDENT OBJECTIVES

The students will commit to learn and establish goals for TRAP

MATERIALS

Poster/PowerPoint with TRAP steps; for each student: short reading passages to find main idea and a blank graph (goal chart)

SET THE CONTEXT FOR STUDENT LEARNING

1. SAY, *"I want to talk with you today about why it's important that we remember what we read."* Discuss why it is important to remember what we read. Solicit specific instances where it is important for students to remember material they have read. Ask for examples from class work (e.g. for a test or quiz, doing homework, answering questions at the end of chapters).

2. SAY, *"I am concerned that you may have a problem remembering what you read."* Hand out the graph of reading comprehension from oral retells or other sources. Discuss the results and consequences (e.g., low grades on assignments or tests).

3. SAY, *"How many of you were happy with how much you remembered? How many of you would like to do better? Today I am going to teach you about a strategy to help you remember what you read. This strategy has been used with lots of kids just like you and it really helped them get much better at remembering what they read."*

DEVELOP THE STRATEGY AND SELF-REGULATION

STEP 1: **Develop background knowledge**

1. SAY, *"The strategy is called TRAP. It's like a trap because it will help you catch information and remember it."* Show the TRAP poster.

2. Put out the mnemonic chart/poster so that only the heading "TRAP" shows. Uncover each part of the strategy as you introduce and discuss it.

   SAY, *"The strategy is easy to remember because the word TRAP is a word you already know. Each letter of TRAP stands for a step that you do. It's really important for you to learn the steps really well. It will help you use the strategy more effectively and that will help you remember what you read."*

"There are four steps to the TRAP strategy. You do all four steps for every paragraph you read. If you use the TRAP strategy it will make it much easier to understand and remember what you just read—it helps us TRAP the important information that we read."

3. Be sure to emphasize that TRAP is a strategy that good readers often use before, during, and after reading.

STEP 2: Discuss TRAP steps

1. Think about what you are going to read. Take the time to consider the reading passage. Think about what students may already know about the passage contents, and what they might need to remember from the reading. At this step, students might scan the title of a reading, and look through a passage for headings and bold words. If they already know something about the passage content that can help them remember it. If they are not familiar with the subject they can expect to definitely learn something new.

2. Read a paragraph. SAY, *"When you begin reading, it is important to remember that you don't try to read the whole passage. Instead you to take one paragraph at a time and make sure you understand that one paragraph before you go on to the next one. It's much easier to remember a small section than a long section such as a whole chapter. How you read is also important. Make sure you read carefully. If you read too fast you won't remember what you've read. You have to understand the words and sentences in the paragraph. While you read, ask yourself if what you read makes sense. If you read a sentence and it doesn't make sense, be sure to go back and reread the sentence to understand it."*

3. Ask yourself what were the main idea and two supporting details.

   SAY, *"When you are done reading the paragraph you should make sure you know the main idea and at least two supporting details from the paragraph. The main idea tells you what the paragraph is mostly about. It's the most important information in the paragraph. You should also find at least two important details about the main idea. Important details back up or help explain that main idea. Knowing those details makes it easier for you to understand and remember the main idea of the paragraph."*

4. Paraphrase the main idea and supporting details.

   SAY, *"This step is where you put the main idea and details into your own words. Thinking about how to put the important information in your own words is really important because that helps you to trap the information in your head. Don't try to remember the main idea or supporting detail sentences word for word; it's easier to remember if you put them in your own words."*

STEP 3: Obtaining commitment

1. SAY, *"I want you to try using the TRAP strategy because it can help you to remember more of what you read. If you use TRAP and try your best you will soon be a much better reader. You will start getting better grades on your assignments and quizzes or tests."*

2. SAY, *"The TRAP strategy works, but it's going to require some effort on your part. I will work with you and help you to learn the strategy, but I need you to promise to learn the strategy and try your hardest."* Get students' commitment.

STEP 4: Set a goal

1. Show the graph. SAY, *"When we practice we will graph the results. This will show you how much better you are getting at remembering what you have read. Let's set a goal for our next practice."* Discuss why goal setting is important and reasons or places students might set goals.

2. SAY, *"Look at what your last score was and decide what you want your goal to be. Then draw a line on the graph to show what your first goal will be."* Help students set realistic goals. Set a goal that is not too high and can easily be met with effort. Be sure all students are setting goals and writing their goals on the goal chart. SAY, *"Okay, I see a lot of very good goals, and if you use the TRAP strategy you are more likely to meet your goals. You might even go higher than your goal on the first day."*

STEP 5: Wrap-up

SAY, *"For next time, I want you to be thinking about some places that you might use the TRAP strategy. Think about the steps I taught you and how you can use the strategy on anything you read. Tomorrow I am going to ask you some places where you might use the strategy. Also, I am going to quiz you on the steps of TRAP. I want you to be able to tell me the steps of TRAP and what you do at each step."*

LESSON 2

Model TRAP

LESSON OVERVIEW

In the lesson the teacher and students will discuss the strategy and practice finding main idea and details (prerequisite for strategy use). The teacher will model strategy use, students will start to memorize the strategy.

STUDENT OBJECTIVES

Students will be able to identify main ideas and supporting details. Students will be able to state the steps of TRAP and the actions at each step.

MATERIALS

For each student: reading passage with two to four paragraphs; graph (i.e., goal chart); main idea and details worksheet.

SET THE CONTEXT FOR STUDENT LEARNING

 1. SAY, *"Yesterday I told you about a strategy. Who can tell me the steps of that strategy? (Pause for responses.) Wow, you remembered a lot of the strategy. Tomorrow I will ask you to write the steps of the strategy from memory. Remember that you need to remember the steps and you need to know what you do at each step."*

 2. SAY, *"Today, we are going to practice using the strategy. Before we practice using it, did you think about some places where you might use the TRAP strategy?"* Solicit student responses and add some of your own (e.g., textbook reading, social studies homework, science homework, reading a story). Write the list on the board and discuss each idea. SAY, *"See, there are a lot of places that the TRAP strategy can be used. I am noticing that anywhere I read to understand or to learn I can use the TRAP strategy."*

DEVELOP THE STRATEGY AND SELF-REGULATION

STEP 1:	Practice finding main idea and details (prerequisite for strategy use)

 1. SAY, *"One really important part of TRAP is finding the main idea. The main idea is what the paragraph is mostly about. It's the most important point that the author is trying to make. There are some tricks that can help you find the main idea."*

- *"First, sometimes the author writes out the main idea for you. The first sentence is often the topic sentence (it tells you what the paragraph is about). But you have to be careful, because sometimes the last sentence is the topic sentence."*

- SAY, *"Sometimes the author does not state the main idea directly. It's implied. You have to figure it out yourself. In this case a good trick is to look for words or ideas that are repeated several times in the paragraph. Often these will give you a clue to the main idea."*

2. SAY, *"We are going to practice finding the main idea. I have a paragraph here, and I want you to try to find the main idea."* Provide students copies or show on the overhead. Read the paragraph aloud while students follow along.

3. SAY, *"What was the main idea of this paragraph?"* If students are struggling, change vocabulary by saying, *"What was that whole paragraph talking about? Great! How did you know that was the main idea?"* Note that it was in the title, the words were written multiple times in the paragraph, or other attributes of the text.

4. SAY, *"This paragraph also gives us additional information about that main idea. Now let's see if you can find at least two important details in this paragraph, just like the TRAP strategy asks us to do."* For student responses, accept anything other than the main idea as a detail and point out how there are often *more* than just two details in the paragraph.

5. SAY, *"Let's practice on another paragraph, and this time, let's write our answers down."* Monitor the students while they find the main idea and details again; help students who are struggling to find the main idea and details.

6. Have the students practice paraphrasing their main idea and details, those identified on the worksheet. This can be done by having students write a paraphrase of the paragraph or passage or by having students pair up and verbally paraphrase what they read.

STEP 2: Think-Aloud: Model use of TRAP and thought process

1. SAY, *"Now I want to show you how to use the TRAP strategy. I am going to use the TRAP strategy on this selection (hold up the selection, which should be at least four paragraphs) and then I am going to ask you to try using the TRAP strategy."*

    • Start by using some self-statements such as: *"Wow, this is really long—but that's okay."*

    • SAY, *"I have my TRAP strategy and that will help me remember what I am reading! I can do this."* Be sure to stress that using TRAP will help them remember.

2. Show students the TRAP self-monitoring sheet. SAY, *"This sheet has the letters for TRAP written out on it. I am going to use this sheet to help me remember to do all the steps of TRAP. Each time I do a step, I will put a check mark in the box. I'll do this for each paragraph. That way I won't forget any steps."*

3. Begin by stating the first step of the TRAP strategy, *"The first thing I need to do is Think about why I'm reading. I am reading to get the main idea and important details. I know the first step, but if I forget a step I can look back at my poster for now."* Point to TRAP poster. *"I need to think about what I am going to read, so that is the first thing I am going to do."*

4. Model the first step including statements such as:

    • I know I am going to have a quiz on this reading, so I need to understand it.

    • I don't know much about this topic, but I bet I'm going to learn a lot about it from this passage.

5. SAY, *"Now that I have some ideas about what I might learn from the reading I can move on to the second step. I know the second step of the TRAP strategy is 'R' which stands for 'read a paragraph,' so that is the first thing I am going to do. I need to remember to read carefully because that will help me remember. After I have finished the second step, it's time to move on to the third step. Okay, I did the 'R' of the TRAP strategy; I read a paragraph and I did a good job. I'll mark it off on the TRAP chart to show that I did it. Now I am on the third step of the strategy, 'A'. I know that 'A' stands for 'ask myself what was the main idea and important details,' so the first thing I am going to do is find the main idea of this paragraph—oh, here it is (say main idea out loud and tell how you knew it was the main idea), and now*

I can find the important details…hmm." Say the details out loud, continuing to use self-statements: *"I did it"* or *"that wasn't bad at all!"* Check off the third step on the TRAP chart and indicate to the students that you have checked it off.

6. State that you have finished the first, second, and third steps. SAY, *"So that leaves only one more step to do! I know that the fourth step of my TRAP strategy is 'P'—'put it into my own words.' I know I can do it because I read the paragraph and I found the main idea and details. I need to be careful to have a good paraphrase because that will help me remember the information. I have to be sure to put the information in my own words."* Model for the class by paraphrasing the main idea and the supporting details. *"Wow! I did it. I did the whole strategy, and it was very easy and it helped me remember what I was reading."*

7. Start the strategy over again. Students need to understand that you do the strategy multiple times in a longer reading. SAY, *"I see that there are still three (or however many are left) more paragraphs to read, and that means that I have to do the TRAP strategy three more times. That's okay; it was easy the last time I did it. Now I need to start the strategy over again. I've already thought about what I'm going to read so I can check that step off. I just need to do the last three steps."* Continue until the section is completed.

STEP 3:   Guided practice

1. After the student has watched the teacher model the strategy for two paragraphs (modeling her or his thought process and self-statements), the students should practice on the remaining paragraphs.

2. SAY, *"Now that you have seen me use the TRAP strategy, it's your turn to try using it. There are two more paragraphs on this page, so how many times will you need to use the TRAP strategy."* Students should respond *"two."* Guide them if necessary. *"Okay, so what is the first thing you do when you are using the TRAP strategy?"* Students should respond: *"'T'—think about what you are going to read."* *"And, what are some things you might think?"* Wait for students' response.

   "Okay, go ahead and read this paragraph. Use the TRAP checklist to make sure that you do every step for each paragraph."

3. When the students are finished reading the paragraph, prompt them for the second step. Students should write down the main idea and two important details for this lesson on the provided worksheet. Ask students to state their main idea and details. When they have done this, prompt them to the third step of the TRAP strategy—ask the students to tell a peer what the paragraph was about. Make sure the paraphrases capture the gist of the paragraph. If not, discuss how the paraphrases could be improved. Repeat the steps for the remaining paragraphs. When the class has completed the passage, ask students to put the passage away and tell a peer whatever they can remember from the entire passage. Praise them and remind them of their goal.

WRAP-UP

SAY, *"Tonight, I want you to be thinking about some places that you might use the TRAP strategy. Think about the steps I taught you and how you can use the strategy on anything you read. Maybe if you have some homework tonight, you could try using the TRAP strategy. Tomorrow I am going to ask you to write whatever you can remember from the strategy and I am also going to ask you whether or not you used the strategy and, if you did, some places where you used it."*

LESSON 3
TRAP Guided Practice

LESSON OVERVIEW

The purpose of this lesson is to provide additional guided practice. The teacher will facilitate transfer of ownership by gradually lessening support while students use instructional materials.

STUDENT OBJECTIVES

The students will use TRAP with teacher support.

MATERIALS

For each student: reading passage, retell checklist for the reading passage, graph (i.e., goal chart)

SET THE CONTEXT FOR STUDENT LEARNING

1. Remove the poster or cover when testing for memorization.

 2. SAY, *"Yesterday we talked about TRAP. I want you to write down each step in TRAP. Remember to put down what you do at each step also."* Provide enough time for students to write, praise what they recall, and fill in what is missing from the steps. *"Great, you remembered a lot/the whole strategy. Today, we are going to practice using the strategy again, and tomorrow I will have you write the steps again to see what you remember and if you have memorized it yet. Before we practice, did you think about some places that you could use the TRAP strategy?"* Solicit student responses and add some of your own: textbook, reading a letter, reading a story, social studies homework, science homework, and so forth. *"Did you use the TRAP strategy in any of those places last night? I would like you to try using the TRAP strategy in other places too, not just with me. The more you use the strategy, the better you will be at it and the closer you will be to your goal."*

SUPPORT THE STRATEGY AND SELF-REGULATION

STEP 1: Guided practice

 1. SAY, *"Today I have a different passage for you to read with a partner."* Allow students time to find a partner. *"Remember to use the TRAP strategy on every paragraph. Use the TRAP checklist to help you remember to do each step. So, how many times will you use the strategy for this passage?"* Responses should be the number of paragraphs. SAY, *"After reading each paragraph, write down the main idea and important details on your scratch paper."*

 2. SAY, *"While you are using the TRAP strategy, I want you to remember that you set a goal. Everyone look to see what your goal is. If you use the TRAP strategy on every paragraph, you will remember more and you will be closer to your goal, or you might even meet or go further than your goal!"*

3. Walk around the room and guide students through strategy use as needed. It is best to intervene only if they are struggling with the main idea and details.

STEP 2: **Do oral retell with students**

 1. SAY, *"Okay, you used the TRAP strategy on that whole passage on every paragraph. Now I want to see how much you remember."* Use the retell procedure for students. Once all the students are finished, show them how to graph their performance.

2. Ask the students if they met their goals. Praise them, and remind them that using the TRAP strategy will make them better readers and help them to continue meeting their goals.

 3. Students who exceeded their goals can set new ones. SAY, *"I can see many of you are working hard, and if you did not meet your goal, review the steps of the TRAP strategy."* You may want to check on the students who did not meet their goals to make sure the goals they set were realistic; help them to lower their goals if necessary so they can meet their goals next time, and provide praise for their effort.

WRAP-UP

 1. SAY, *"Tonight, I want you to think about the steps I taught you and how you can use the strategy on anything you read. Maybe if you have some homework tonight, you could try using the TRAP strategy. Tomorrow I am going to ask you to write out the steps in the strategy and I am also going to ask you whether or not you used the strategy and, if you did, some places where you used the strategy."*

2. Remind students that they will need to come to the next session, write out TRAP, and tell what it means from memory.

LESSON 4
Fade TRAP Checklist

LESSON OVERVIEW

The teacher will provide guided practice in students' use of TRAP while supporting the students as they learn to create their own TRAP checklist.

STUDENT OBJECTIVES

Students will create their own TRAP checklist and use this while reading a passage.

MATERIALS

For each student: reading passage; retell checklist on reading passage; graph (i.e., goal chart)

SET THE CONTEXT FOR STUDENT LEARNING

1. Remove the poster or cover when testing for memorization.

2. SAY, *"I want you to write out the steps in the strategy I taught you. Put down each step and what you do at each step."* Allow students to write, praise what they recall, and fill in what is missing from the steps. *"Wow, you remembered a lot/the whole strategy. Today, we are going to practice using the strategy, and tomorrow I will have you write the steps again to see what you remember and if you have memorized it yet. But before we practice using it, did you use the TRAP strategy last night?"* Solicit student responses and add some of your own: textbook, reading a letter, reading a story, social studies homework, science homework, and so forth.

3. SAY, *"I would like you to try using the TRAP strategy in other places too, not just with me. The more you use the strategy, the better you will be at it and the more you will remember important information from what you read."*

SUPPORT THE STRATEGY AND SELF-REGULATION

1. SAY, *"Today I have a different passage for you to read. While you are using the TRAP strategy, I want you to remember that you set a goal. Everyone look to see what your goal is. Today you are going to work without the checklist. Instead, of using the checklist, you will write down T-R-A-P in the margins as you do each paragraph. Writing down the steps will help to remind you to do each step. If you use the TRAP strategy on every paragraph, you will remember more and you will be closer to your goal, or you might even go further than your goal! So, if this passage has eight (or however many) paragraphs, how many times will you need to do the TRAP strategy (eight)?"*

2. Encourage students to use their paper and pencil to write main idea and details.

   • Some students may choose to circle main idea and underline details or may choose to use a highlighter.

   • Walk around the room and guide students through strategy use as needed. It is best to intervene only if they are struggling with the main idea and details.

3. Do retells with students, have students calculate the percent correct and fill in their goal sheets. Do retells individually with the students. Remind students how to graph their performance. Walk around providing assistance on graphing. Ask the class if they met their goals. Praise them and remind them that using the TRAP strategy will make them better readers and help them to continue meeting their goals. Students who exceeded their goals can set new ones, as appropriate.

You may want to check on the students who did not meet their goals to make sure the goals they set were realistic, to help them to lower their goals if necessary so they can meet their goals next time, and to provide praise for their effort.

WRAP-UP

Make sure to note which students are still struggling with the strategy. They will need extra instruction. Thank the students for working hard. Encourage students to use the strategy on their homework.

TRAP without Visual Reminders

LESSON OVERVIEW

The teacher will support student use of TRAP without visual reminders.

STUDENT OBJECTIVES

Students will use TRAP without checklists or visual reminders while reading a passage.

MATERIALS

For each student: reading passage, retell checklist on reading passage, graph (i.e., goal chart)

SET THE CONTEXT FOR STUDENT LEARNING

1. Remove the poster or cover when testing for memorization.

2. SAY, *"We have been talking about a strategy all week. By now, you should know the steps of this strategy. I want to play a game to see how well you remember the steps of the strategy (e.g., ball toss, 'concentration' in pairs). Today, we are going to continue using our strategy, but before we practice using it, did you think about some places that you could use the TRAP strategy?"* Solicit student responses and add some of your own: textbook, reading a letter, reading a story, social studies homework, science homework, and so forth. *"And, did you use the TRAP strategy in any of those places last night?"*

3. Discuss any changes students have made to the strategy (e.g., do they write main idea and details, or do they highlight the main ideas as they read a text?).

4. SAY, *"I would like you to try using the TRAP strategy in other places too, not just with me. Remember, the more you use the strategy, the better you will be remembering important information from what you read."*

5. Discuss why it is important to remember and understand what we read—tests, assignments, and learning new information in classes.

SUPPORT THE STRATEGY AND SELF-REGULATION

STEP 1: Guided practice without visual reminders

1. SAY, *"Today I have a different passage for you to read. While you are using the TRAP strategy, I want you to remember that you set a goal. Everyone look to see what your goal is. Using your TRAP strategy will help you remember more information from this reading passage. So, if this passage has eight paragraphs, how many times will you need to do the TRAP strategy (eight)?"*

2. Encourage them to use their paper and pencil to write main idea and details.

3. Walk around the room and guide students through strategy use as needed. It is best to intervene only if they are struggling with the main idea and details.

STEP 2: **Do retell, calculate performance, and fill in goal sheet**

 1. SAY, *"Okay, you used the TRAP strategy on that whole passage, on every paragraph. Now, I want you to retell what you can remember about the passage. Try to retell the passage without looking back."*

2. Allow time for students to retell. Once all students are finished, ask students to graph their performance. Walk around providing assistance on graphing.

3. Ask the class if they met their goals. Praise them and remind them that using the TRAP strategy will make them better readers and help them to continue meeting their goals. Students who exceeded their goals can set new ones.

4. SAY, *"I can see many of you are working hard, and if you did not meet your goal, review the steps of the TRAP strategy."* You may want to check on the students who did not meet their goals to make sure the goals they set were realistic, to help them to lower their goals if necessary so they can meet their goals next time, and to provide praise for effort.

WRAP-UP

Tell the students they have been doing an excellent job learning and using the TRAP strategy. Encourage them to use the strategy on other reading or homework (e.g., social studies text, science text, language arts homework).

LESSON 6
Independent Practice

LESSON OVERVIEW

The teacher provides the students with independent practice in using TRAP.

STUDENT OBJECTIVES

The students will use TRAP independently without the use of checklists or visual reminders.

MATERIALS

For each student: reading passage, retell checklist on reading passage, graph (i.e., goal chart)

SET THE CONTEXT FOR STUDENT LEARNING

1. Remove or cover the poster when testing for memorization.

2. SAY, *"First, let's review the steps."* Call on students to give the steps in TRAP and what is done at each step. Ask students "why" questions about each step (e.g., *Why do we think about what we are going to read? Why do we make paraphrases?*).

3. SAY, *"Today will be our last day to practice using the strategy in class, but before we practice using it, did you use the TRAP strategy last night or in other classes?"* Solicit student responses and add some of your own: textbook, reading a letter, reading a story, social studies homework, science homework, and so forth.

SUPPORT THE STRATEGY AND SELF-REGULATION

STEP 1: Guided practice without visual reminders

1. SAY, *"Today I have a different passage for you to read. While you are using the TRAP strategy, I want you to remember that you set a goal. Everyone look to see what your goal is. If you use the TRAP strategy on every paragraph, you will remember more and you will be closer to your goal, or you might even go further than your goal! So, if this passage has eight paragraphs, how many times will you need to do the TRAP strategy (eight)?"*

2. Encourage them to use the strategy however they want (e.g., they can write notes; they can highlight as they read).

3. Walk around the room and guide students through strategy use as needed. It is best to intervene only if they are struggling with the main idea and details.

Do retells with students and graph performance

1. Do retells with students and show them how to graph their performance. Walk around providing assistance on graphing.

2. Ask the class if they met their goals. Praise them and remind them that using the TRAP strategy will make them better readers and help them to continue meeting their goals. Students who exceeded their goals can set new ones.

3. SAY, *"I can see many of you are working hard. If you did not meet your goal, review the steps of the TRAP strategy."* You may want to check on the students who did not meet their goals to make sure the goals they set were realistic, to help them to lower their goals if necessary so they can meet their goals next time, and to provide praise for their effort.

4. SAY, *"Now, I want you to tell a partner what you can remember from what you just read. Tell your partner as if he or she had never read this passage."*

WRAP-UP

1. Discuss with the class how the passages that they have been using to practice may look different from other types of reading they have to do in school (e.g., chapter books like those in the novels unit, textbooks).

2. Explain that you can modify the TRAP strategy to fit the type of text you are reading. For example, if you are reading a novel and there is a lot of dialog and short paragraphs, it may be better to paraphrase a chapter instead of each paragraph.

REFERENCE

Schumaker, J.B., Denton, P.H., & Deshler, D.D. (1984). *The paraphrasing strategy.* Lawrence: University of Kansas.

TRAP Mnemonic Chart

T Think before you read

R Read a paragraph

A Ask "What is the paragraph mostly about? What is the most important information?"

P Paraphrase the important information

How much can I remember?

Write your goal at the top. Draw a line to show your goal. After you read, fill in your chart to show how much you remembered.

Goal								
100								
90								
70								
60								
50								
40								
30								
20								
10								
	Quiz 1	Quiz 2	Quiz 3	Quiz 4	Quiz 5	Quiz 6	Quiz 7	Quiz 8

Name: _____

Practice Paragraphs for Lesson 2

For the early pioneers, the trip west along the Oregon Trail was very dangerous. Many people died along the way. Some wagon trains were attacked by hostile Indians. Others became trapped in the mountains without food and many of their members starved to death. People drowned in dangerous river crossings. Because the pioneers were crossing open country, the violent storms that occur frequently on the great plains were a serious danger. Illness was a constant threat, and many people died of diseases. Even a minor injury such as a small cut could become infected and result in death. Only the strongest and the luckiest were able to complete the journey.

Jupiter is the fifth planet from the sun. It is much bigger than the earth. You could put more that 1,400 planets the size of earth inside Jupiter. Because Jupiter is so much bigger, you would weigh more that 10 times what you weigh on earth. Because it is much farther from the sun, it is very cold on Jupiter. In fact, it is so cold that most of Jupiter is made of frozen gases. Jupiter does not have oceans and continents like the earth. The only solid part of Jupiter is a small rocky core. The surface of Jupiter is a violent place which is constantly covered by clouds and where winds can sometimes blow at nearly 600 km per hour. Huge storms rage over the surface of Jupiter. Some are so large that they can be seen from earth. One storm called the Great Red Spot has lasted for over 300 years. In sum, Jupiter is very different from the earth.

When computers were just invented they were as big as a small house and it took dozens of people to make them work. The first computer used vacuum tubes, which were about the size of your fist and were very hot. In fact, early computers had to have their own air conditioning systems. If the air conditioning failed, the computer would shut down or even catch fire. To use the computer you could not simply sit down at a keyboard and type. Instead, you had to use punch cards, which were fed to the machine. There was no monitor to watch. The only output device was a printer. Early computers were not nearly as powerful as they are now, either. For example, there is more computing power in the average cell phone than there were in all the computers used in the first manned mission to the moon!

Flesch-Kincaid grade level: 6.36

TRAP Checklist

Paragraph	T	R	A	P
1				
2				
3				
4				
5				
6				

Finding the Main Idea

Start by reading the paragraph. If you can't figure out the main idea, here are some suggestions:

1. Look at the first sentence of the paragraph. This might be the main idea.

2. Look for repetitions of the same word or words in the paragraph. The main idea should be mentioned several times in the paragraph.

Now let's summarize the main idea and supporting details!

What is this paragraph about? _____

_____

_____

_____

_____

What are some details in this paragraph? _____

_____

_____

_____

_____

Chapter 6

TRAP IDEAS for Summarizing

TRAP

Think before your read

Read a paragraph

Ask "What is the paragraph mostly about? What is the most important information?"

Paraphrase the important information

IDEAS

Identify important details to support the main idea

Delete trivial details

Eliminate redundant details

Add a term for a list of words or concepts

Summarize

MATERIALS

Six-paragraph TRAP Notes Checklist and Outline

TRAP IDEAS Mnemonic Chart

TRAP IDEAS Checklist

Notes Outline (a)

IDEAS Checklist

Notes Outline (b)

Peer Checklist—Summary Evaluation

TRAP IDEAS are strategies to help students develop written summaries. Lessons for teaching students to use information learned, after developing the main idea with TRAP, and to write summaries are presented in this chapter. These lessons are an extension of TRAP (**T**hink before your read, **R**ead a paragraph, **A**sk "What is the paragraph mostly about? What is the most important information?"; **P**araphrase the important information). In Lesson 2, students are explicitly taught how to transition from oral retells, taught in Chapter 5, to writing notes while using the TRAP strategy. The teacher models how to use the TRAP strategy to create a notes outline. These notes are then used to create a written summary with IDEAS (**I**dentify important details to support the main idea, **D**elete trivial details, **E**liminate redundant details, **A**dd a term for a list of words or concepts, **S**ummarize). Prior to beginning instruction in TRAP IDEAS, it is suggested that students learn TRAP.

Introduce and Discuss Using TRAP for Writing Summaries with IDEAS

LESSON OVERVIEW

IDEAS summary strategy will be introduced.

STUDENT OBJECTIVE

Students will learn the steps of IDEAS.

MATERIALS

TRAP IDEAS mnemonic chart, TRAP IDEAS worksheet

SET THE CONTEXT FOR STUDENT LEARNING

Tell students that they will be learning a new strategy today. The strategy will work with the TRAP strategy that they previously learned. Orally test for student knowledge of the steps of TRAP and tell the students that the new strategy will expand on TRAP.

DEVELOP THE STRATEGY AND SELF-REGULATION

STEP 1: Introduce IDEAS

1. SAY, *"I am going to teach you a strategy for summarizing something you read. The strategy is called 'IDEAS' and we use it with our TRAP strategy. We will learn how to use the steps of IDEAS while using our TRAP strategy to 'TRAP' main ideas and details in textbooks."*

2. SAY, *"IDEAS is a strategy that we use after we read a passage or a chapter. And while we are reading the passage, we should be using our TRAP strategy on every paragraph."*

Brainstorm reasons why summarizing what we read is important or how it can help us:

* It makes us check for understanding.
* We have to put what we read into our own words.
* If we can't summarize, then we probably didn't understand what we read.

Brainstorm places that summarizing might be necessary:

* on a test
* to show what you know or understand
* in language arts class
* for a paper
* for a book report

3. SAY, *"Summarizing is an important skill that you will need in many content areas and classes, such as science, social studies, and language arts. This strategy will help you to understand what you read and write summaries."*

Remind students that they already know the steps of TRAP. Tell them that they will be learning IDEAS today.

STEP 2: I—Identify important details to support the main idea

1. Give each student the IDEAS mnemonic chart. Tell them that they will need to look at each step on their sheet as you are talking about the steps. Point to the letters I, D, E, A, and S as you discuss each step.

2. Cover your paper so only the first step shows. SAY, *"The first step of the IDEAS strategy is to identify important details that support the main idea of the section or passage you just read using the TRAP strategy. Sometimes when we are reading a textbook, there will be sections within a chapter that all have a similar main idea—this means that all of the paragraphs in the section will be providing specific details on that same main idea. Our first step is to go back over our outline we made with our TRAP strategy and identify what the main idea is and the details that support that main idea. We do that using a highlighter."*

3. Discuss different formats of content textbooks to ensure students understand that this strategy can be used on whole chapters or smaller sections. For example, a science text may have a chapter on the scientific method. Within that chapter, there will be several sections discussing each step of the scientific method. Individual summaries could be created for each section of the chapter.

STEP 3: D—Delete trivial details

Uncover the second step on the IDEAS worksheet. SAY, *"Once I have identified the main idea of the passage and important, supporting details, I need to see if my notes outline has some details that aren't that important or do not support the main idea. In other words, you want to go through your notes and delete or cross out details that don't relate to the main idea; the word we use for these details is trivial."*

STEP 4: E—Eliminate redundant details

Point out that this step is similar to the previous step. SAY, *"After you have deleted trivial details, you may notice that there are some details in your notes outline that are very similar or redundant. These details should also be crossed out, or eliminated, because we will not want to include the same details multiple times in our summary."*

STEP 5: A—Add a term for a list of words of concepts

SAY, *"Once I have finished crossing out details that I won't need for my summary, I need to go through my notes outline one more time to see if there are some lists or concepts that can be combined. For example, when I created my outline using TRAP, maybe I wrote a list of terms that are all related such as: 'The pioneers traveled with horses, oxen, cattle, and donkeys.' This list could be shortened or combined by using the word 'animals' in my outline. I can add that term to my notes outline"*:

The pioneers traveled with ~~horses, oxen, cattle, and donkeys~~ animals.

STEP 6: S—Summarize

SAY, *"When I finish making changes to my notes, I need to create a written summary of what I read. Creating a summary means I have to take what I have read and put it into my own words, and because I created a notes outline and highlighted important details, it should be easy for me to create a summary."*

> This passage was about the pioneers traveling west to begin new lives. They traveled in covered wagons as a group. These groups of wagons were called wagon trains. The wagons contained all the belongings of the pioneers. The pioneers traveled west with their whole family and their animals. It took months to travel west.

STEP 7: Use IDEAS until the entire chapter or selection is summarized

SAY, *"Once I have finished the last step in IDEAS, I need to make sure I summarized everything I read. Sometimes this means I will have to use the IDEAS strategy multiple times in a chapter."*

WRAP-UP

Quickly check for memorization of strategy steps.

SAY, *"In the next lesson I am going to show you how to use TRAP and IDEAS together to read a passage or chapter and create a written summary."*

Remind students that you will check next time to see if they remember TRAP and IDEAS.

Writing Notes Using TRAP

LESSON OVERVIEW

This lesson provides a transition from the oral activities completed in the TRAP lessons in Chapter 5 to writing notes. The teacher will model writing notes after using the TRAP strategy.

STUDENT OBJECTIVE

Students will complete a TRAP outline while following the teacher-led modeling lesson.

MATERIALS

"California Gold Rush" (*see* Appendix); TRAP outline overhead or PowerPoint, TRAP outline/checklist for each student

SET THE CONTEXT FOR STUDENT LEARNING

Review the TRAP strategy. Demonstrate using TRAP with IDEAS. Tell students that you will be teaching them how to use the TRAP strategy to take notes. Taking notes makes writing a summary easier because you don't have to reread the whole passage or chapter to write your summary.

DEVELOP THE STRATEGY AND SELF-REGULATION

STEP 1: Model writing notes with TRAP

1. Tell the students that you will show them how to write notes with TRAP when reading a passage. Tell them that you will first review the steps of TRAP with the "California Gold Rush" passage. Quickly go through all TRAP steps. Encourage students to support you in this process.

2. After reading a paragraph and completing a collaborative oral retell, SAY, *"I did a good job using my TRAP strategy, but I'm going to write the main idea and details down because I'm taking notes as I read."* Model how you write notes for the main idea and details in outline format:

    1. Main idea

        a. Detail

        b. Detail

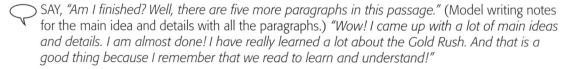 SAY, *"Am I finished? Well, there are five more paragraphs in this passage."* (Model writing notes for the main idea and details with all the paragraphs.) *"Wow! I came up with a lot of main ideas and details. I am almost done! I have really learned a lot about the Gold Rush. And that is a good thing because I remember that we read to learn and understand!"*

STEP 2: Model a retell

Model how you will use the outline to help you with the oral retell of the entire passage. Ask the students, in pairs, to practice using the outline for an oral retell.

WRAP-UP

Tell the students that in the next lessons they will use the outline for writing a written retell or summary.

Repeat this lesson with another passage for students having difficulty taking notes.

LESSON 3

Model Creating a Summary

LESSON OVERVIEW

The teacher will model how to use TRAP IDEAS together using a Think-Aloud.

STUDENT OBJECTIVE

Students will complete a written summary.

MATERIALS

"Jefferson is Chosen as President of the United States" (or other reading passage), TRAP notes checklist, TRAP IDEAS mnemonic chart, TRAP IDEAS worksheet

SET THE CONTEXT FOR STUDENT LEARNING

Orally test for student knowledge of the steps of TRAP IDEAS. Tell the students that they will watch the teacher use the TRAP IDEAS strategies together to identify main ideas and create written summaries.

DEVELOP THE STRATEGY AND SELF-REGULATION

STEP 1: Discuss the modeling

SAY, *"Today I am going to show you how to use TRAP IDEAS. First, I am going to read through the whole passage using the TRAP strategy. Then, I am going to create my notes outline. Finally, I will write a summary of what I have read. While I am doing this, I want you to follow along."*

STEP 2: Model TRAP

Start by getting out the reading passage, the TRAP notes checklist, the mnemonic chart, and the TRAP IDEAS worksheet.

SAY, *"What am I supposed to be doing? I have this passage that I need to read. Well, I know my TRAP strategy helps to make sure I understand what I'm reading. I've used my TRAP strategy a lot, so this should be easy. First step, think about what I'm about to read. Well, the title of this passage is 'Jefferson is Chosen as President of the United States.' That doesn't really tell me a lot, but it makes me think I will be learning about Thomas Jefferson."*

SAY, *"Okay. Step 1 of TRAP is done. Step 2 is to read a paragraph. Easy enough."* Read the first paragraph aloud. Have students follow along.

SAY, *"Now I need to ask myself what was the main idea and important details. Well, I remember learning how to find the main idea. One way is to check the first sentence of the paragraph because that can be where the main idea is stated....Yes! I think that's it! The main idea is definitely that Thomas Jefferson became the president."* Highlight, underline, or circle the main idea in the paragraph. Then, write the main idea on the notes worksheet. Do the same with two details.

SAY, *"Phew! One more step of TRAP! The last step is 'paraphrase.' I'm going to look at my paragraph."* Orally paraphrase the paragraph, praise yourself, then continue to think aloud as you read the remainder of the passage.

STEP 3: Model IDEAS

SAY, *"Now that I have read the whole passage and created my notes outline, I'm ready to use my IDEAS strategy to write a summary. This passage had a few headings. I think I'll have to write more than one summary."*

"The first step is 'Identify important details to support the main idea.'" Look at your notes outline. *"I think the main idea of the passage is the main idea from the first paragraph, Thomas Jefferson being president and all the things he did."* Put a star next to the main idea on the worksheet.

SAY, *"Now I should go through my notes with a highlighter and highlight details that are related to the main idea."* Go through the notes outline, highlighting details related to the main idea. Think aloud as you read and highlight.

SAY, *"The next step is 'Delete trivial details.' If the main idea is Thomas Jefferson's presidency, I should go through my notes page to see if there are details I don't need for my summary or details that aren't really related."* Go through the notes outline; cross out any trivial details.

SAY, *"The next step in IDEAS is to 'Eliminate redundant details.' For this step I need to go through my notes outline again to see if I have details that are the same or similar."* Go through the notes outline, cross out redundant details. Praise yourself.

SAY, *"Wow. I only have two more steps of my IDEAS strategy left. I'm doing great and I feel like I know a lot about the things Thomas Jefferson did when he was the president. I need to keep going. The next step is 'Add a term for a list of words of concepts.' I remember that this is the last time I'm going to go through my notes outline before I create my summary. Well, this detail says 'small farms were important in Tennessee, Kentucky, Georgia, and Alabama.' I wonder if there is a term or word I can use instead of this list… I think all those states are in the South. So I'm going to change the list to say 'Southern states'—so now my detail reads: 'Small farms were important in the Southern states.' Awesome! Now I'm ready to write my summary!"*

SAY, *"My final step in IDEAS is to 'Summarize.' I can do that. It should be fairly easy because I read the chapter using the TRAP strategy and took notes."*

On chart paper or on an overhead, write a summary of the chapter. Think aloud as you write. Ask for student participation as appropriate. Refer to your notes as you write the summary.

STEP 4: Discuss the strategy

Brainstorm with students how using TRAP IDEAS can help us remember more from what we read (e.g., while we are reading and writing and summarizing, we are constantly checking for understanding).

WRAP UP

Quickly check for memorization of strategy steps.

SAY, *"In the next lesson you will write a summary of a passage you have already read. It should be easy because you've already read the chapter using your TRAP strategy!"*

Remind students that you will check next time to see if they remember TRAP and IDEAS.

LESSON 4

Guided Practice

LESSON OVERVIEW

To focus on creating summaries with the IDEAS worksheet, a passage previously read with TRAP will be used. The teacher will circulate, closely monitoring each student's ability to write in note form and to summarize in writing.

STUDENT OBJECTIVE

Students will practice summarizing a previously read passage.

MATERIALS

Passage from previous TRAP lesson ("The Battle of Gettysburg," "Volcanoes"), blank TRAP outline, IDEAS worksheet, Peer checklist—summary evaluation

SET THE CONTEXT FOR STUDENT LEARNING

Orally test memorization of TRAP and IDEAS.

SUPPORT THE STRATEGY AND SELF-REGULATION

STEP 1: Create notes

Give each student a passage that has been previously read (and/or marked) for main ideas and details. Tell students to transfer the information to the TRAP outline in note form.

STEP 2: IDEAS

1. Tell the students that will write a summary of the passage. Tell them to use their notes and the IDEAS worksheet to guide the creation of their summary. Optional: Students can create summaries in pairs.

2. Circulate and provide assistance as needed.

STEP 3: Peer feedback

1. Tell students that they will be reading their summary to a peer. They will use a checklist to ensure they complete the necessary steps (Peer Checklist Summary Evaluation).

2. Have students pair up. Each student should read his or her written summary aloud. Their partner should give them feedback (following the checklist).

WRAP-UP

Tell students that they will be using the TRAP IDEAS strategy again tomorrow on a longer passage. Repeat this lesson for students having difficulty creating summaries with IDEAS.

LESSON 5

Independent Practice with TRAP IDEAS

LESSON OVERVIEW

Students will apply the TRAP IDEAS strategies to read and summarize a passage. The teacher will circulate, closely monitoring each student's ability to use TRAP for reading, to create a notes outline, and to create a written summary of what they have read.

STUDENT OBJECTIVES

Students will read with TRAP, write notes on an outline, and write a summary using IDEAS.

MATERIALS

"Christopher Columbus" reading passage, blank TRAP outline worksheet (optional), IDEAS checklist (optional)

SET THE CONTEXT FOR STUDENT LEARNING

Orally test memorization of TRAP IDEAS. Have students get in pairs and "quiz" each other on strategy steps.

SUPPORT THE STRATEGY AND SELF-REGULATION

STEP 1: Read with TRAP

Give each student a new passage to read ("Christopher Columbus"). Tell students to use TRAP to read the passage. Tell them to create their own check sheet to monitor all the steps. Students can identify main ideas and details by marking the passage lightly with a pencil or by highlighting.

STEP 2: Write notes

Tell students to transfer the information from the passage to the TRAP outline in note form or to create their own notes outline.

STEP 3: IDEAS

Tell the students that they will write a summary based on the reading. Tell students to use their notes and the IDEAS worksheet to guide their summary. Students may choose to write a summary on a blank piece of paper if they do not require the worksheet as a support.

WRAP-UP

Ask students to get in pairs and read their partner's summary. Remind students that you will check next time to see if they remember TRAP IDEAS. **Scaffold by gradually using longer, more difficult passages with multiple sections as students demonstrate mastery in using TRAP IDEAS to create written summaries. Scaffolding can also be done by changing the materials students use. For example, students start by using the TRAP Notes checklist and outline, then the IDEAS checklist, and finally use only the notes outline.**

TRAP IDEAS Checklist Worksheet

☐ **T**hink about what you are about to read

☐ **R**ead a paragraph

☐ **A**sk myself "What is this paragraph mostly about? What is the most important information?"

☐ **P**araphrase

☐ **I**dentify important details to support the main idea

☐ **D**elete trivial details

☐ **E**liminate redundant details

☐ **A**dd a term for a list of words or concepts

☐ **S**ummarize

TRAP IDEAS Mnemonic Chart

1. Use **TRAP** to read the passage

T Think before you read

R Read a paragraph

A Ask "What is the paragraph mostly about? What is the most important information?"

P Paraphrase the important information

2. Create a notes outline

3. Use **IDEAS** to create your summary

I Identify important details to support the main idea

D Delete trivial details

E Eliminate redundant details

A Add a term for a list of words or concepts

S Summarize

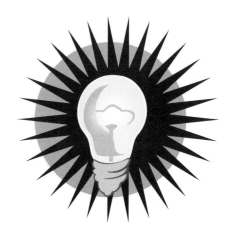

Building Comprehension in Adolescents: Powerful Strategies for Improving Reading and Writing in Content Areas by Linda H. Mason, Ph.D., Robert Reid, Ph.D., and Jessica L. Hagaman, Ph.D.

Notes Outline (a)

1. _____

    a. _____

    b. _____

2. _____

    a. _____

    b. _____

3. _____

    a. _____

    b. _____

4. _____

    a. _____

    b. _____

5. _____

    a. _____

    b. _____

6. _____

    a. _____

    b. _____

IDEAS Checklist Worksheet

After TRAP, I need to use my IDEAS strategy to create a written summary.

1. Go through your notes page

2. Use IDEAS

☐ **I**dentify important details to support the main idea

    ☐ Highlight or put a star next to the important details

☐ **D**elete trivial details

    ☐ Cross out trivial details on your notes outline

☐ **E**liminate redundant details

    ☐ Cross out redundant details on your notes outline

☐ **A**dd a term for a list of words or concepts

    ☐ If there are lists, combine them. Add this to your notes outline

☐ **S**ummarize

_____

_____

_____

_____

_____

_____

_____

_____

_____

_____

_____

_____

_____

_____

_____

_____

_____

_____

Notes Outline (b)

Main idea	
Detail	
Detail	

Main idea	
Detail	
Detail	

Main idea	
Detail	
Detail	

Main idea	
Detail	
Detail	

Main idea	
Detail	
Detail	

Main idea	
Detail	
Detail	

Main idea	
Detail	
Detail	

Peer Checklist Summary Evaluation

☐ Listen to your partner read their summary or read your partner's summary

Questions to evaluate your partner's summary

1. Was the summary written in his or her own words?

  ☐ Yes   ☐ No

2. Was the whole chapter/passage summarized?

  ☐ Yes   ☐ No

☐ Give your partner two positive comments about the summary

☐ Give your partner feedback/ways to improve their summary

☐ Switch! Now it's your turn to read your summary!

TRAP Notes Checklist and Outline

1. ☐ **T**hink about what you are reading

    ☐ **R**ead a paragraph

    ☐ **A**sk myself, "What is this paragraph mostly about? What is the most important information?"

Main idea	
Detail	
Detail	

    ☐ **P**ut it into my own words

2. ☐ **T**hink about what you are reading

    ☐ **R**ead a paragraph

    ☐ **A**sk myself, "What is this paragraph mostly about? What is the most important information?"

Main idea	
Detail	
Detail	

    ☐ **P**ut it into my own words

3. ☐ **T**hink about what you are reading

    ☐ **R**ead a paragraph

    ☐ **A**sk myself, "What is this paragraph mostly about? What is the most important information?"

Main idea	
Detail	
Detail	

    ☐ **P**ut it into my own words

(continued)

CHAPTER 6

TRAP
&
IDEAS

4. ☐ **T**hink about what you are reading

☐ **R**ead a paragraph

☐ **A**sk myself, "What is this paragraph mostly about? What is the most important information?"

Main idea	
Detail	
Detail	

☐ **P**ut it into my own words

5. ☐ **T**hink about what you are reading

☐ **R**ead a paragraph

☐ **A**sk myself, "What is this paragraph mostly about? What is the most important information?"

Main idea	
Detail	
Detail	

☐ **P**ut it into my own words

6. ☐ **T**hink about what you are reading

☐ **R**ead a paragraph

☐ **A**sk myself, "What is this paragraph mostly about? What is the most important information?"

Main idea	
Detail	
Detail	

☐ **P**ut it into my own words

Chapter 7

Think About Reading with TWA

TWA

Think before reading

think **W**hile reading

think **A**fter reading

MATERIALS

TWA Mnemonic Chart

Learning Contract

Self-monitoring Checklist

Self-statement Sheet

Passages for Modeling and Teaching the Strategy:

>Gum

>Man Walks on the Moon

Passages for Peer Practice:

>Pesticides

>Yellowstone

Passages for Independence and Generalization:

>A Letter to a Father

>In Search of Chimpanzees

A blank journal for vocabulary, not included in Chapter 7 materials, should be available for each student.

TWA (**T**hink before reading, think **W**hile reading, think **A**fter reading) is a nine-step multi-component reading comprehension strategy (Mason, 2004). In TWA lessons explicit instruction for self-regulation and for vocabulary development is embedded throughout each lesson. For example, unfamiliar content text vocabulary, and words the author uses to support meaning (e.g., connectors), are noted prior to each lesson, discussed, and recorded in a vocabulary journal.

Initial TWA lessons take time! Given this, we recommend using short simple text (i.e., three to four paragraphs of descriptive or classification text) below the students' independent reading level for teacher-led modeling, group collaborative practice, and initial peer practice. Guided practice lessons can then be scaffolded to include longer passages and a variety of text types. In addition, we have provided retell passages and scoring sheets in the Reading to Learn Appendix. To illustrate instruction, we have provided sample adapted text for each lesson. Teachers have noted that once the procedures are learned, students can apply the strategies efficiently and quickly to meet a number of reading purposes (Mason, in press; Mason, Meadan-Kaplansky, Corso, & Hedin, 2004).

TWA Strategies

Three steps are included in each of the three reading phases (before reading, while reading, and after reading). In "Think before reading," three steps for prior knowledge acquisition are taught. The students examine text structure while completing the first step, "Think about the author's purpose." Using procedures developed from Ogle's (1989) K-W-L strategy (what I Know, what I Want to learn, what I Learned), students develop statements and questions for steps two and three—"think about what you know" and "think about what you want to learn." The three "think While reading" TWA steps are developed from Hansen and Pearson's (1983) (discuss students' previous experience, connect this experience with the text, and share ideas for expanding knowledge), and Graves and Levin's (1989; comprehension monitoring and rereading parts) strategies. Students are taught to monitor their "reading speed," to monitor their understanding by "rereading" when something is not understood and to "link knowledge" by making connections between prior knowledge and the text.

"Think after reading" has two strategy steps developed at the paragraph level ("think about the main idea," and "think about summarizing information"), followed by the final step, an oral retelling of the complete passage ("think about what you have learned"). Procedures similar to those noted in Chapter 5 ("TRAP for Reading Comprehension") and Chapter 6 ("TRAP IDEAS for Summarizing") are used for main idea and summarization development. To reinforce locating the main idea in each paragraph, students use yellow highlighters to mark sentences and phrases related to the main idea in each paragraph, and highlight the important details in blue and trivial details in pink (or cross them out with pencil). Once students have developed main ideas and summaries, they orally retell what has been read and learned in the passage.

Goal setting, self-monitoring, self-instructions, and self-reinforcement are explicitly taught in TWA lessons. Students establish goal setting by committing to learn and use all nine TWA steps by signing a contract; prior to each reading, the students establish goals to use all nine TWA steps. Each student is taught to self-monitor completion of each before and while reading strategy step at the passage level; the main idea and summarization reading steps at the paragraph level; and the final retell at the passage level. Following a teacher-led modeling lesson, students create a list of personal self-instructions. Students are taught to self-reinforce for completing steps on their monitoring sheets. Students are given the opportunity to revisit goals and self-instructions at the end of each lesson.

PRIOR TO INSTRUCTION

A teacher should consider collecting students' retell performance prior to TWA instruction. This information can be used by both the teacher and the students to monitor performance after the strategies have been learned. We have provided a number of passages and scoring sheets for this purpose in the Reading to Learn Appendix.

LESSON 1

Introduce TWA

LESSON OVERVIEW

The purpose of the first lesson is to discuss the TWA strategy as a good strategy for getting information from content text for the purpose of understanding and remembering what was read. The teacher will explain and discuss how to use the TWA strategy before, during, and after reading. The teacher will set the purpose for the vocabulary journal.

STUDENT OBJECTIVES

The students will commit to learning and applying TWA when reading text. The students will orally state how the nine steps of TWA are used before, during, and after reading.

MATERIALS

TWA mnemonic chart (overhead or PowerPoint and paper copy chart for each student), TWA learning contract, journal for vocabulary

SET THE CONTEXT FOR STUDENT LEARNING

Tell the students that the class will be learning about reading from informational text. Discuss briefly what good readers do while reading passages that provide information in science and/ or social studies. For example, they reread a part or word if they do not understand, look for the main ideas, and summarize information. Tell the students that you are going to teach them a "strategy" for reading. Tell them that the strategy will help them understand more about what they have read and will help them remember the things they read.

DEVELOP THE STRATEGY AND SELF-REGULATION

STEP 1:   Introduce TWA

Display a TWA mnemonic chart overhead or PowerPoint so that only the heading "TWA" shows. Uncover each part of the strategy as you introduce and discuss it. Be sure to emphasize that TWA is a strategy that good readers often use before, during, and after reading. Use the analogy of an airplane taking off. For example, SAY, *"With TWA we can take off with reading! Just like a pilot of a plane, we are the pilots and in control of our reading. Just like a pilot who does specific things before, during, and after a plane trip, we need to do things before, during, and after reading."*

STEP 2:   Introduce "Think before reading"

1. Tell the students that there are three steps to complete when you "Think before reading." The first step is to "think about the author's purpose" (uncover this). Use the pilot analogy—a pilot thinks about his or her purpose and then has an understanding of where he or she is to go. The author often uses a structure or map. Thinking about the author's purpose works in the same way. It lets you know where you are going.

2. Ask the students what they know about this step. Be sure to include that authors write to inform, write to persuade, and write for personal expression, and use a variety of structures to convey meaning. SAY, *"When we know the author's purpose, it helps us understand what we are about to read."* Describe and discuss together how this helps reading. For example, if the author has written for personal expression, you know to look for certain things and words. The author may have written a story or personal narrative (you may want to say a personal event). You know to look for characters, places, times, and so forth. If the author has written to inform, you know to look for information such as main ideas and details about real people, places, or events.

3. Uncover "think about what you know." Use the pilot analogy—the pilot of a plane knows a lot about flying. When pilots know where they are going, they begin to think about what they know—the flight path, the airport, and similar information. When reading, thinking about what you know also helps you understand what you are reading. Like a pilot, you create a map with some detail in your head about the topic.

4. Uncover "think about what you want to learn." Use the pilot analogy—a pilot wants to know if there are storms in the flight path, other planes in the flight path, etc. This helps the pilot look for things while flying, making the trip easier. Thinking about what you want to learn helps you look for things while reading, therefore making reading easier. For example, if you want to learn from a passage about Bob Dylan about where Bob Dylan got his start singing, you would focus on finding that information.

STEP 3: Introduce "Think While reading"

1. Tell the students that there are three things good readers do while reading.

2. Uncover "think about reading speed." Use the pilot analogy—a pilot must constantly check his or her speed. Going too fast or too slow can have disastrous results. When reading, checking reading speed or pace is something good readers do as well. Reading speed is important because reading too fast or too slow can make it harder for you to understand and remember what was read. We need to read at different speeds sometimes. For example, we might need to read our science text very carefully so we would slow down, but a novel we might read very quickly.

 3. Uncover "think about linking what you know." Use the pilot analogy—pilots link what they know about a new situation with what they already know about flying. For example, if a pilot comes upon a storm he or she links how to fly in stormy weather with all the times he or she flew in stormy weather before. It is easier to understand and remember something that is linked to what you already know. Provide another example. For example, SAY, *"If I am reading about football, I link all new information about football with what I know—and that's a lot! When I come to the word 'touchdown,' I think of the meaning of the word in my head; if I do not know the meaning, I try to learn it!"*

4. Uncover "rereading parts." Use the pilot analogy—a pilot must constantly check his or her instruments. If a pilot does not understand what the instruments say, he or she keeps reading them. Good readers also check their understanding. When they do not understand, they reread.

STEP 4: Introduce "Think After reading"

Tell students that there are three things good readers do after reading.

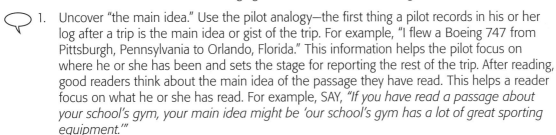

1. Uncover "the main idea." Use the pilot analogy—the first thing a pilot records in his or her log after a trip is the main idea or gist of the trip. For example, "I flew a Boeing 747 from Pittsburgh, Pennsylvania to Orlando, Florida." This information helps the pilot focus on where he or she has been and sets the stage for reporting the rest of the trip. After reading, good readers think about the main idea of the passage they have read. This helps a reader focus on what he or she has read. For example, SAY, *"If you have read a passage about your school's gym, your main idea might be 'our school's gym has a lot of great sporting equipment.'"*

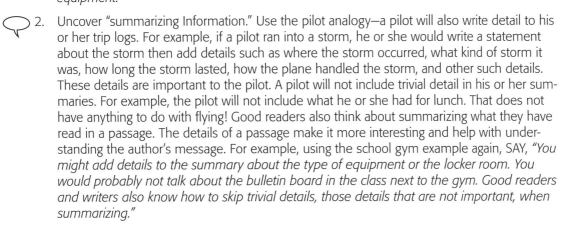

2. Uncover "summarizing Information." Use the pilot analogy—a pilot will also write detail to his or her trip logs. For example, if a pilot ran into a storm, he or she would write a statement about the storm then add details such as where the storm occurred, what kind of storm it was, how long the storm lasted, how the plane handled the storm, and other such details. These details are important to the pilot. A pilot will not include trivial detail in his or her summaries. For example, the pilot will not include what he or she had for lunch. That does not have anything to do with flying! Good readers also think about summarizing what they have read in a passage. The details of a passage make it more interesting and help with understanding the author's message. For example, using the school gym example again, SAY, *"You might add details to the summary about the type of equipment or the locker room. You would probably not talk about the bulletin board in the class next to the gym. Good readers and writers also know how to skip trivial details, those details that are not important, when summarizing."*

3. Uncover "what you learned." Use the pilot analogy—after finishing a trip a pilot shares details of the trip with other pilots, or with his or her family. The pilot may write about the trip for the boss or company. The pilot starts at the beginning and tells what happened with some details included. Using only what has actually happened during the flight, the pilot retells the events of the flight. Good readers can tell what they have learned from reading a passage. Retelling what you have learned in reading helps you understand and remember the information.

STEP 5: Vocabulary journal

Hand each student a journal to be used for vocabulary study. Tell the students that they will record two types of vocabulary words for the passages read. The first vocabulary word types will be words that relate directly to the topic of the passage. Use an appropriate example word. For example, if your class will be reading about the history of space travel, a vocabulary word may be something like "Sputnik." Briefly note the meaning of the word. The next type of words are those words used by an author to help tell the reader understand what is written. For example, if you see words such as "another" in the passage, you know that at least two things, reasons, and so forth are noted. Tell the students that you will explain and show them how to use the journal in the next lessons.

STEP 6: Commitment to learn the strategy

Ask the students to "sign up" to learn the strategy and to use the vocabulary journal. Introduce the TWA learning contract. Give each student a learning contract and have them complete it and sign it. After they have signed the contract, you sign it. Be sure to tell the students that you are committing to do your best in teaching them the TWA strategy and to help them identify important words in text to be read.

STEP 4: Introduce "Think After reading"

STEP 4: Introduce "Think After reading"

STEP 7: Memorization practice

1. Have the students write out the mnemonic for TWA with spaces for the three steps on scratch paper. Ask the students to check off spaces as they orally state each step.

    Students only write the following:

    T _____ _____ _____

    W _____ _____ _____

    A _____ _____ _____

2. Ask students to explain what TWA stands for and why it is important to use TWA before, while, and after reading. Help the students as needed to ensure that each student knows what TWA stands for and why it is important.

3. Review the nine steps orally. As each is identified, the students can check the blank spot. Use peer practice to support memorization if needed.

4. Stress that using TWA helps reading, and give an example.

WRAP-UP

Tell students that they will need to come to the next class and write out the TWA mnemonic (as shown earlier) and tell what it means from memory. Have each student take the scratch paper with TWA and the spaces and the TWA mnemonic chart to study.

Modeling TWA

LESSON OVERVIEW

The purpose of the second lesson is to develop background knowledge, to model the strategy and self-regulation procedures, and to establish students' self-instructions. The teacher models, while talking aloud, using all steps of TWA. Select a simple and short text with three to four paragraphs. Use simple text to insure that students are focused on the strategy process, not trying to process difficult content. The example text, "Gum," could be used for science (discoveries or inventions), social studies (Central America), or health (food products) class.

STUDENT OBJECTIVES

The students will add words and definitions to their vocabulary journals. The teacher will model using the TWA strategy and self-regulation procedures before, during, and after reading. The students will develop a list of self-instructions for using TWA.

MATERIALS

Information passage sample "Gum," vocabulary journal, TWA mnemonic chart, self-monitoring checklist; graphing sheet, yellow, blue, and pink highlighters

---

ESTABLISH THE CONTEXT FOR STUDENT LEARNING

Give each student a piece of paper and ask them to write out the strategy reminder, TWA, with spaces as done in Lesson One. Ask them what each letter stands for. Orally practice the nine steps of TWA. If students have trouble with the parts, give them a few minutes to practice together in pairs.

Ask the students if they remember why it is important to use TWA. Let them (or you) give examples of how TWA can help in reading.

DEVELOP THE STRATEGY AND SELF-REGULATION

STEP 1: Vocabulary journal

Tell the students that in this lesson you will use the vocabulary journal for new vocabulary words in preparation for text reading. Select four important and generalizable words from the passage "Gum" (e.g., chicle, rubber, latex, mixture). Provide and discuss the links between the words and the students' world knowledge. Ask students to write definitions with an example sentence in their vocabulary journal.

STEP 2: Model TWA, goal setting, self-monitoring, self-statements

1. Tell the students that you will show them how TWA works when reading a passage. Tell them that TWA works especially well for passages that contain information about people,

places, and things. Tell them that you will go through all the steps of TWA with a passage, "Gum." Let them know that you will be reading and thinking aloud so that they can see all the TWA steps. Students can assist you when appropriate, but remember that you are the one in charge.

2. Introduce the checklist. Show the students the self-monitoring checklist that you will use when reading the passage. Tell the students that you will be showing them how to use the checklist.

3. Model the whole reading process using TWA with self-statements to guide you. Be sure to use all the types of self-instructions discussed in Chapter 3. Tell the students that in the next lessons they will be getting a lot of practice in each step. Be sure to check each step off as it is completed. A model script follows:

SAY, *"I have a passage to read. Using TWA will help me understand and remember the passage. What is the first thing I should do? The first thing I need to do is to think about three things before reading. First, I need to think about the author's purpose. Well, I can do this. The title is 'Gum.' I should read the first sentence to be sure.* (Read the first sentence.) *I'm still not sure. I'll read the second sentence.* (Read the second sentence.) *Okay. The author is stating that some things are discovered accidentally; gum is one of those things. I noticed that the word 'chicle' was in the first couple of sentences. We learned what chicle means in our vocabulary lesson. What does chicle mean?* (Briefly discuss the meaning of chicle.) *The author's purpose is to tell us about, or to describe, the discovery of gum. I know that when an author writes to provide and describe information, he will be writing information with main ideas and details.* (Check off monitoring sheet.) *The next thing I need to do is to think about what I know. I know a lot about gum."* Share some information with the students. Include & briefly discuss the targeted vocabulary words. Check off monitoring sheet. SAY, *"Next, I need to think about what I want to learn.* (Share your questions. Check off monitoring sheet.) *I have checked the three steps to think before reading. I am ready to read."*

Start reading at a normal speed, then, speed up. SAY, *"Whoa, slow down, this is not making sense. I see on my TWA check sheet that I need to think about reading speed; I will slow down so I can understand what I am reading."* Note that stopping at punctuation is a good way to monitor this.

Then, read at an acceptable speed, stopping when you come to something to link knowledge (model how to link information).

Read until you come to something you do not understand. SAY, *"This doesn't make sense."* (Re-read and tell the students to check the vocabulary journal if they don't remember the meaning of a word.) *"Oh, I understand now. Using the strategy is really helping me understand this information."* Finish reading the passage, modeling each of these steps again. **Follow these procedures for reading the entire passage. Be sure to note all vocabulary words.**

SAY, *"I really think I know a lot more about gum now. What do I need to do next? After reading, think about…. Well, the first step is to think about locating the main ideas and summarizing each paragraph?* (Introduce markers.) *I will use these markers to help me identify main ideas and important details. I will start this with the first paragraph in the passage."* Using the yellow marker, highlight phrases and sentences critical to the main idea. Check off monitoring sheet for the main idea. Then model how to highlight supporting details in blue. *"What do I need to do next? I also need to take out any information that is not important."* Cross out with pencil or highlight in pink the details you want to eliminate. Model summarizing the information. Check off monitoring sheet for details. **Follow these procedures recursively for summarizing each paragraph in the passage.** Use coping statements such as *"This is taking a long time, but I know I will get faster with practice,"* throughout modeling.

SAY, *"Now I can retell what I read and learned in this passage. This will be easy as I have all the main ideas and details highlighted!"* Model how to state a retell. Check off the monitoring sheet.

STEP 3: Reinforce performance

Review the TWA checklist with the students. Ask if all parts are complete. If so, model writing a star or other symbol on your checklist paper to reinforce yourself for a "job well done!"

STEP 4: Develop self-instructions

1. Give each student a blank copy of the self-instruction sheet. Explain that they will use the paper for recording some things they can say to themselves when reading with TWA. Ask them if they remember things you said to yourself when thinking before, while, and after reading. Stress that the things you said to yourself helped you remember the TWA strategy and how to use it.

2. Have the students record one or two things they could say to themselves when thinking before, while, and after reading. Be sure to tell them that these are things they can say inside their head. If students resist, they can always write down some of the things you said.

WRAP-UP

Review the lesson and ask each student to explain what TWA stands for and why it is important to use TWA before, while, and after reading. Update the learning contract to include a statement to use TWA when reading. Review the words in students' vocabulary journals.

Group Collaborative Practice

LESSON OVERVIEW

The teacher will introduce using the vocabulary journal for four new vocabulary words and for words that connect the author's ideas. The class will collaboratively practice TWA reading. The teacher will discuss and remodel the main idea and summarization strategies, if needed. The group will collaboratively retell orally what they have learned. The example passage "Man Walks on the Moon" could be used in science (space travel) or social studies (historical event). The teacher should demonstrate to the students how to extract key information pertinent to class objectives.

STUDENT OBJECTIVES

The students will collaboratively practice, with their teacher and peers, using TWA to read a passage. The students will use their vocabulary journals for writing words used in the passage.

MATERIALS

TWA mnemonic charts; information passage sample "Man Walks on the Moon"; TWA checklists; TWA self-instruction sheets; yellow, blue, or green, and pink markers; vocabulary journals

SET THE CONTEXT FOR STUDENT LEARNING

Orally practice the nine steps of TWA. Discuss and give examples of how TWA helps with reading assignments. If the students are having trouble with the parts, give them a few minutes to practice together in pairs.

SUPPORT THE STRATEGY AND SELF-REGULATION

STEP 1: Vocabulary journal

1. Introduce and teach new vocabulary words in preparation for reading of the text. Select four important and generalizable words from the passage "Man Walks on the Moon" (e.g., lunar, gravity, adhere, module). Provide and discuss the links between the words and world knowledge. Ask students to write definitions with an example sentence to their vocabulary journal.

2. Tell the students that today you will look at how the author uses connector words to link information in text. Ask the students to write the words "and," "but," and "however." Ask them to look out for when these words appear in sentences.

STEP 2: Collaboratively complete "Think before" and "While reading" steps

1. Give each student a copy of the passage "Man Walks on the Moon" and a TWA checklist. Ask the students to get their TWA self-instruction sheets, and remind them to refer to the

self-instructions, especially when they have difficulty with one of the steps. Tell the students that you will complete the steps of TWA together. Set a goal to use all steps of TWA and tell the students you expect them to help monitor using the strategy by checking their own TWA checklist for each step.

2. Collaboratively decide "the author's purpose." The author's purpose is to inform and to provide information about when a man walked on the moon. Ask the students what kind of things should be looked for in informational writing. Note that you will be looking for main ideas and details about the topic. Check off the TWA checklist.

3. Collaboratively complete "think about what you know" and "what you want to learn" steps. Let the students take the lead on what they know about the moon and someone walking on the surface. Guide the students to think about things they may want to know and learn from the text. Check off TWA checklist.

STEP 3: Collaboratively read the passage

Read the passage "Man Walks on the Moon" together. Remind students to refer to the TWA self-instruction sheet. Discuss reading speed, and note that stopping at punctuation is a good way to monitor this. Evaluate students' reading speed after each paragraph. Ask the class, *"Is there any part we should reread?"* If there is no response, select a section to reread to demonstrate this step. After each paragraph, orally practice linking knowledge for content and the vocabulary words written in the journals. Ask the students about other words that could be added to the journal. Add words, discussing and providing definitions as needed. Tell the students to look at the connecting words and note how the author used them to connect ideas. Discuss how difficult it would be to read the passage without these connectors! Check off the TWA checklist.

STEP 4: Main idea strategy and summary for each paragraph

1. Tell students that in the last lesson you used highlighters to help locate the main idea and develop summaries. Explain that for TWA you want the main idea to give you the "gist" of each paragraph. Explain that this will help when developing the paragraph summaries and retelling what you learned.

2. Give each student a yellow highlighter. Read the first paragraph in "Man Walks on the Moon." Together find the sentence in the paragraph that tells the gist of the paragraph. Highlight this sentence in yellow. Look at the other sentences in the paragraph and SAY, *"Are any others important for the gist? Highlight these in yellow."*

3. Develop a main idea statement. Tell the students that these are best if they are in their own words.

4. Give each student a blue or green and a pink (or pencil for crossing out) highlighter. Tell the students that the blue or green and pink markers serve a special purpose. The markers will help identify which sentences have important details and which have not so important details. Discuss each sentence and decide *as a group* if the sentence has an important detail if so, highlight it in blue or green. If not, highlight it in pink. Note that for the passage "Man Walks on the Moon" important details may differ for science and social studies.

5. Tell the students that you are now ready to develop the summary together. Model how to develop the summary for the first paragraph. Be sure to note that the main idea should be the first part of the summary. Tell the students that summaries are best and will be easiest to understand and remember if they are in their own words. Check off the TWA checklist.

6. Collaboratively develop main idea statement and summaries for each paragraph. Check off the TWA checklist as you do this.

STEP 5: Collaboratively think about what you learned

Tell the students the class is going to retell the passage in their own words, and tell it just like the person listening knows nothing about states of matter. Collaboratively retell. Be sure to include self-instructions to help you with retelling. Note that a good way to remember all the information is to think of the main ideas and then think about the important details for each main idea. Spend time talking about *your* thought process in doing a retell. You may want to write down the students ideas on the board or overhead so that you can review them after the retell is complete. Check off the TWA checklist.

STEP 6: Add to self-instruction sheet

Now that the students have had an opportunity to try the strategy, have them look over their TWA self-instruction sheets and add any other statements that may help them in using the strategy.

STEP 7: Reinforce performance

Ask students to look at the TWA checklist. Did they complete all parts? If so, they may make or write a star or other symbol on their checklist paper.

WRAP-UP

Update learning contracts if needed. Review words in vocabulary journals. Remind students that they will need to come to the next session and write out TWA and tell what it means from memory. **If the students need another day or two of group collaborative practice, repeat the lesson with a new passage.**

Peer Practice

> ## LESSON OVERVIEW
>
> The teacher will monitor pairs of students to assess students' fluency in using TWA and to determine if additional individual instruction is needed. The example passage adapted from Rachel Carson's *Silent Spring* ("Pesticides") could be used for social studies, science, or health classes.
>
> ## STUDENT OBJECTIVE
>
> Pairs of students will collaboratively practice TWA while reading a passage.
>
> ## MATERIALS
>
> TWA mnemonic charts, information passage "Pesticides," TWA self-instruction sheets, TWA checklist, highlighters

SET THE CONTEXT FOR STUDENT LEARNING

Orally practice the nine steps of TWA. Discuss and give examples of how TWA helps with reading assignments. The majority of students will have the strategy steps memorized by this lesson. If individual students are having trouble with the parts, provide them an opportunity to practice at home or school.

SUPPORT THE STRATEGY AND SELF-REGULATION

STEP 1: Pair practice

Tell the students that they will use the steps of TWA with a partner. Stress that you will assist them as much as you need to!

STEP 2: Vocabulary journal

1. Introduce and teach new vocabulary words in preparation for reading the text. Select four important and generalizable words from the passage "Pesticides" (e.g., pesticides, contamination, lingered, exposure). Provide and discuss the links between the words and world knowledge. Ask students to write definitions with an example sentence to their vocabulary journal.

2. Note the words "also" and "thus." Discuss how the author will use these words to make connections in thoughts while writing. Tell the students to look for these words when reading, and have them write these words in the journal.

STEP 3: Complete "Think before reading" and "While reading" steps

1. Give each student a copy of the passage "Pesticides" and a TWA checklist. Tell students to get out their TWA self-instruction sheet and remind them to refer to the statements when needed. Tell the students that you want them to complete the first three steps of TWA with their partner. When they finish these steps, they should be ready to report back to you as you circulate through the room. Tell students to set a goal to use TWA and to use the TWA checklist as they complete the steps. Monitor the students' use of the before reading steps.

2. Tell the students that you want them to take turns while reading—one will practice the three steps for "while reading" with the first paragraph, then the other will practice the three steps with the next paragraph, and so on. Stress that they will need to consider the three steps and that they should check off the sheet when they have finished reading. Also note that the students should attend carefully to the vocabulary words while reading by noting them after reading a sentence or paragraph. Monitor what the students do while reading.

STEP 4: Pair practice of main idea and summaries for each paragraph

Tell students to work with their partner to develop main idea statements and summaries for *each* paragraph to report back to you. Tell them that you want them to take turns—one will practice the strategy with the first paragraph, then the other will practice the strategy with the next paragraph, and so forth. They should check off the main idea and summary as it is completed.

STEP 5: Pair practice of "think about what you learned"

Tell students to "think about what you learned" and be ready to report back to you. Be sure to help them by giving examples of how you can use the main ideas, details, and summaries to develop a great retell.

STEP 6: Reinforce performance

Ask students to look at the TWA checklist. Did they complete all parts? If so, they may write a star or other symbol on their checklist paper.

WRAP-UP

Ask students if they need or want to add or change anything on their self-instruction sheet. Update the learning contract if needed. Review words in vocabulary journals. Remind students that you will quiz them on TWA. **Repeat this lesson with a new passage until students have demonstrated that they can complete the strategy steps independently.**

Fading Instructional Supports

LESSON OVERVIEW

The teacher will tell students that most times when they are reading they will not have access to the TWA chart, check sheet, or self-instructions; nor will they be able to use highlighters. Although we are presenting this "fading materials" lesson as a single lesson, many students will need to have support materials reduced gradually. We recommend using a simple text for this lesson and begin by fading the mnemonic chart first, followed by fading the highlighters and self-statements. Procedures for fading each support type are noted in the lesson below.

STUDENT OBJECTIVES

Pairs of students will practice TWA while reading a passage without the use of instructional support materials.

MATERIALS

Information passage "Yellowstone", vocabulary journal

SET THE CONTEXT FOR STUDENT LEARNING

Orally quiz students on the nine steps of TWA. Discuss and give examples of how TWA helps with reading assignments.

SUPPORT THE STRATEGY AND SELF-REGULATION

STEP 1: Vocabulary journal

1. Introduce and teach new vocabulary words in preparation for reading the text. Select four important and generalizable words from the passage "Yellowstone" (e.g., settlers, wilderness, roam, geysers). Provide and discuss the links between word and world knowledge. Ask students to write definitions with an example sentence in their vocabulary journal.

2. Note the words "such as." Discuss how the author will use these words to make connections in thoughts while writing. Tell the students to look for these words when reading. Have the students write these words in the journal.

STEP 2: **Wean off materials**

1. Tell the students that today you will show them how to use TWA without support materials. The first step is to for them to each create their own check sheet. This sheet can be created in the same way that they created the memorization practice sheet in earlier lessons. Show the students how to do this on a blank sheet of paper.

T _____

_____

_____

W _____

_____

_____

A _____

_____

_____

2. Using a sample text paragraph (e.g., one from a prior lesson), model how you will not highlight but write, lightly in pencil, "MI" for main idea sentences and "D" for sentences with important details on the appropriate sentences in the text.

3. Tell the students that they will not have their self-instructions to refer to while reading. They should think about the statements that help them use TWA and continue to use them in their heads.

STEP 3: **Pair practice**

Tell the students that they will set a goal to practice all the steps of TWA with a partner, using their new check sheets and pencils. Let them know that you will be listening carefully to monitor each thing they do and that you want them to report back to you as they are working. Stress that you will assist them as much as you need to! Circulate around the room, checking on students' performance.

STEP 4: **Complete "Think before" and "While reading" steps**

1. Give each student a copy of the passage "Yellowstone." Tell the students that you want them to complete the first three steps of TWA with their partner.

2. Tell the students to use their handwritten TWA checklist. The students should write check marks in the space by "T" as they finish the "Think before reading" steps.

3. Let students work in pairs to read the passage. Tell them that you want them to take turns— one will practice the three steps for "While reading" with the first paragraph, then the other will practice the three steps with the next paragraph, and so on. Stress that they will need to check off spaces by the "W" when they have finished reading. Carefully monitor what the students do while reading.

STEP 5: Pair practice main idea and summaries for each paragraph

Let students work in pairs to develop main idea statements, and summaries for each paragraph. Tell them that instead of highlighting they can write "MI" for main ideas or "D" for details. Tell them that you want them to take turns—one will practice the strategy with the first paragraph, then the other will practice the strategy with the next paragraph, and so on. They should check off the main idea and summary spaces by "A" as they are completed for each paragraph.

STEP 6: Pair practice of "think about what you learned"

Let students work together for "think about what you learned" and retelling the passage. Check off space.

STEP 7: Graph performance

Ask students to look at their check sheets. Did they complete all parts? Support self-reinforcement.

WRAP-UP

Remind students that they will need to come to the next session and write out TWA and tell what it means from memory. Ask students if they need or want to add or change anything on their self-instruction sheet. Update the learning contract if needed. Review words in vocabulary journals. **Repeat this lesson with a new passage until students have demonstrated that they can complete the steps of the strategy independently by creating their own support materials.**

LESSON 6

Independence and Generalization

LESSON OVERVIEW

The teacher will monitor pairs of students to assess students' fluency in using TWA with a different, more difficult text. Two adapted example passages have been provided.

STUDENT OBJECTIVES

Pairs of students will collaboratively practice TWA while reading a passage.

MATERIALS

Information passages: "A Letter to a Father," "In Search of Chimpanzees."

SET THE CONTEXT FOR STUDENT LEARNING

Orally, briefly review the nine steps of TWA. Tell the students that they will be applying TWA for reading a letter or a journal and answering a question about the text to be read.

SUPPORT THE STRATEGY AND SELF-REGULATION

STEP 1: Pair Practice

Tell the students that they will use the steps of TWA with a partner. Let them know that you will be listening carefully to each thing they do and that you want them to report back when they finish each step. Stress that you will assist them as much as needed!

STEP 2: Vocabulary journal

1. Introduce and teach new vocabulary words in preparation for reading the text. Select four important and generalizable words from the selected passage. Provide and discuss the links between word and world knowledge. Ask students to write definitions with an example sentence to their vocabulary journal.

2. Note connecting words in the passage. Discuss how the author will use these words to make connections in thoughts while writing. Tell the students to look for these words when reading. Have the students write these words in the journal.

STEP 3: Complete "Think before reading" steps

Give each student a copy of the selected passage. Tell the students that you want them to complete the first three steps of TWA with their partner. When they finish these steps, they should be ready to report back to you as you circulate through the room. Tell students to check off their handwritten TWA checklist as they complete the steps.

STEP 4: Pair practice of "Think While reading" steps

Tell the students that you want them to take turns while reading—one will practice the three steps for "while reading" with the first paragraph, then the other will practice the three steps with the next paragraph, and so on. Stress that they will need to consider the three steps and that they should check off their check sheet when they have finished reading. Also note that the students should attend carefully to the vocabulary words while reading by noting them after reading a sentence or paragraph. Carefully monitor what the students do while reading.

STEP 5: Pair practice of main idea and summaries for each paragraph

Tell students to work with their partner to develop main idea statements and summaries for each paragraph. Tell them that you want them to take turns—one will practice the strategy with the first paragraph, then the other will practice the strategy with the next paragraph, and so on. They should check off the main idea and summary as it is completed.

STEP 6: Pair practice of "think about what you learned"

Tell students to "think about what you learned" and to use the information from their main idea statements and summaries to orally answer the passage question. (Procedures for linking TWA to writing to learn instruction is addressed in Chapter 11, TWA + PLANS for Informative Writing.)

WRAP-UP

Ask students to look at the TWA checklist. Did they complete all parts? If so, they may write a star or other symbol on their checklist paper. Verbally reinforce the students for using TWA for the new passage.

Ask students if they need or want to add or change anything on their self-statement sheet. Update the learning contract if needed. Review words in vocabulary journals. **Repeat this lesson with different, longer, more complex passages until students have demonstrated that they can complete the steps of the strategy independently across passage types.**

REFERENCES

Graves, A.W., & Levin, J.R. (1989). Comparison of monitoring and mnemonic text-processing strategies in learning disabled students. *Learning Disabilities Quarterly, 12,* 232–36. doi:10.2307/1510693

Hansen, J., & Pearson, P.D. (1983). An instructional study: Improving the inferential comprehension of good and poor fourth-grade readers. *Journal of Educational Psychology, 75,* 821–829.

Harris, K.R., Graham, S., Mason, L.H., & Friedlander, B. (2008). *Powerful writing strategies for all students.* Baltimore, MD: Paul H. Brookes Publishing Co.

Mason, L.H. (in press). Teaching students who struggle with learning to think before, while, and after reading: Effects of SRSD instruction. *Reading and Writing Quarterly.*

Mason, L.H. (2004). Explicit self-regulated strategy development versus reciprocal questioning: Effects on expository reading comprehension among struggling readers. *Journal of Educational Psychology, 96,* 283–96. doi:10.1037/0022-0663.96.2.283

Mason, L.H., Meadan-Kaplansky, H., Hedin, L., & Corso, L. (2006). Self-regulated strategy development instruction for expository text comprehension. *Teaching Exceptional Children. 38,* 47–52.

Ogle, D.M. (1989). The know, want to know, learn strategy. In K.D. Muth (Ed.), *Children's comprehension of text,* (pp. 205–223). Newark, DE: International Reading Association.

CHAPTER 7

TWA

TWA Mnemonic Chart

T Think before reading

Think about:

    The Author's Purpose

    What You Know

    What You Want to Learn

W While reading

Think about:

    Reading Speed

    Linking Knowledge

    Rereading Parts

A After reading

Think about:

    The Main Idea

    Summarizing Information

    What You Learned

From Harris, K.R., Graham, S., Mason, L.H., & Friedlander, B. (2008). *Powerful writing strategies for all students.*
Baltimore, MD: Paul H. Brookes Publishing Co., Inc.; adapted by permission.

In *Building Comprehension in Adolescents: Powerful Strategies for Improving Reading and Writing in Content Areas* by Linda H. Mason, Ph.D., Robert Reid, Ph.D., and Jessica L. Hagaman, Ph.D. (2012, Paul H. Brookes Publishing Co., Inc.)

TWA Checklist Worksheet

☐ **T** Think before reading

Think about:

☐ The author's purpose

☐ What you know

☐ What you want to learn

☐ **W** While reading

Think about:

☐ Reading speed

☐ Rereading parts

☐ Linking what you know

☐ **A** After reading (main ideas and summarizing should be check for each paragraph!)

Think about:

☐ The main idea

☐ Summarizing information

☐ What you learned

✓

From Harris, K.R., Graham, S., Mason, L.H., & Friedlander, B. (2008). *Powerful writing strategies for all students.* Baltimore, MD: Paul H. Brookes Publishing Co., Inc.; adapted by permission.

In *Building Comprehension in Adolescents: Powerful Strategies for Improving Reading and Writing in Content Areas* by Linda H. Mason, Ph.D., Robert Reid, Ph.D., and Jessica L. Hagaman, Ph.D. (2012, Paul H. Brookes Publishing Co., Inc.)

Learning Strategies Contract

Strategy: _____

Student: _____ Date: _____

Teacher: _____

- -

Target completion date: _____

Goal: _____

_____

_____

How to meet this goal: _____

_____

_____

Signatures: Student _____

Teacher _____

- -

_____ has successfully completed instruction on

_____ and agrees to use it in

_____ .

Date: _____ Student: _____

Teacher: _____

From Harris, K.R., Graham, S., Mason, L.H., & Friedlander, B. (2008). *Powerful writing strategies for all students.* Baltimore, MD: Paul H. Brookes Publishing Co., Inc.; adapted by permission.

In *Building Comprehension in Adolescents: Powerful Strategies for Improving Reading and Writing in Content Areas* by Linda H. Mason, Ph.D., Robert Reid, Ph.D., and Jessica L. Hagaman, Ph.D. (2012, Paul H. Brookes Publishing Co., Inc.)

96

Reading Self-Instruction Sheet

Before reading

_____

_____

_____

_____

_____

While reading

_____

_____

_____

_____

After reading

_____

_____

_____

_____

From Harris, K.R., Graham, S., Mason, L.H., & Friedlander, B. (2008). *Powerful writing strategies for all students.*
Baltimore, MD: Paul H. Brookes Publishing Co., Inc.; adapted by permission.

In *Building Comprehension in Adolescents: Powerful Strategies for Improving Reading and Writing
in Content Areas* by Linda H. Mason, Ph.D., Robert Reid, Ph.D., and Jessica L. Hagaman, Ph.D.
(2012, Paul H. Brookes Publishing Co., Inc.)

97

Gum

Sometimes things are discovered by accident. For example, chewing gum was accidentally discovered in the 1860s by United States workers in Central America. A company was searching for materials to use as rubber when they found chicle in some trees. Chicle was used for the first chewing gum! However, because chicle was expensive and hard to get, a substitute product for gum was invented.

The new man-made gum is made in the same way as the chicle chewing gum. Once the mixture is made, it is heated and then cooled. Then the gum mixture is put on a large belt, rolled to the right thickness, cut, wrapped, and packaged. Bubble gum is made the same way. The difference is rubber latex is added to the mixture to give it more strength. This helps the gum stretch when making bubbles.

The first bubble gum was accidentally created by W.E. Diemer in 1928. He discovered how to make bubble gum while testing gum recipes. After he made the first bubble gum, Dubble Bubble, he taught others how to blow bubbles. He invited kids into his home to talk about his invention. His wife told a New York newspaper, "He would say to me, 'I've done something with my life. I've made kids happy around the world.'"

Flesch-Kincaid grade level: 5.44

From Harris, K.R., Graham, S., Mason, L.H., & Friedlander, B. (2008). *Powerful writing strategies for all students.* Baltimore, MD: Paul H. Brookes Publishing Co., Inc.; adapted by permission.

In *Building Comprehension in Adolescents: Powerful Strategies for Improving Reading and Writing in Content Areas* by Linda H. Mason, Ph.D., Robert Reid, Ph.D., and Jessica L. Hagaman, Ph.D. (2012, Paul H. Brookes Publishing Co., Inc.)

98

Man Walks on the Moon

Astronaut Neil Armstrong's first steps on the moon were the beginning tests of the lunar soil's firmness. He was also testing his ability to move in his bulky white spacesuit and backpacks under the influence of lunar gravity. "The surface is fine and powdery," the astronaut reported. "I can pick it up loosely with my toe. It does adhere in fine layers like powdered charcoal to the sole and sides of my boots. I only go in a small fraction of an inch, maybe an eighth of an inch. But I can see the footprints of my boots in the treads in the fine sandy particles."

Mr. Armstrong's initial moonwalk lasted 19 minutes, before Colonel Aldrin joined him outside the lunar module spacecraft. To test their ability to walk on the moon's surface, the two men performed some simple tasks. They scooped up samples of rock and soil, set up a television camera farther away from the lunar module, rooted an American flag to the ground, performed scientific experiments, and hopped and jumped around to display their ability to walk on the lunar surface. They noticed that walking and working on the moon was not as difficult as what others predicted. Mr. Armstrong even stated that he was "very comfortable."

The people back on earth thought that the black-and-white television pictures of the lunar module and the men walking about it were too precise and clear that they almost seemed unreal. The pictures appeared more like a toy and toy-like figures than human beings on the most daring and far-reaching space expedition thus far undertaken. However, the people back on earth knew that the moon landing was a triumph of modern technology and personal courage.

Flesch-Kincaid grade level: 9.5

Adapted from Wilford, J.N. (1969, July, 21). "Men Walk on Moon: Astronauts Land on Plain; Collect Rocks, Plant Flag." *The New York Times.* Retrieved from http://www.nytimes.com/learning/general/onthisday/big/0720. html#article

In *Building Comprehension in Adolescents: Powerful Strategies for Improving Reading and Writing in Content Areas* by Linda H. Mason, Ph.D., Robert Reid, Ph.D., and Jessica L. Hagaman, Ph.D. (2012, Paul H. Brookes Publishing Co., Inc.)

99

Pesticides

The most alarming of all man's assaults upon the environment is the contamination of air, earth, rivers, and sea with dangerous and even lethal chemical materials. These poisons circulate mysteriously by underground streams until they emerge and combine into new forms that kill plants, sicken animals, and work unknown harm on those who drink from once pure wells. The poisons travel from link to link of the food chain.

People developed these poisons, also called pesticides. Some pesticides have the power to kill every insect, the good and the bad. The use of these pesticides has stopped the song of birds and the leaping of fish in the streams, and coated the leaves with a deadly film, and has lingered on in the soil. How can anyone believe it is possible to put down these pesticides on the surface of the earth without making it unfit for all life?

We're on a pesticide treadmill. The insects adapt to the particular pesticide used, forcing people to find ever deadlier new ones. Thus the chemical war is never won, and all life is caught in a violent cycle. Health effects for people depend on exposure over time. Some pesticides have toxic effects in very small quantities. In the ecology of the human body small amounts can cause powerful effects.

Flesch-Kincaid grade level: 9.06

Adapted from Carson, R. (2002). *Silent spring.* New York, NY: Houghton Mifflin.

In *Building Comprehension in Adolescents: Powerful Strategies for Improving Reading and Writing in Content Areas* by Linda H. Mason, Ph.D., Robert Reid, Ph.D., and Jessica L. Hagaman, Ph.D. (2012, Paul H. Brookes Publishing Co., Inc.)

Yellowstone

Yellowstone was the first national park named by the United States government. The park was established to keep the land in its natural condition. In 1872, more than two million acres were set aside for the park. The new park covered land in the states of Montana, Idaho, and Wyoming.

Before Yellowstone became a park, settlers pushed into the wilderness near Yellowstone. They killed off many of the animals and cleared the land for farming. As more people followed, more animals, grasslands, and trees were destroyed. The U.S. government decided that the park should be a safe place for animals such as bison, bighorn sheep, mountain goats, elk, coyotes, and bears. These animals roam freely through the park today.

People love to visit this beautiful, natural park. Yellowstone has a variety of attractions such as geysers and hot springs. This is the only place on earth with so many of these natural wonders. One of the most famous sights is a geyser that erupts every 30 to 60 minutes. It spits boiling water and steam about 150 feet into the air. The largest active geyser in the world is Steamboat Geyser. It was asleep for nine years. Then everyone was surprised; Steamboat erupted! It shot hot water up to 500 feet high.

Yellowstone has a major mountain range, the Rocky Mountains. Volcanoes made this mountain range. The Continental Divide in the mountain range crosses the park. The Continental Divide is important. It divides the rivers that flow east from the waters that flow west. Yellowstone National Park has so many things to see that visitors are never disappointed.

Flesch-Kincaid grade level: 6.78

From Harris, K.R., Graham, S., Mason, L.H., & Friedlander, B. (2008). *Powerful writing strategies for all students.* Baltimore, MD: Paul H. Brookes Publishing Co., Inc.; adapted by permission.

In *Building Comprehension in Adolescents: Powerful Strategies for Improving Reading and Writing in Content Areas* by Linda H. Mason, Ph.D., Robert Reid, Ph.D., and Jessica L. Hagaman, Ph.D. (2012, Paul H. Brookes Publishing Co., Inc.)

101

A Letter to a Father

Prior to the start of the Civil War, on April 21, 1861, General Ulysses S. Grant wrote a letter to his father. The following text paraphrases what General Grant wrote. What was Grant asking and/or telling his father?

Dear Father,

    We are now in the middle of hard times when everyone must be for or against his country, and show the side they are taking by every choice they make. I feel that since I was educated for such an emergency as in this war, at the expense of the Government at West Point, that this is especially important. However, I do not wish to act quickly or without advice about joining the U.S. army for this war. What I ask now is your approval of the action I am taking, or advice in the matter.

    Whatever may have been my political opinions before the war, I have but one opinion now. That is, we have a U.S. Government, and laws and a flag, and they must all be protected and sustained. Now, there are two parties, traitors and patriots. I want, hereafter, to be ranked with the patriots, and I trust, the stronger party.

    I do not know but my decision may put you in an awkward position, and a dangerous one. But the costs of my decision cannot now be counted. My advice would be to leave where you are if you are not safe. I would never change my opinion for the sake of a little security.

Yours truly,
U.S. Grant

Adapted from Grant, U.S. (1861, April 21). *Personal letter from Ulyssis S. Grant to his father.* [Personal letter]. Letters of Ulysses S. Grant to his father and youngest sister 1857-1878. Project Gutenberg ebook. Retrieved from http://www.gutenberg.org/files/13471/13471-h/13471-h.htm

In *Building Comprehension in Adolescents: Powerful Strategies for Improving Reading and Writing in Content Areas* by Linda H. Mason, Ph.D., Robert Reid, Ph.D., and Jessica L. Hagaman, Ph.D.
(2012, Paul H. Brookes Publishing Co., Inc.)

102

In Search of Chimpanzees

The following text is a paraphrase from Jane Goodall's journal about her effort and work to help chimpanzees in East Africa. What does her journal entry tell you about the very first day in her journey to help these endangered animals?

14th July, 1960

    We finally managed to get off today. We woke at dawn, left about 9 and arrived at the beach on Lake Tanzania about 11. All along the beach fishermen were frying fish. Above our campsite, the mountains rose up steeply behind the beaches. The lake water was so clear I could scarcely believe it. Every so often a stream cascaded down the valleys between the ridges, with its thick fringe of forest. This was the home of the chimps.

    Our tent was up in no time, in a clearing up from the fishermen's huts on the stony beach. We had some lunch together, and then Ma and I spent an exhausting and hot afternoon setting things in order. I say exhausting because I had a foul sore throat, turning into a cold.

    Then, about 5 o'clock, someone came along to say some people had seen a chimp. So off we went and there was the chimp. It was quite a long way—too far to see properly what it looked like—but it was a chimp. It moved away as we and the fisherman were looking at it. And, though we climbed the neighboring slope, we didn't see it again. However, we went over to the trees and found a fresh chimp nest there. We could not tell if it was from today or yesterday. We then returned to our camp on the beach, had dinner together, and went to bed.

Jane Goodall

Flesch-Kincaid grade level: 5.64

Adapted from J. Goodall. (2010, July 13). Jane's Journal: Excerpt from July 14, 1960. [web log post]. Retrived from http://www.janegoodall.org/blogs/janes-journal-excerpt-july-14-1960

In *Building Comprehension in Adolescents: Powerful Strategies for Improving Reading and Writing in Content Areas* by Linda H. Mason, Ph.D., Robert Reid, Ph.D., and Jessica L. Hagaman, Ph.D. (2012, Paul H. Brookes Publishing Co., Inc.)

103

Section III

Writing to Learn

Chapter 8

Writing to Learn

As a group, American students perform poorly in the area of written expression. Results of the National Assessment of Educational Progress (Salahu-Din, Persky, & Miller, 2008) showed that 75% of participating high school students were unable to meet the requirements for the *proficient* standard in written expression. For student who are at-risk or who qualify for special education the situation is even more serious; 95% of these students were at or below the *basic* level for writing performance. These data do not reflect a sudden drop in performance; rather they are indicative of a chronic problem in secondary schools.

The need for proficient written expression does not stop at high school; effective writing skills are necessary for an ever increasing number of American graduates (College Entrance Examination Board, 2004; National Center for Education Statistics, 1998). Without competence in written expression it may be difficult or impossible to pursue post-secondary education in college or technical schools. This need also extends to the workplace. Companies now commonly expect salaried employees to have proficient writing skills, and even hourly employees are likely to have some writing responsibilities (College Entrance Examination Board, 2004). For these reasons it is critical that teachers be able to supply students with effective strategies to help them develop proficiency in written expression.

In this chapter we discuss how teachers can help students to become more effective and efficient writers. First we discuss factors that affect written expression and the major problems students commonly experience in learning to become proficient writers. Next we introduce each of the writing strategies. The C-SPACE strategy was developed by MacArthur, Schwartz, and Graham. The STOP and DARE strategies were developed by De La Paz and Graham. An example of how each strategy might be used in the classroom is included. Finally, we provide suggestions on how the writing strategies can be integrated with the reading comprehension strategies presented in previous chapters.

WRITTEN EXPRESSION PROBLEMS

It is not surprising that many students have difficulty with written expression. Writing is a difficult and demanding task even for accomplished writers. Writing is not like other academic skills. For example, most students can easily and effortlessly call up and apply math facts; the process is rapid and automatic. In contrast, writing rarely becomes automatic. Students who struggle with written expression often experience problems with: 1) content generation, 2) creating and organizing structure for compositions, 3) formulation of goals and higher level plans, and 4) knowledge of text structures (Graham & Harris, 2003). Additionally, during writing one must constantly monitor and evaluate the text that is being produced and maintain effort. Struggling writers often have problems in all of these areas. Note that in practice these problems interact with one another. For example, lack of knowledge of text structure (e.g., that a narrative must have characters, setting, and action) will affect content generation. Students who do not know that there should be a setting are unlikely to include one. These problems can be boiled down to two broad areas: 1) planning to write, and 2) organization.

Planning to Write

Struggling writers typically do little if any planning. When given a writing task, they tend to simply start writing immediately before doing any sort of planning (e.g. Jacobson & Reid, 2010). Any information relevant to the topic is written down without regard to organization, goals, or audience; there is little if any thought about the relevance of the content or how it is presented (Graham & Harris, 2003). As soon as an idea comes into the student's head, it is immediately put down on paper. Scardamalia and Bereiter (1987) termed this behavior "knowledge telling." As a result, struggling writers often produce compositions that are little more than a mishmash of disjointed ideas. There is no focus on the purpose of the composition, which is to express an idea or thought through written communication to a particular audience. Another planning-related problem struggling writers may experience is difficulty with generating content. Some students may have deficits in background knowledge. These students may complain that they don't know what to say.

Strategy instruction directly addresses these problems. One of the major thrusts of strategy instruction for students who struggle at writing is to engender a writing process that begins with a well-defined planning activity. Students are taught, through direct instruction in specific step-by-step planning strategies, to use the same types of planning strategies that skilled writers utilize. Planning is supported through the use of graphic organizers that serve to cue specific steps in the planning strategy and guide the planning activities. This planning also helps students to activate their background knowledge by cueing them to focus on specific content that should be included in a composition. For example, knowing that a narrative includes a setting can help a student draw on existing background knowledge of settings.

Organizing

After students have planned a composition they must be able to organize their thoughts. Struggling writers often have difficulty with organization (Englert & Mariage, 1991). One major reason is that struggling writers are often unaware of or fail to understand the importance of *text structures*. Skilled writers are aware of and recognize the importance of text structures. These structures serve as a blueprint for compositions. For example, persuasive text contains a topic sentence with a position clearly stated, reasons for the position, elaboration on the reasons, and a conclusion. Skilled writers recognize these structures and understand that using these structures is crucial to production of a successful composition. Unfortunately, struggling writers are often unaware of patterns or structures in text. Thus, they do not utilize these patterns or structures while producing their own compositions. Rather than organize their thoughts, they simply start writing letting each thought prompt the next; little if any effort is made to assess text organization (Graham & Harris, 2003).

The strategies presented in this section help students to better organize their compositions. The students are taught text structures that are specific to the genre (i.e., narrative, informative, or persuasive writing). The students are also taught why these structures are important and how using them results in better compositions. They are also provided with specific strategies for outlining and organizing compositions. This is done through the use of mnemonics which remind the students of steps in the organizational process, and through graphic organizers. Directly teaching organizational patterns and strategies has proven to be highly effective in improving academic performance of struggling writers (Graham & Harris, 2003).

STRATEGIES

In this section we provide an overview of the written expression strategies included in this book along with a brief vignette on how the strategy might be used in practice.

C-SPACE

The ability to produce a narrative (i.e., tell a story) is a critical skill. It is a skill that many students develop while they are very young without formal instruction. Students are exposed to narratives through bedtime stories and in daily social interactions, and thus are exposed to the genre and internalize the elements of narrative at an early age. Difficulty producing coherent narratives, however, is a serious concern. An inability to produce coherent narratives puts students at an increased risk for academic failure, because narrative production is a central element in many students' academic activities, not to mention high-stakes testing situations. Additionally, narratives play a central role in many daily social interactions (Renz et al., 2003). To relate to a peer what one did over the weekend or to describe an interesting event (e.g., watching monster trucks or going to a flower show) requires students to produce coherent narratives.

Strategy instruction is an effective means of helping students become more proficient in producing narrative text. Research shows that strategy instruction can significantly increase the length, quality, and completeness of students' narratives (Graham & Harris, 2003). One effective strategy for improving narrative production is the "story grammar" approach (MacArthur, Schwartz, & Graham, 1991; Reid & Lienemann, 2006). This approach is based on the concept that all narratives have a kind of grammar. That is, there are certain elements that are consistently included in high quality narratives (e.g., character, setting, plot). In this approach, students are taught the "grammar" of narratives and then taught how to take these elements and create a complete and coherent narrative. C-SPACE is a story grammar strategy. Each letter in the C-SPACE mnemonic stands for a critical element of a complete narrative: **C**haracters—Who are the characters in the story? **S**etting—Where and when did the story take place? **P**urpose—What does the main character try to do? **A**ction—What does the main character do to achieve the goal? **C**onclusion—What is the result of the action? **E**motions—What are the reactions and feelings of the main character? The order of the mnemonic also provides an organizational cue to help the student to place the elements in an order that makes sense. C-SPACE can be used for many types of narrative forms, including, stories, personal narratives, and biographies. The following illustrates how C-SPACE might be used in the classroom.

Mrs. Fisher is worried about Doug. The class is working on personal narratives. Doug has not handed in his assignment. It is three days late and he keeps saying that he forgot it. When Mrs. Fisher asked the class to write a personal narrative in class, Doug handed in a two-sentence paper. Mrs. Fisher schedules a meeting with Doug to talk about the problems he is having. Doug is very upset. He tells her that he just doesn't know what to say. It also comes out that he is very worried about the writing demonstration exam that the district requires for graduation. Mrs. Fisher decides that the C-SPACE strategy would be perfect for Doug; she also identifies two other students who appear to be struggling with personal narratives.

To begin, Mrs. Fisher tells the students that she can teach them a strategy that will help them learn to write narratives much more easily. She stresses that she has taught this to students just like them and these students got much better. She notes that if they try their best and use the strategy, she believes that they will do much better too. In the initial lessons, Mrs. Fisher teaches the students the C-SPACE elements. Students practiced identifying them in narratives. She also stresses the need to include all the elements in a good narrative. The students quickly memorize the C-SPACE elements. After a few lessons, they are able to use the C-SPACE organizer to plan their narratives, and can write narratives that contain all the required elements. She also wants the students to write longer narratives with more detail and description. She has students self-monitor the length of their narratives. They count the number of words in their narratives and graph the result. To help students see their progress, Mrs. Fisher asks the students to compare their narratives written before they learned the strategy to the ones they produced after. The students can easily see the improvement!

STOP & DARE

Persuasive writing has long been valued in our society. The ability to articulate a position clearly and persuasively is one of the skills expected of a literate and educated citizen (Crowhurst, 1990). Persuasive writing is commonly required in schools. It has academic value because writing persuasive essays can help students to acquire new knowledge (Driver, Newton, & Osborne, 2000) and can enhance knowledge in content areas (De La Paz, 2005). Results of national assessments show that persuasive writing is very difficult for many students (Persky, Daane, & Jin, 2003). This is due in part to the fact that persuasive writing has established conventions. Good persuasive writing requires the author to take a position and to attempt to convince the reader of the validity of this position. To do this, writers must: a) adopt a position, b) support the position, c) present reasonable alternative positions, and d) rebut the opposing positions (Ferretti, MacArthur, & Dowdy, 2000). Additionally, the writer must do all these with audience in mind.

One reason persuasive writing is difficult for many students is that they have not been exposed to these conventions, and thus are unaware of how to structure an effective persuasive essay. The STOP & DARE strategy is a very effective means of helping students learn to produce a complete persuasive essay (De La Paz & Graham, 1997). The "STOP" mnemonic stands for: **S**uspend judgment, **T**ake a side, **O**rganize your thoughts, **P**lan more while you write; the "DARE" mnemonic is: **D**evelop the topic sentence, **A**dd supporting ideas, **R**eject possible arguments for the other side, **E**nd with a conclusion. Using this approach ensures that students include all the required elements, and have organized their essay correctly. The following illustrates how STOP & DARE might be used in the classroom.

Mr. Nelson's History class is studying the Iraq war. Mr. Nelson wanted to see how well the class could apply the content so, as a part of the unit, Mr. Nelson assigned a short in-class paper on whether or not we should have invaded Iraq. He was very surprised with what he received. None of the papers had all the elements of a good persuasive essay. Most had a topic sentence stating a position, but little more. Very few had some supporting reasons. Some papers were literally blank. Mr. Nelson knew from class discussions that students were aware of reasons (both pro and con) and of rebuttals for the Iraq war. He decided that the students needed a strategy to help the structure their essays. He decided to use the STOP & DARE strategy. He talked with the class about the problems with the essay, and told them that he would teach a strategy that would help them write a good essay. Mr. Nelson taught the strategy to the class in six lessons. He repeated one lesson because some students still were not fluent with the strategy. Then he repeated the in-class assignment on the Iraq war. After the students were finished, he gave them their original essay and asked them to compare the two. The students were pleasantly surprised at their improvement.

TWA + PLANS

Students' competence at demonstrating that they can extract and expound on information gained from informational text has been referred to as the "quiet crisis" in American education (Gunning, 2003). The problem is two-pronged. Students experience difficulty both in comprehending text (i.e., identifying main ideas and important details) and in generating text to demonstrate comprehension; as a result, around 30% of students are unable to perform competently in content area classes (Mason, Snyder, Sukhram, & Kedem, 2006). The problem is even more serious among struggling learners. One reason students experience difficulty with informational writing is that it is difficult for them to express their knowledge. Informational text structure is more complex and does not follow the more familiar conventions of narrative text (Englert & Raphael, 1988). Another reason is more basic—schools often fail to instruct students in how to write informational text (Mason et al., 2006).

One effective way to improve students' skill at producing expository text is to use TWA + PLANS. This approach combines an effective reading comprehension strategy TWA (see Chapter 7) with PLANS, a strategy to help students plan and organize their compositions. Teaching reading comprehension strategies and composition strategies together is a powerful approach that has demonstrated effectiveness in several studies (Mason, in press). The PLANS mnemonic stands for: **P**ick goals, **L**ist ways to meet goals, **A**nd, make **N**otes, **S**equence your notes. Students are then taught to Write and Say More and Test Goals (Graham, MacArthur, Schwartz, & Page-Voth, 1992). The following illustrates how TWA + PLANS might be used in the classroom.

Mr. Taft has just talked to his earth science class about a series of three of reports that they will be assigned. The reports will require the students to do a series of readings, synthesize the results, and write a three-page paper on each of the topic areas. The class did not react well. Judging by the questions that they asked, many of the students didn't have any idea of how to attack this task. Mr. Taft is worried that some students may have trouble picking out main ideas and important supporting details. He noted that several students had problems with this on their responses to the study questions in their text. If students can't locate this information they will do poorly on the assignment. He decides to use the TWA + PLANS strategy because this will help with both reading comprehension and the expository writing required for the reports.

Mr. Taft tells the class that because they were so concerned about the reports, he will work with them to show them a way that will help them find important information and then use it to write their reports. He also tells them that it will probably help them with the study questions in the text. He begins by teaching the TWA strategy. He uses the earth science text for examples. He begins with chapters that students have previously read and answered questions on. Using familiar material makes it easier for the students to focus on applying the TWA strategy. Students can also compare their performance before they learned the strategy to when they used the strategy. Most students see a real improvement. Then Mr. Taft introduces the PLANS strategy. Once again he uses familiar material from their text to model strategy use and for collaborative practice. He begins with short informative essays and gradually increases the length. For his final lesson, he gives students a longer passage of new material. He tells them that this will be practice for the actual reports. Most of the students work independently. Three students, who have some difficulty, are paired with a peer. Mr. Taft instructs them to work cooperatively on the project. In each pair, the student who has mastered the strategy helps the student who is still experiencing some difficulty. The students are happy with the results. Moreover, they notice that when they used TWA + PLANS they remembered more of the material in greater detail. They realize that this would also help them on exams.

POW for Quick Writes

Classroom writing activities in which students write about a specific topic can facilitate learning, promote critical thinking, and benefit students' comprehension and vocabulary by encouraging students to make connections throughout the writing process (Deshler, Palinscar, Biancarosa, & Nair, 2007; Tierney & Shanahan, 1996). One way to incorporate writing in the classroom in content areas is through Quick Writes. Quick Writes are brief, generally no more than 10-minute, informal writing activities that require students to produce a written response to a specific question (Mason, Benedek-Wood, & Valasa, 2009). Quick writes are very flexible and can be used in a variety of written language genres. For example, in a social studies unit on the evolution of voting laws, students could write: a) an informative response to "Describe the voting rights law of 1964," b) a narrative response to "Describe how they will feel when they vote for the first time," or c) a persuasive response to "Should the voting age be lowered to 16?"

To teach Quick Writes, we combine the POW strategy (**P**ick my idea, **O**rganize my notes, **W**rite and say more), a general writing strategy, with three genre-specific strategies:

1) C-SPACE (**C**haracter, **S**etting, **P**urpose, **A**ction, **C**onclusion, **E**nding) for narrative Quick Writes; 2 TIDE (**T**opic sentence, at least three **I**mportant **D**etails, and an **E**nding) for informative Quick Writes; and 3) TREE (**T**opic sentence, at least three **R**easons, at least three **E**xplanations, and an **E**nding) for persuasive Quick Writes. Students are first taught to use POW plus one of the three genre specific strategies. After mastery of the first genre-specific strategy, students can be taught additional genre-specific strategies. The following illustrates how Quick Writes might be used in the classroom.

> Tom is a ninth grade student with ADHD. He is in inclusive classrooms for his content area classes, and gets resource support for one hour a day as needed. He is having problems in his American History class. His teacher uses short constructed written response tests and Tom has only taken multiple-choice tests. Tom has problems with organizing his thoughts. It wasn't a problem on multiple-choice tests but it is a huge problem on tests that require a paragraph response. Tom seems to understand the content, but he can't seem to convey it on the tests. Mr. Power, the resource teacher, thinks that POW + TIDE might be a solution for Tom. Mr. Power picked TIDE because it is appropriate for informative writing. He met with Tom to discuss the problems he was having. Tom said that he had a problem organizing information and then when he wrote he would forget things. It took him so long to get organized that he could not finish the test.
>
> Mr. Power told Tom that he thought he could help. He told Tom that what he needed was a way to quickly organize his thoughts and then get them down on paper. Tom was eager to learn how to get better organized. Over the next week, Mr. Power worked with Tom on the POW + TIDE strategy. Tom grasped the steps quickly. For practice, Mr. Power used the exam questions from prior American History tests. Tom had a tendency to rush through his answers and sometimes skipped steps in the strategy. Mr. Power suggested that he remember to write the POW + TIDE mnemonic at the top of each page on his test to help him remember. Tom also practiced monitoring the time spent on each question to be sure that he would be able to finish all the questions on an exam. After six lessons, Tom was fluent in the strategy. His next test score was a B+!

INTEGRATING READING COMPREHENSION AND WRITING STRATEGIES

Reading comprehension strategies and written composition strategies make a powerful combination. In practice the two can be easily combined with synergistic results. Reading comprehension strategies help students develop richer background knowledge. This improves the store of content material that a student can draw on. Written composition strategies allow students to more easily express their thoughts and to meet the expectations of the genre (e.g., narrative, expository, persuasive) they are expected to use. It benefits comprehension, because writing about a topic tends to improve the depth of knowledge about the topic. In the lesson plans that follow, two of the reading comprehension strategies are linked with writing strategies. Teachers may also wish to combine different strategies. To do this effectively, we would make the following recommendations.

- Teach the reading comprehension strategy to a high degree of mastery before introducing the writing strategy. Students need a strong foundation before moving to the writing strategy.

- We recommend that teachers use only the one reading comprehension strategy (TRAP, TRAP IDEAS, or TWA,) that is best suited to their students and the content. Changing between different strategies could be confusing.

- Teachers should choose a writing strategy carefully. There is a limit to the number of strategies that can be taught and mastered by students. Teachers should choose writing strategies that will provide maximum benefit to the students. For example, if students will have a number of major assignments that require reports, an informational text strategy might be most beneficial. On the other hand, if students will be focusing primarily on narrative writing, then a strategy such as C-SPACE would be most appropriate.

REFERENCES

Achieve. (2006). *Closing the expectations gap 2006: Annual 50-state progress report on alignment of high school policies with the demands of college and work.* Washington, DC: Author.

Center on Education Policy. (2007). *State high school exit exams: Working to raise test scores.* Washington, DC: Author.

Center of Education Policy. (2008). *State high school exit exams: Students with disabilities.* Washington, DC: Author.

Crowhurst, M. (1990). Teaching and learning the writing of persuasive/argumentative discourse. *Canadian Journal of Education, 15*(4), 348–359.

Daniels, H. & Bizar, M. (2005). *Teaching the best practice way.* York, ME: Stenhouse Publishers.

De La Paz, S., & Graham, S. (1997). Strategy instruction in planning: Effects on the writing performance and behavior of students with learning difficulties. *Exceptional Children, 63*, 167–181.

De La Paz, S. (2005). Effects of historical reasoning instruction and writing strategy mastery in culturally and academically diverse middle school classrooms. *Journal of Educational Psychology, 97*, 139–156.

Deshler, D. Palincsar, A. Biancarosa, G. & Nair, M. (2007). *Informed choices for struggling adolescent readers: A research-based guide to instructional programs and practices.* Newark, DE: International Reading Association.

Driver, R. Newton, P. & Osborne, J. (2000). Establishing the norms of scientific argumentation in classrooms. *Science Education, 84*, 287–312.

Englert, C.S., & Mariage, T.V. (1991). Shared understandings: Structuring the writing experience through dialogue. *Journal of Learning Disabilities, 24*, 330–342.

Englert, C.S., & Raphael, T.E. (1988). Constructing well-informed prose: Process, structure and metacognitive knowledge. *Exceptional Children, 54*, 513–520.

Ferretti, R.P., MacArthur, C.A., & Dowdy, N.S. (2000). The effects of an elaborated goal on the persuasive writing of students with learning disabilities and normally achieving peers. *Journal of Educational Psychology, 92*, 694–702.

Graham, S., MacArthur, C., Schwartz, S., & Page-Voth, V. (1992). Improving the compositions of students with learning disabilities using a strategy involving product and process goal setting. *Exceptional Children, 58*, 322–334.

Graham, S., Harris, K.R. (2003). Students with learning disabilities and the process of writing: A meta-analysis of SRSD studies. In H.L. Swanson, K.R. Harris, & S. Graham (Ed.), *Handbook of learning disabilities.* New York, NY: The Guilford Press.

Gunning, T.G. (2003). *Building literacy in the content areas.* Boston, MA: Allyn & Bacon.

Jacobson, L. & Reid, R. (2010) Improving the persuasive essay writing of high school students with ADHD. *Exceptional Children, 76*, 157–174.

MacArthur, C.A., Schwartz, S.S., & Graham, S. (1991). A model for writing instruction: Integrating word processing and strategy instruction into a process approach to writing. *Learning Disabilities Research and Practice, 6*, 230–236.

Mason, L.H. (in press). Teaching students who struggle with learning to think before, while, and after reading: Effects of SRSD instruction. *Reading and Writing Quarterly.*

Mason, L.H., Benedek-Wood, E., & Valasa, L. (2009). Quick writing for students who struggle with writing. *Journal of Adolescent and Adult Literacy, 53*, 313–322.

Mason, L., Snyder, K., Sukhram, D., & Kedem, Y. (2006). TWA + PLANS strategies for expository reading and writing: Effects for nine fourth-grade students. *Exceptional Children, 73*, 69–89.

Persky, H.R., Daane, M.C., & Jin, Y. (2003). *The nation's report card: Writing 2002.* (NCES 2003–529). U.S. Department of Education. Institute of Education Sciences. National Center for Education Statistics. Washington, DC: Government Printing Office.

Reid, R., & Lienemann, T. O. (2006). Improving the writing performance of students with ADHD. *Exceptional Children, 71*, 361–377.

Renz, K., Lorch, E.P., Milich, R., Lemberger, C., Bodner, A., & Welsh, R. (2003). On-line story representation in boys with attention deficit hyperactivity disorder. *Journal of Abnormal Child Psychology, 31*, 93–104.

Salahu-Din, D., Persky, H., and Miller, J. (2008). *The Nation's Report Card: Writing 2007* (NCES 2008-468). National Center for Education Statistics, Institute of Education Sciences, U.S. Department of Education, Washington, DC: Government Printing Office.

Scardamalia, M., & Bereiter, C. (1987). Knowledge telling and knowledge transforming in written composition. In S. Rosenberg (Ed.), *Advances in applied psycho-linguistics: Vol. 2. Reading, writing, and language learning* (pp. 142–175). Cambridge, MA: Cambridge University Press.

Tierney, R.J., & Shanahan, T. (1996). Research on the reading-writing relationship: Interactions, transactions, and outcomes. In R. Barr, M.L. Kamil, P.B. Mosenthal, & P.D. Pearson (Eds.), *Handbook of reading research: Volume II* (pp. 246–280). White Plains, NY: Longman.

Chapter 9

C-SPACE for Narrative Writing

C-SPACE

Characters
Setting
Problem
Action
Conclusion
Emotion

MATERIALS

C-SPACE mnemonic chart

C-SPACE graphic organizer

C-SPACE self-monitoring sheet

C-SPACE feedback sheet

Reliable resources for biographies

Note: It is suggested that students keep a folder for their written work and writing resources while learning the C-SPACE strategy.

The C-SPACE strategy was developed by MacArthur, Schwartz, and Graham (1991). C-SPACE (**C**haracters, **S**etting, **P**roblem, **A**ction, **C**onclusion, **E**motion) is a story-writing strategy that can also be used to help students plan and write personal narratives and biographies. In C-SPACE lessons, explicit instruction for planning, self-regulation, and peer feedback is embedded throughout each lesson. For example, students are taught to plan prior to writing, use checklists to ensure all steps are complete, and give peers positive and constructive feedback.

Goal setting, self-monitoring, self-instructions, and self-reinforcement are explicitly taught in C-SPACE lessons. Students establish goal setting by committing to learn and use all six C-SPACE steps; following each written narrative, students check for each of the steps and graph the results. Each student is taught to self-monitor completion of each step before and while writing a narrative. Following a teacher-led modeling lesson, students begin to use the strategy on their own. Students are taught to self-reinforce for completing steps on their monitoring sheets. Students are given the opportunity to revisit goals at the end of each lesson.

Prior to beginning C-SPACE instruction, the teacher should collect a sample of each student's writing performance in the task (e.g., story, narrative, or biography) to be taught. These pre-instruction assessments will be used in Lesson 2.

Materials included:

Lesson 1: Introduce the strategy
Lesson 2: Discuss current performance and set goals
Lesson 3: Model the strategy
Lesson 4: Collaborative practice
Lesson 5: Practice the strategy
Lesson 6: Practice the strategy
Lesson 7: Practice the strategy without prompts
Lesson 8: Optional lesson instructing students how to give peer feedback
Lesson 9: Optional lesson instructing students how to use the C-SPACE strategy for writing biographies. This lesson includes instruction on how to use the graphic organizer to research facts for writing the biography.

REFERENCE

MacArthur, C.A., Schwartz, S.S., & Graham, S. (1991). A model for writing instruction: Integrating word processing and strategy instruction into a process approach to writing. *Learning Disabilities Research and Practice, 6,* 230–236.

Introduce the Strategy

LESSON OVERVIEW

The teacher will introduce and describe the C-SPACE strategy to students, identify story parts, and begin strategy memorization.

STUDENT OBJECTIVE

The student will review the parts of a story and practice the parts of a story using the C-SPACE acronym.

MATERIALS

Mnemonic chart/paper, short biography, graphic organizer

SET THE CONTEXT FOR STUDENT LEARNING

Explain to the students that they are going to learn a method for writing personal narratives or biographies.

DEVELOPING THE STRATEGY AND SELF-REGULATION

STEP 1: Explain C-SPACE

1. SAY, *"I want to talk with you today about writing."* Discuss the different types of writing we use (e.g., essay versus narrative) and the different audiences we write for.

    SAY, *"We are going to be focusing on a specific type of narrative writing—personal narrative writing. This means that you will be writing about experiences you have had. While we learn about writing personal narratives, I have a strategy that will help make sure we include all the important parts of a good narrative. The strategy is called C-SPACE."* (Show C-SPACE mnemonic chart)

2. Put out the mnemonic chart/poster so that only the heading "C-SPACE" shows. Uncover each part of the strategy as you introduce and discuss it .

3. SAY, *"The strategy is easy to remember because the word SPACE is a word you already know—and all you have to do is add a 'C' in front of SPACE. Each letter of C-SPACE stands for a step that you do. It is very important for you to learn the steps well. It will help you use the strategy more effectively and that will help you become a better writer."*

    *   Explain the steps of the strategy. Start with *character* and *setting*. Explain that personal narratives have an interesting main character and a good description of the setting that involves both time and place.

    *   Discuss *problem*. Note that the main character in a biography or narrative may have a problem or something that he or she wants to accomplish or overcome. A biography will be about what the main character does to solve the problem or get what he or she wants—*action*.

- Discuss *conclusion*—at the end of a biography, there will be a conclusion. The character may or may not solve the problem or get what he or she wants. Finally, it is important to include *emotion*—how the character or character(s) feel in the story.

STEP 2: Read the narrative and identify parts (prerequisite for strategy use)

 1. SAY, *"Let's practice using C-SPACE by identifying components in a story."*

2. SAY, *"I have a sample narrative and I want you to try to identify the story parts as I read aloud. Please follow along."* Provide students with copies, or show them the narrative on an overhead. Read the story aloud while students follow along—using the mnemonic chart as necessary.

3. Have students use planning chart or organizer to write each story part as it is identified.

STEP 3: Memorizing the strategy

Have students turn over their mnemonic chart. Rehearse the strategy steps.

Go around the room and have students say a strategy step and its meaning. Have students get in pairs and "quiz" each other on the steps.

WRAP-UP

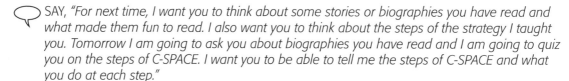 SAY, *"For next time, I want you to think about some stories or biographies you have read and what made them fun to read. I also want you to think about the steps of the strategy I taught you. Tomorrow I am going to ask you about biographies you have read and I am going to quiz you on the steps of C-SPACE. I want you to be able to tell me the steps of C-SPACE and what you do at each step."*

Discuss Current Performance and Set Goals

LESSON OVERVIEW

The teacher will discuss the C-SPACE strategy, discuss students' current performance, obtain students' commitment to learn and use the strategy, set initial performance goals, practice finding components in written work, and support strategy memorization.

STUDENT OBJECTIVES

The students will practice rehearsing the parts of a story and the mnemonic C-SPACE. Students will set goals.

MATERIALS

One copy for each student: previously written narrative or biography, graph, mnemonic chart

SET THE CONTEXT FOR STUDENT LEARNING

1. SAY, *"Yesterday I told you about a strategy. Who can tell me the steps of that strategy?"* Pause for responses. *"Wow, you remembered a lot of the strategy. Tomorrow I will ask you to write the steps of the strategy from memory. Remember that you need to remember the step and you need to know what you do at each step."* SAY, *"Today, we are going to continue learning about the strategy. Before we practice using it, did you think about some biographies you have read?"*

2. Solicit student responses. Write the list on the board and discuss each idea.

   Discuss what made the stories or biographies memorable, e.g., they were about interesting people, the characters had an interesting or relatable problem to solve.

DEVELOP THE STRATEGY AND SELF-REGULATION

STEP 1: **Discussing current performance and identifying story parts**

1. SAY, *"Let's take a look at a personal narrative that you previously wrote."*

   Give each student a personal narrative that he or she wrote previously. Ask them to read it to themselves and see which parts their narratives contain and which parts are missing.

2. Conference briefly with each student, making note of what parts he or she has and what parts are missing.

3. Give each student a graph. Have them graph the number of parts their story had. For students who had all parts, remind them that they can make components better.

STEP 2: Obtaining commitment

SAY, *"I want you to learn the C-SPACE strategy because it can help you to write better, more complete narratives. Writing good, complete narratives is important in many of your classes—many classes have assignments that require you to write a narrative.*

The C-SPACE strategy is a great trick to make sure your narratives have all the necessary components. For you to get the most out of the strategy, we are going to make sure you learn it well and practice it." Get students' commitment.

STEP 3: Set a goal

SAY, *"Each time we practice we will graph the results. This will show you how much better and more complete your narratives are. Let's set a goal for our next practice."* Discuss why goal setting is important and reasons or places we might set goals.

Examples to guide discussion:

- Goals give us something to work towards (i.e., they focus our energy).

- Goals help us see our improvement and progress.

- Goals are motivating.

- Many successful people/learners set goals.

- We might set goals such as "finish my homework" or "write two pages."

SAY, *"Look at what your last score was and decide what you want your goal to be. Then draw a line on the graph to show what your first goal will be."* Help students set realistic goals. Set a goal that is not too high and can easily be met with effort. Be sure all students are setting goals and writing their goals on the goal chart. SAY, *"Okay, I see a lot of very good goals, and if you use the C-SPACE strategy you are more likely to meet your goals."*

WRAP-UP

SAY, *"Tomorrow I am going to show you exactly how to use the C-SPACE strategy. I am also going to quiz you on the steps of the strategy because it's important that you know the steps of the strategy by memory."*

LESSON 3

Model the Strategy

LESSON OVERVIEW

The teacher will continue to discuss the strategy, model strategy use, and support strategy memorization.

STUDENT OBJECTIVE

The students will listen to the C-SPACE strategy being modeled.

MATERIALS

One copy for each student: mnemonic chart, graphic organizer, graph, paper and pencil

---

SET THE CONTEXT FOR STUDENT LEARNING

Ask the students if they remember the strategy and story parts. Have each student take out a piece of paper and write the steps of the strategy (and what they mean). Check for understanding. Go through steps as a class.

DEVELOP THE STRATEGY AND SELF-REGULATION

STEP 1: Model the strategy

1. Get out the graphic organizer and mnemonic chart.

2. Start by modeling how to pick an interesting or funny event from your life to write a narrative about (e.g., winning a big game, moving to a new house, getting a new pet).

3. Discuss why it's important to start with an interesting or funny event (e.g., it will keep the audience interested).

4. Model the entire strategy, including the planning and writing. Use the graphic organizer so that students can see your planning—use an overhead projector or large chart paper if necessary. Plan the story you will model in advance, including what you will say and write.

    Here are some general guidelines:

    (1) Verbalize each step in planning and writing.

    (2) Include general problem definition ("Let's see. What do I do first?", "What do I do next?"), creativity ("Let my mind be free and good ideas will come to me"), and self-evaluation statements ("Wow! I did a good job").

    (3) Work at a pace so that students can follow what you are doing, but quick enough so you do not lose their interest.

    (4) Get started by yourself, but to keep the group involved, ask for student assistance when necessary.

SAY, *"What I am doing? Oh yes, I'm going to write a personal narrative—that's a story about something that has happened to me. A good story has all the parts and is interesting to read. What's the first thing I'm supposed to do? I remember that strategy we've been talking about—C-SPACE. What's the first step? The first step is 'C' which I remember means I have to think about characters—or who and what this story will be about. Well, since this is a personal narrative, I know the story will be about me. Wow! That was easy. I'll write 'me' on the graphic organizer under 'characters.'"*

SAY, *"What is the next step? I'm going to plan before I write my story by writing my ideas on this graphic organizer. What do I have to do next? Setting."* Talk out your ideas and make brief notes on the organizer. Finish by reviewing the parts of the strategy and saying that you have good ideas for all the parts and that all the ideas make sense.

SAY, *"Now I have to write the story. I can add more ideas and details as I am writing."* Talk yourself through writing the story on chart paper or on the overhead. Keep thinking aloud, refer to your plan, and add ideas. Allow students to assist.

STEP 2: Graph performance

1. Have the students assist you in counting the number of story parts you have in your story.

2. Demonstrate how you would graph the number of story parts.

WRAP-UP

Have the students put any work from the day in their folders. Remind them that they will be asked to remember the mnemonic and story parts for the next class. Tell them that they will be writing a story in the next class.

LESSON 4

Collaborative Practice

LESSON OVERVIEW

The students and teacher will collaboratively write a story using C-SPACE.

STUDENT OBJECTIVES

The students will orally rehearse the parts of a story and the mnemonic C-SPACE. Collaboratively, students will write a story that has all the parts of C-SPACE.

MATERIALS

One copy for each student: mnemonic chart, graphic organizer, graph, paper and pencil

---

SET THE CONTEXT FOR STUDENT LEARNING

Ask the students if they remember the strategy and the story parts. Have them write the mnemonic. Check for understanding.

SUPPORT THE STRATEGY AND SELF-REGULATION

STEP 1: Practice strategy with group

1. Explain that you will plan and write a story together as a group. The students should use the mnemonic chart. Together you will complete the graphic organizer and write the story on chart paper.

2. Explain that you will be working on a personal narrative and that many of you will have similar experiences—for example, everyone has experienced a "first day of school." You may want to brainstorm experiences that everyone/most students have had, (e.g., a time they felt very embarrassed; a fun experience with friends or family) and choose which to write about.

3. After deciding on an experience, follow these general guidelines as you work together:

    •   Prompt the students to verbalize each step of the strategy and each part of C-SPACE.

    •   Give feedback on students' responses. If a student gives an inappropriate response, work to develop a better or more appropriate response.

    •   Provide help as needed.

    •   Prompt students to "let their minds be free" as they think of ideas and check whether their plan makes sense.

4. SAY, *"What is the first step in the strategy?"* Students should answer, *"character."* Ask *"What does that mean we should do?"* Students should answer, *"Identify a main character for our narrative."* Ask, *"Who is the main character in a personal narrative?"* Students should answer, *"Me!"* SAY, *"What is the next step?"* Continue to lead students through the process, write students' responses, and have them record ideas on their graphic organizer.

SAY, *"After we have planned and brainstormed, what do we need to do?"* Students should respond, *"It's time to write our narrative."* Take turns with the students, adding to the story as you write. Ask for student assistance as appropriate.

STEP 2: **Graph performance**

1. Have students count the number of parts in the story you wrote together.

2. Have the students graph the number of parts on their graph.

WRAP-UP

Have students put all work from the day into their folders. Remind them that they will be asked to remember the mnemonic and story parts for the next class.

LESSON 5

Practice the Strategy

LESSON OVERVIEW

With assistance from the teacher, the students will begin to write stories that include all story parts.

STUDENT OBJECTIVES

The students will write the parts of a personal narrative and the mnemonic C-SPACE. The students will plan and write stories with all six parts of C-SPACE.

MATERIALS

One copy for each student: mnemonic chart, graphic organizer, graph, paper and pencil

SET THE CONTEXT FOR STUDENT LEARNING

Ask the students if they remember the strategy and story parts. Have them write the mnemonic as review. You may also have students pair up and "quiz" each other on the steps.

SUPPORT THE STRATEGY AND SELF-REGULATION

STEP 1: Group and individual practice

1. Explain to the students that they will plan a story together, and then each student will write his or her own version. Each student (and the teacher) will complete a graphic organizer.

2. Have students pick an event from their lives. **Make sure the event has been experienced by all or most students.**

3. Lead the students through the strategy. Follow the same general guidelines as before:

    • Prompt the students to verbalize each step of the strategy and each part of C-SPACE.

    • Give feedback on students' responses. If a student gives an inappropriate response, work to develop a better or more appropriate response.

    • Provide help as needed.

    • Prompt students to "let their minds be free" as they think of ideas and check whether their plan makes sense.

4. Remind students that they need not write all the same things on their own organizer, but they must write something appropriate for each part.

5. Tell each student to write a story using the graphic organizer to plan. As they plan and write, monitor to ensure they are using all the story parts. Provide help only as necessary.

STEP 2: Read stories and graph performance

1. Have the students share stories by reading them aloud. Stories can be read to the whole class, in small groups, or in pairs. Students may revise their narrative if they are missing parts.

2. Have students graph the number of parts for their own story on their graph.

STEP 3: Discuss improving narratives

Briefly discuss how students can improve narratives once they have included all story parts.

*   Additional characters can be added.

*   Tension/uncertainty can be created through word choice.

*   For example, they can use "million dollar words." Instead of "surprised," the word "flabber-gasted" could be used.

*   Remind students that even if they have all the necessary story parts, they can still find ways to make their narratives better.

WRAP-UP

Have students put all their work into their folders. Remind them that they will be asked to remember the mnemonic and the story parts for the next class.

LESSON 6

Practice the Strategy

LESSON OVERVIEW

Students will memorize the mnemonic and parts of C-SPACE. With the teacher's assistance, the students will plan and write their own stories.

STUDENT OBJECTIVES

The students will write the parts of a story and the mnemonic C-SPACE. The students will independently write a story that has all the parts of C-SPACE.

MATERIALS

One copy for each student: mnemonic chart, graphic organizer, graph, paper and pencil

SET THE CONTEXT FOR STUDENT LEARNING

Ask the students if they remember the strategy and story parts. Have them write the mnemonic.

SUPPORT THE STRATEGY AND SELF-REGULATION

STEP 1: Individual practice

1. Tell the students that they will plan and write their own story. Have students brainstorm some events from their lives that could be interesting to write about. Brainstorming can be done as a whole class or in pairs.

2. Remind students to use all the steps of the strategy. Tell them that they can use their mnemonic charts if necessary and that you will check on them as they use the strategy.

3. Monitor the students' use of the strategy and confer with them as they work. Provide as much help as necessary, but encourage students to work on their own. Make sure each student plans for and has all six parts prior to writing the narrative.

STEP 2: Read stories and graph performance

1. Have students share stories by reading them out loud. Allow revising if necessary.

2. Have students graph the number of parts in their own story on their graph.

WRAP-UP

Repeat this lesson until the students demonstrate that they can plan by using the graphic organizer and mnemonic chart to write a story that contains all six parts of C-SPACE. Some students may need more time, practice, and assistance than others to complete this lesson. *Optional: Some students can work independently while those that require more assistance may still brainstorm and plan together prior to writing their narrative.*

LESSON 7

Practice the Strategy Without Prompts

LESSON OVERVIEW

The students will memorize the mnemonic C-SPACE. With the teacher's assistance (as necessary) students will plan a narrative, create their own notes, and write their own narrative.

STUDENT OBJECTIVES

The students will write a narrative that has all the parts of C-SPACE. They will make their notes on a blank piece of paper.

MATERIALS

One copy for each student: mnemonic chart, paper and pencil

SET THE CONTEXT FOR STUDENT LEARNING

Ask the students if they remember the strategy and story parts. Review as necessary.

SUPPORT THE STRATEGY AND SELF-REGULATION

STEP 1: Individual Practice

1. Tell the students that they will plan and write another personal narrative. Remind them that they will not always have a graphic organizer to plan their narratives, but they can use a blank piece of paper. Briefly demonstrate how this is done.

    Discuss how you already know the steps of the strategy C-SPACE, and that those steps ensure you have all the parts of a narrative.

     SAY, *"Without your graphic organizer, you can write the letters of C-SPACE on a piece of paper—Write C, S, and P on the top half of the paper, evenly spaced. Then write A, C, and E on the bottom half of the paper, parallel to C, S, P."*

2. Discuss some possible events that students could write about in their personal narrative. Remind students of the steps of the strategy. Tell students that they can use the mnemonic chart as necessary.

3. Monitor students' use of the strategy. Provide assistance as needed, but encourage students to work on their own.

STEP 2: Read stories and graph performance

1. Have students share their stories. Allow revising if necessary.

2. Have students graph the number of parts in their narrative on their graph.

WRAP-UP

Repeat this lesson until students demonstrate that they are able to plan and write a narrative with six story parts without using the graphic organizer.

LESSON 8

(Optional): Instructing Students How to Give Peer Feedback

LESSON OVERVIEW

The students learn how to work with a partner while planning a story. This lesson could be used before or after Lesson Five to help students who are having difficulty.

STUDENT OBJECTIVES

Students will learn to work with a partner to plan a narrative.

MATERIALS

One copy for each student: mnemonic chart, Directions for Peer Feedback sheet, graphic organizer or blank piece of paper, paper and pencil

SET THE CONTEXT FOR STUDENT LEARNING

Review the purpose of the strategy. The students will be helping each other with their stories before they write them. Ask about ways in which the students have worked together on writing in class (e.g., brainstorming ideas, working in pairs). This will depend on the amount of peer revising that has been previously implemented in the classroom.

DEVELOP PEER FEEDBACK

STEP 1: Describe the strategy

1. Explain that the students will plan their narratives alone, and then they will share their plan with a partner before they begin writing. Partners will discuss how to make their stories better. Each student will then write his or her narrative alone.

2. Explain that they will learn the steps for helping one another improve their story plans. Show them the Peer Feedback sheet.

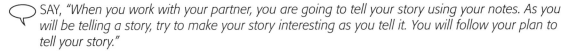 SAY, *"When you work with your partner, you are going to tell your story using your notes. As you will be telling a story, try to make your story interesting as you tell it. You will follow your plan to tell your story."*

"After you tell your story, your partner will tell you what he or she likes best. Why is it important to tell something positive first?" You should always start with a positive. It is easier to listen to feedback and suggestions for improvements if you have already heard some positive things about your narrative.

SAY, *"In the next step, the author and his or her partner will discuss ways to make the story better. To do this, they will use the C-SPACE strategy. They will think about each part of the narrative and come up with ways to make some parts better."*

"The last step is to write your partner's changes on your graphic organizer or planning sheet. Any new ideas or suggestions that they give you should be written down so you do not forget to use them when you write your story."

"Then, you switch and the other student is the author, and you follow the same steps."

STEP 2: Explain questions

1. SAY, *"Let's talk about the questions to ask each other about each step of C-SPACE. The questions will help you think about how to make your narrative better. What makes characters and settings interesting?"* The students should discuss such things as descriptions, good details, and expressions of their personalities. Discuss how it should be easy to adequately describe the main character, because in a personal narrative, the main character is themselves and they are expert at knowing themselves.

2. SAY, *"What is the next part of a narrative after the character and setting? Yes. It is the problem. What is a problem?"* The students should say that the main character has a problem or something he or she wishes to accomplish. *"The problem is very important; it is like the main idea of the narrative. The story should be all about what the main character does to solve the problem, so the author should be sure that everyone recognizes the problem when reading the narrative. The questions we want to ask about the problem are: 'What is the problem? Can you tell what it is? Does it make sense?'"*

3. SAY, *"What is the next part of a story? The next part is action."* Discuss what makes for interesting action in a narrative. Remind students that the action should fit the problem. Discuss how the *problem* can set off a "chain of events." For example, if the problem was that you lost your dog, the actions would be: 1) You made posters with your dog's picture and posted them in the neighborhood, 2) You walked around yelling your pet's name, and 3) You called the humane society to see if anyone found a lost dog.

4. SAY, *"What is next? We have to reach a conclusion. What is the conclusion? It's what happens at the end of a story or narrative."* The students should understand that the problem may be solved, or that the characters sometimes fail to solve the problem. The question to ask about the conclusion is: *"Is the problem solved?"*

5. SAY, *"What about emotions? What is important about emotions in stories?"* Discuss with students that we should ask, "Can we tell how the character feels about the problem and the conclusion?"

STEP 3: Model the strategy

Start by identifying an interesting event from your life about which you will write a short narrative. Complete a graphic organizer (or make notes on a blank piece of paper). Work out your story ahead of time. It should be a mostly complete story with room for improvement (e.g., lacks emotion, poor descriptions of character or setting). Tell the story to the group and prompt them to ask questions and make suggestions for improvement. Follow all of the steps for working with a partner. Make notes and think aloud about how you would change your narrative when you write it. Write the narrative later and share it on another day. Be sure to point out how much better the narrative is. Optional: have students help you write the narrative.

Here are some general guidelines for this modeling and guided practice:

1. Prompt students to identify steps of the C-SPACE strategy.

2. Provide clear feedback and help as necessary for students to use peer feedback appropriately.

3. Take suggestions from students.

STEP 4: Pair practice

Have students plan a short narrative. Then have students pair up and give each other feedback on their plan. Students should then write the narrative and graph the number of story parts.

WRAP-UP

Make sure all students have copies of the new charts. Have the students put their work in their folders. Repeat this lesson (or components of this lesson) as necessary.

(Optional): Using the C-Space Strategy to Write Biographies

LESSON OVERVIEW

The students will learn how to use the C-SPACE strategy to plan and write biographies. This lesson could be included any time after Lesson Three.

STUDENT OBJECTIVES

The students will listen to a modeled lesson about using C-SPACE to plan and write biographies.

MATERIALS

One copy for each student: mnemonic chart, graphic organizer, "Planning for My Biography" sheet, paper and pencil

SET THE CONTEXT FOR STUDENT LEARNING

Review the purpose of the strategy. The students will be using the C-SPACE strategy to help them plan and write a biography.

DEVELOP THE STRATEGY AND SELF-REGULATION

STEP 1: Describe the strategy

Explain that the students will be planning and writing a biography. Discuss how the C-SPACE strategy can help ensure their biography has all the necessary components. Review what a biography is and how it is different from a personal narrative or story—e.g., it is based on factual events from someone else's life.

SAY, *"This time when you use the C-SPACE strategy, the first step will be to pick a person. This person will be the main character of the biography. However, because this person will be real and we may not know a lot about them, we will have to do some research to complete the rest of our graphic organizer."*

STEP 2: Explain the research component

1. Explain that the students will be using the C-SPACE planning sheet to record facts about their main character. This will help them plan their biography prior to writing it.

2. Discuss appropriate places to find information, such as textbooks, the library, and reliable Internet sources.

3. Tell students that they will have to record where they found the information to include in the biography.

STEP 3: Model the strategy

 1. SAY, *"Now I am going to show you how to use the C-SPACE strategy to plan and write a biography."*

2. Start by choosing a person to research. Pick someone that all or most students will know, such as the president). You should work out the biography ahead of time. Start by writing your chosen person on the graphic organizer under "Character." Include self-statements— e.g., "That was easy. I already have one step done!"

3. Then model how to find additional information for your biography.

 SAY, *"Well, now that I have picked my main character, I need to find some reliable information about them. I have this sheet that helps me with the steps in finding reliable information. I am going to use this. I'm going to start by seeing if I can use any of my textbooks, because I know they will have reliable information in them."* The instructor should model finding some information in a textbook. Then the instructor should model using another source, perhaps a library book or Internet source.

4. Fill in the graphic organizer as you find information. Include self-statements, for example, *"Okay, only four more steps and then I can write my biography!"* Continue thinking aloud.

5. Once you have completed the graphic organizer, begin to write the biography.

 SAY, *"Now I have to write my biography. I know I can add more details as I write."*

Ask for student help as appropriate. Talk yourself through writing the story (on chart paper or overhead), refer to the plan, and add ideas as you go.

STEP 4: Practice

Have students pick someone to be the main character of their biography. Students should spend some time researching facts to complete the graphic organizer prior to writing the biography. Have students graph the number of story parts on their graph.

WRAP-UP

Have students put all of their work into their folder. Repeat this lesson or components from this lesson as needed.

C-SPACE Mnemonic Chart

C Character

S Setting

P Purpose

A Action

C Conclusion

E Emotions

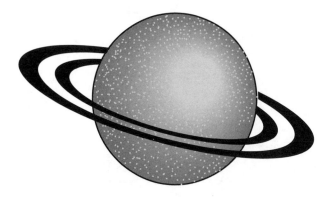

From Harris, K.R., Graham, S., Mason, L.H., & Friedlander, B. (2008). *Powerful writing strategies for all students.* Baltimore, MD: Paul H. Brookes Publishing Co., Inc.; adapted by permission.

In *Building Comprehension in Adolescents: Powerful Strategies for Improving Reading and Writing in Content Areas* by Linda H. Mason, Ph.D., Robert Reid, Ph.D., and Jessica L. Hagaman, Ph.D. (2012, Paul H. Brookes Publishing Co., Inc.)

135

C-SPACE Graphic Organizer

Story Parts	*	*	*	*	*	*
6						
5						
4						
3						
2						
1						
	Narrative 1	Narrative 2	Narrative 3	Narrative 4	Narrative 5	Narrative 6

Planning Your Personal Narrative

Characters Who will this story be about?	Setting Time and place	Purpose What the main character tries to do
Action What is done to achieve the **purpose**	Conclusion Results of the **action**	Emotions The main character's reactions and feelings

From Harris, K.R., Graham, S., Mason, L.H., & Friedlander, B. (2008). *Powerful writing strategies for all students.*
Baltimore, MD: Paul H. Brookes Publishing Co., Inc.; adapted by permission.
In *Building Comprehension in Adolescents: Powerful Strategies for Improving Reading and Writing
in Content Areas* by Linda H. Mason, Ph.D., Robert Reid, Ph.D., and Jessica L. Hagaman, Ph.D.
(2012, Paul H. Brookes Publishing Co., Inc.)

Author's Peer Feedback Guide

☐ Brainstorm a topic.

☐ Plan your narrative using your graphic organizer.

☐ Using your notes, tell your story to your partner.

☐ Listen to your partner's feedback.

☐ Make notes on your plan sheet.

☐ Write your narrative; include any feedback from your peer.

Partner's Peer Feedback Guide

☐ Listen to your partner's story.

☐ Tell them what you liked about their narrative.

Discuss ideas using C-SPACE

☐ C – Characters

☐ S – Setting

☐ P – Problem

☐ A – Action

☐ C – Conclusion

☐ E – Emotion

From Harris, K.R., Graham, S., Mason, L.H., & Friedlander, B. (2008). *Powerful writing strategies for all students.* Baltimore, MD: Paul H. Brookes Publishing Co., Inc.; adapted by permission.

In *Building Comprehension in Adolescents: Powerful Strategies for Improving Reading and Writing in Content Areas* by Linda H. Mason, Ph.D., Robert Reid, Ph.D., and Jessica L. Hagaman, Ph.D. (2012, Paul H. Brookes Publishing Co., Inc.)

138

Finding Reliable Sources

Here are some steps to help you with your research.

1. Where did you find your information?

    ☐ textbook

    ☐ library book

    ☐ television

    ☐ newspaper

    ☐ magazine/journal

    ☐ Internet

2. Determine whether the information comes from a reliable source:

    ☐ the book/article is published

    ☐ there is an author listed.

        ☐ verify that the author is knowledgeable on the topic (find his/her web site, determine if they have a degree or work for a university)

        ☐ the web site ends with .edu, .gov, .org

3. Write down where you found your information

    _____

    _____

    _____

    _____

    _____

    _____

    _____

    _____

    _____

    _____

    _____

    _____

    _____

    _____

    _____

    _____

Chapter 10

STOP & DARE
for Persuasive Writing

STOP

Suspend judgment

Take a side

Organize ideas

Plan more as you write

DARE

Develop a topic sentence

Add supporting ideas

Reject an argument

End with a conclusion

MATERIALS

Essay topics/prompts

Word count graph

Linking words

STOP & DARE directions

Goal Setting

Brainstorming Sheet

The STOP and DARE strategies were developed by De La Paz and Graham (1997). STOP and DARE are strategies that help students plan and write persuasive essays. In the following lessons, the persuasive/opinion essay planning strategy STOP (**S**uspend judgment, **T**ake a side, **O**rganize ideas, **P**lan more as you write) is introduced. Then, the essay writing strategy DARE (**D**evelop a topic sentence, **A**dd supporting ideas, **R**eject an argument, **E**nd with a conclusion) is introduced. Explicit instruction in self-regulation is incorporated into each of the lessons. Specifically, goal setting, self-monitoring, self-instructions, and self-reinforcement are components in the STOP and DARE lessons. In addition, students are asked to sign a learning contract, committing to learning and using the STOP and DARE strategies.

Prior to beginning STOP and DARE instruction, the teacher should collect a sample of students' writing performance in the task (i.e., persuasive essay, opinion essay) to be taught. These preinstruction assessments will be used in Lesson 1.

Introduce STOP and DARE

LESSON OVERVIEW

The teacher will introduce and describe the STOP and DARE strategies in the first lesson. The teacher will also support students as they identify parts of an essay, and obtain students' commitment to learn and memorize the strategy.

STUDENT OBJECTIVES

Students will orally state the parts of the essay planning strategy STOP, the parts of a good essay in DARE, identify essay parts included in a sample essay and one of their baseline essays, and graph the number of parts found in their own essay.

MATERIALS

STOP and DARE mnemonic chart, STOP and DARE direction sheet, sample essays for identifying parts, previously written individual student essays, chart paper or chalkboard, pencil

SET THE CONTEXT FOR STUDENT LEARNING

1. Introduce writing essays. This introduction to the strategy emphasizes what makes a good persuasive essay. Explain to the students that for this writing class they will learn how to compose good essays. Good essays can persuade someone to change her or his point of view. Good writers plan before they write. Good essays have several parts.

2. SAY, *"I know that you've had to write essays for your classes over the last few years. Writing essays is difficult, and over the next few weeks I am going to be teaching you a trick to help you compose a good essay. To write a good essay you need to plan your essay. Good writers plan before they write. Also, good essays have a few basic parts. You will learn the parts of a good essay."*

3. Why should students learn to write essays? The components of essays can be found everywhere: on TV, radio, newspaper editorials, letters to the editor, at home, and so forth. People who can write good essays know how to convince and persuade others. Students can share if they have tried to convince their parents, teachers, or friends to believe their side of an issue before, and what those issues were.

4. ASK, *"What is one reason that someone has to learn to write an essay?"* Respond positively to any logical answer or acknowledge the student's response and go on. SAY: *"People who can write good essays know how to convince and persuade others. Good essays can persuade someone to change his or her point of view. I'm sure you've tried to convince one of your parents or teachers to believe your side of an issue before. Tell me about a time you tried to convince someone of your position before."* Respond positively to student answers. If they do not provide am answer, provide an example of your own. *"So, we know that we need to know how to convince others. We often need to do this in essays too."*

DEVELOP THE STRATEGY AND SELF-REGULATION

STEP 1: Describe and discuss the strategy STOP

1. In this first step of instruction the teacher should discuss the writing process with students, emphasizing that most "expert" writers plan before starting to compose. Give each student the STOP and DARE chart. Explain that the chart will help them learn and remember the planning process they will be learning. The chart should be covered so that only the first step, "Suspend Judgment," shows.

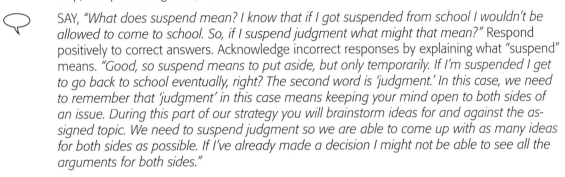   SAY, *"What does suspend mean? I know that if I got suspended from school I wouldn't be allowed to come to school. So, if I suspend judgment what might that mean?"* Respond positively to correct answers. Acknowledge incorrect responses by explaining what "suspend" means. *"Good, so suspend means to put aside, but only temporarily. If I'm suspended I get to go back to school eventually, right? The second word is 'judgment.' In this case, we need to remember that 'judgment' in this case means keeping your mind open to both sides of an issue. During this part of our strategy you will brainstorm ideas for and against the assigned topic. We need to suspend judgment so we are able to come up with as many ideas for both sides as possible. If I've already made a decision I might not be able to see all the arguments for both sides."*

2. Uncover "Take a Side."

   SAY, *"In this step you will evaluate what you've brainstormed up to this point. You need to look at both sides of the issue, the arguments that you have for each side, and make a decision about which side you believe in. This is an important part of the planning process. Why might it be important to take a side before you start to plan?"* (It will help you pick the ideas that you will use in your essay.) SAY, *"Okay, so once you have chosen a side to support you will need to try to convince your reader to agree with you. You'll use the ideas that you brainstormed to help you make your point."*

3. Uncover "Organize Ideas." The third step will help students to select ideas they feel will support their belief, and to select at least one argument they can refute.

   SAY *"In this step you will pick ideas that you feel will support your belief. Additionally, you'll pick one argument that you can refute. 'Refute' means that you have to be able to oppose it, shoot it down, but with support. 'That argument is stupid' doesn't work here. For a persuasive essay to be strong it needs to have supporting ideas as well as explanations of the counter arguments. These counter arguments have to be dealt with carefully. We want to show that they are not the side people should believe or our readers might think they are better than our real argument. How might we be able to refute an argument that goes against our point?"* (For example, thinking of a contrasting reason or a condition that would make an exception to the argument.) *"Why is that important?"* (For example, we need to show that the idea isn't good, or not as good as ours.)

   SAY, *"Now I want you to select three ideas for the side you're supporting and one from the side that you're refuting. Number the arguments from one to three in the order you think they should be presented in your essay. This will help you organize your essay. Deciding the order of your arguments is similar to using a map. Why do we use a map when we travel? What purpose does it serve? When a traveler uses a map, he or she looks first for her or his destination and chooses a route to that place. Taking a side is like deciding your destination, and your essay will guide others to accept the side you believe in."*

4. Uncover "Plan More as You Write."

   SAY, *"'Plan more as you write' means that while you're writing you should still be thinking about your arguments for and against the topic. Your plan is a guide but it can change. If you come across roadwork when you're traveling you don't just stop and wait until it's done. You take a detour. Writing can be like that too. Maybe you realize one of your ideas isn't as strong as you thought, or maybe you have thought of something new to add. You might come up with a great idea while you're writing. You just need to be sure it clearly relates to your position."*

STEP 2: Parts of an essay

In this step the teacher and student will brainstorm parts of a good essay.

SAY, *"What are the parts of a good essay? What words have you learned or heard your teachers use when they talk about good essays?"* Respond positively to all student answers; write down any answers that correspond to the essay parts below, such as main idea, reasons, examples, arguments, end, and so forth. Prompt as necessary.

SAY, *"When we talk about essays and the parts that make up an essay there are certain words that we should use. I want you to use these words and get used to them if you aren't already. These words are: topic sentence, supporting ideas, argument(s), and conclusion."* Write these parts on the chart paper or chalkboard as you label each. Make sure these terms are clearly understood by the students. Note any parts that students have previously generated.

STEP 3: Essay parts reminder: DARE

This step will introduce students to the essay parts reminder DARE.

SAY, *"Now I'm going to show you a reminder to help you remember the important parts of a good essay. We'll practice using it, but remember that you need to memorize it."*

1. Uncover the essay part reminder DARE chart & read it aloud:

    Develop a topic sentence.

    Add supporting ideas.

    Reject an argument.

    End with a conclusion.

2. Give the sample essay to the students.

    SAY, *"Let's practice finding these parts. Read along silently as I read the essay aloud. Raise your hand when you hear the topic sentence, supporting ideas, arguments, and conclusion."* Respond positively and provide encouragement as you go along.

3. After all the essay parts have been identified, ask for another example of each part for the same topic (for example, an opposing idea). Write down student responses on chart paper or chalkboard or highlight responses in essay on overhead.

STEP 4: Chart current level of performance

For this step, the students' current level of performance will be reviewed. **If time is running short, however, proceed to Step 5 and complete this step during the next session.**

SAY, *"Remember the purpose of knowing a strategy is to help you become a better writer. Right now we're going to set some goals for writing a good essay and I'm going to have you sign a contract."*

1. Hand out one of the pretest (baseline) essays.

    SAY, *"This is one of the essays that you wrote for me before we started learning our strategy. I want you to read through it to see which parts of a good essay you included and which ones you didn't. Remember, it's okay if your essay doesn't have all the parts of a good essay, because you didn't know the trick yet."*

2. Briefly note which parts each student has and what is missing.

 SAY, *"Okay, let's underline all the essay parts that you included and make a list of those that are missing. This gives a good idea about what we need to work on.* (Note included and excluded parts.) *Now we're going to graph how many essay parts we included, along with the number of words that were used in your essay. We are also looking at how long your essay is, because we know that often a longer essay is a better essay. We're going to use this to keep a running record of your improvement. That means we'll do this each time that you write an essay."*

3. Even if a part is present, students may be able to make that part better in subsequent essays. Give examples for improvement such as:

   - can tell your point of view
   - can have several reasons
   - can give examples
   - can consider an argument
   - can reject an argument by countering it or dealing with it in some way
   - can have a clear ending

4. Spend a few minutes explaining the STOP and DARE checklist. Give the student a checklist and ask him or her to mark the number of essay parts written in his or her pretest.

5. Explain the goal—to write better essays. Remind the students that good essays have all STOP *and* DARE parts, and that good essays make sense. The goal is to have all the parts and "better" parts next time.

6. Have the students set a goal for the next time they write and note the goals on the graphing sheet (length & essay parts).

7. Have students record goal on learning contract and sign the contract.

STEP 5: Practice STOP and DARE

Practice the mnemonic STOP.

 SAY, *"It is important that you memorize this so you don't have to think about it to use it. If it is memorized you can use it automatically and just think about the assignment you're working on rather than the parts of the reminder. Remember that you also have to know what each step means. It's important that you understand what you do at each step."*

Options for practicing STOP and DARE:

- Turn over the chart and ask the students to tell you the essay-planning reminder. (They should tell you STOP, and tell you what each letter means.)

- Ask each student to write the reminder on paper. If students have trouble, turn the chart over and allow them to look. Keep doing this until all students can tell you the reminder and explain each letter from memory.

Have students pair up and "quiz" each other on the steps.

- Go around the room and have each student say a step (and explanation) for STOP and DARE.

WRAP-UP

Give the students a reminder sheet to keep with them. Announce that there will be a nongraded "quiz" in the beginning of the next class.

LESSON 2

Model the Strategies

LESSON OVERVIEW

The teacher will review STOP and DARE, test for memorization, model the strategy, and develop self-statements.

STUDENT OBJECTIVES

The students will verbally state the part of the essay-planning strategy STOP and the parts of a good essay as in DARE. The students will demonstrate an understanding of how to use the STOP and DARE strategies.

MATERIALS

STOP and DARE cue sheet (directions), STOP and DARE brainstorming sheet (brainstorm), sample essays for identifying parts, previously written individual student essays, chart paper or chalkboard, pencil

SET THE CONTEXT FOR STUDENT LEARNING

Quiz the students to see if they remember the word that will help them remember how to plan (STOP) and what the letters stand for. Give them a piece of paper and ask them to write down the word and any details about the strategy step. Help as necessary. Test to see if they remember the word that will help them remember the parts of a good essay (DARE). Give them a piece of paper and ask them to write down the word and any details about the strategy step. Ask students to tell you what each word means. Help as necessary.

DEVELOP THE STRATEGY AND SELF-REGULATION

STEP 1: Identify essay parts and elaborations

Give the sample essay to the students.

SAY, *"Remember how we read through an essay together yesterday? Here is another sample essay. Read along as I read aloud. Let me know when you hear each of the essay parts."* Underline each in the text as they are identified. *"Now that we found all the parts included in this essay I want us to think about other examples of each essay part. It is important to notice that good writers often elaborate their reasons, topic sentence, argument, and conclusions. These elaborations provide support for the reasons, arguments, and so forth. Let's look back at the two essays that we've already read and see how the authors did this."* Have an example from each essay already identified.

STEP 2:   Model the strategy

In this step the teacher will model how to use the strategy to plan and write a good essay. It is important that the teacher has memorized the procedure so that it will be fluent. In order to provide an example of modeling this strategy, a sample script has been provided below.

1. Keep the STOP and DARE chart to the side during modeling.

    SAY, *"Today, I am going to show you how to use STOP and DARE together to plan and write a good essay. I will talk out loud as I go. You might be able to help me, if I ask you, but what I really want you to do is to listen and watch me work. I want you to see how I use this strategy to write my essay. It will make it easier for you to understand how to think your way through the strategy."*

2. Model the entire process using the cue sheet and the list of linking words.

    SAY, *"Okay, first I need to 'suspend judgment.' That means don't make up my mind about the topic yet. I need to brainstorm ideas for and against my topic. I need to have my ideas ready before I make any decisions about which side I'm going to take. By not taking a side now I'll be better at finding arguments for both sides. I'm going to write my ideas on this brainstorm sheet so I won't forget them. I like that there are columns, plus, my STOP reminder is listed right there if I need it. This will definitely help me keep my ideas organized while I plan."*

3. Refer to the cue sheet.

    SAY, *"I'm going to use my cue sheet now, to help me plan. There are three questions listed with Suspend Judgment. These must be things I need to think about before I move on to the next step. I'll go through them one at a time to be sure I'm following all the steps. I need to be sure to follow all the steps so I can write a good essay. The first question says, 'Did I list ideas for both sides? If not, do this now.' Let me see... I did that!"*

    "Okay. What does the second question say? 'Can I think of anything else? Try to write more.' All right, I need to think of more reasons. What other reasons can I think of?" Add at least one idea to the FOR side. *"What about AGAINST? Why wouldn't I support this idea?"* Pause, then add another idea to the AGAINST side. Add one more idea to one side. *"Okay, do those make sense? Are they listed on the right side? Yes? Okay, what's next?"* Pause, then SAY, *"One more question for this step. It says, 'Another point I haven't yet considered is.... Think of possible arguments.' Do I have any arguments? Yes, I do."* Pause. *"Okay, are there any points I haven't considered yet?"* Pause. *"This is a hard because I have so many ideas already. I need to take my time and think of something someone else would say."* Add at least one idea, preferably for the side that you will take.

4. Step 2, "Take a Side"

    SAY, *"Wow, that's great. I'm done with Step 1 and have done a lot of good work. Now I need to do Step 2, 'Take a Side.' That means I really have to pick one side as my argument. Which one do I really believe?"* Provide answer. *"I think this is the right one to choose because I like the reasons for this one better."*

    Pause. *"Let me see what the cue sheet for Step 2 says. It says, 'Place a + at the top of one box to show the side you will take in your essay. Okay, I chose this side so I'll write my + up here. Okay, have I done everything for that step? Let me look back at my cue sheet and see. Yes, I have. Good. I'm halfway done. What's next?"*

5. Step 3, "Organize ideas"

    "Step 3 is 'Organize ideas.' It says I should decide which ideas are strong and which ideas I can dispute. That means I should think about the ideas I have for my argument." Read each idea that is on the side you have chosen aloud and decide if it is a good idea. Be sure

to verbalize why you think an idea is or is not strong enough to use. You should note at least one idea that is not strong, decide out loud to skip it, and explain why it is being skipped (for example, I don't know enough about it, it isn't clear, or some other reason).

"Okay, now I have strong ideas for my argument. I need to decide which ideas I can dispute. That means I need an argument that I can reject, one that I know how to deal with in some way. I have to be able to make my reader see why I think the argument isn't as good an idea as the one I've chosen." Choose one argument from the reasons on the other side. Pause. Choose one more argument.

SAY, *"I have to choose my arguments carefully so I don't confuse my reader about which side I am on. I'm really doing well with this plan. I like my ideas; let me look at the cue sheet for this step. It says, 'Put a star next to ideas you want to use.' I need to choose at least three ideas to use that support my point. I'll start with three but I know that I can always choose more if I think I can support them and they make sense."* Make choices of which arguments to use. Put a star next to them. *"Okay, I picked three that I think are the strongest. What is my next step? Let me look at my cue sheet."*

"What does the second 'Organize Ideas' direction say? 'Did I star ideas on both sides? Choose at least one argument you can dispute.' Well I decided that I had two arguments that I can dispute. I'll pick the one I think is the easiest. Okay, what is the last direction for Step 3? It says, 'Number your ideas in the order you will use.'" (Pause.) *"I'd better think about this—what makes sense? I need to remember that the order of these will help guide my readers so they agree with what I believe. It's like the map we talked about earlier. I have to remember that the point of this essay is to make the reader agree with me. This should help."*

"This is going to be a good essay, I'm really taking my time to plan it out. The last step is, 'Plan more as you write. Remember to use all four essay parts and continue planning.' Okay, that means I should still think of ideas as I write my essay. Let me look at my cue sheet and see what I need to think about next."

"Well, I already finished all the STOP steps. Nice, I'm making progress! The next thing listed on my cue sheet is DARE. That means I'm ready to start actually writing this essay. I know what DARE means (read cue). So, I'm ready to write my essay, I'll just think of DARE as I go."

6. Verify each part that you write by telling that you have your topic sentence, and so forth. Point out that you can add supporting ideas after you reject your argument.

   Be sure to elaborate on two or three ideas as you write, and try to revise something as you go. Give a strong, summary conclusion by restating your premise using different words.

7. After you finish, compliment yourself for the work you have done and then demonstrate graphing. Mark the checklist for each part; write down the number of ideas selected on the line under the column. If you met a goal over three, you "busted" the chart and can draw a star on top of the column. Thank the students for their help (which may have simply been to pay attention).

STEP 3:   Development of self-statements

1. The teacher should ask whether students noticed the positive things being said before, while, and after modeling the strategy.

2. Briefly discuss the purpose of self-statements.

   SAY, *"Sometimes the things we say to ourselves while we are working influence how well we work. For example, if I keep saying things like, 'I hate writing. This is so stupid. Why do I have to do this?' Will I feel like sitting down and writing my essay? Probably not. When I catch myself saying those negative things to myself, I can stop and find something positive to say like: 'It's okay, I have my strategy and that is going to make writing this essay so much easier!' When I do that, it can make it easier for me to keep working and I usually write better essays!"*

3. Ask students to identify some of the statements used by the teacher (for example, "It's okay," "I can do this") and why they think the teacher said them. Ask students to identify when the teacher used these statements (e.g., when frustrated or confused, to stay on track).

4. Have students brainstorm some self-statements they might use when writing a persuasive essay. Students should record their self-statements on the *Writing Self-Statements Sheet* (in Chapter 12, Quick Writes, pg. 209)

STEP 4: Rehearsal of STOP and DARE

Students should verbally rehearse STOP and DARE until mastery has been achieved. Students must be able to recite all steps and essay parts from memory. Wording doesn't have to be exact, but meaning should be the same.

1. Review all four steps—read STOP off the chart as you go. Tell students they need to memorize the steps.

2. Have students practice. Practice any way you think helpful. For example, mnemonic chart facing up, turn sheet and cards over, write, cover, say, repeat.

Students can paraphrase the four steps and DARE from memory.

WRAP-UP

Remind students that you will check next time to see if they can remember on their own the essay planning reminder (STOP) and the essay parts reminder (DARE).

LESSON 3

Collaborative Practice and Linking Words

LESSON OVERVIEW

Students will collaboratively write an essay using the essay-planning (STOP) and essay parts (DARE) strategies. The linking word list will be explained in this lesson.

STUDENT OBJECTIVES

The students will verbally state the part of the essay-planning strategy STOP and the parts of a good essay as in DARE. The students will collaboratively practice writing an essay using STOP and DARE. Using this essay and their previously written essay evaluated in Lesson One, the students will set a goal for writing essays.

MATERIALS

STOP and DARE mnemonic chart (chart), STOP and DARE cue sheet (directions), STOP and DARE brainstorming sheet (brainstorm), linking/transition word sheet, sample essays from Lessons 1 and 2, paper, pencil

SET THE CONTEXT FOR STUDENT LEARNING

Quiz the students to see if they remember the planning steps and essay parts. Ask the students if they've been thinking about what they've learned. Briefly discuss where and why it would be appropriate to use STOP and DARE.

DEVELOP THE STRATEGY AND SELF-REGULATION

STEP 1: Introduce linking words

1. Give each student a list of linking/transition words.

 SAY, *"I'm going to show you some words that will help make your ideas go together. These probably aren't new words to you but you might not use them as often or as well as you could. Let's look at the list together. Let's think for a minute about transition or linking words. What does 'transition' mean? How about 'linking?'"* Pause. Discuss their answers or ask where they might have heard those words before. *"Yes, transition means moving from one thing to another, and linking means connecting things together. Why might we use words that we call transition or linking words? How might these types of words help make our essay better?"*

2. Ask the students to get the previously read sample essays from their folders.

 SAY, *"Okay, let's look at this essay we talked about before. Take a minute and look it over and see if you can find any transition or linking words in this essay. Use your list to help you."* Give them one minute to locate any transition words they can find. *"Okay, now, let's look at our list and see if we can find any different or better words that we could use instead*

of the ones used here." Have the students explain their choices. *"Transition words join the ideas we're discussing in our essay together. When we choose good transition words we are helping the reader follow our ideas and see how they connect to support our position. They are important! We want our ideas to make sense to the reader, right?"*

STEP 2: Criterion setting

1. Ask each student to take the checklist out of his or her folder. Explain that today you will write an essay together. This essay will be put on the checklist.

SAY, *"Before we start on the essay, though, we want to set a goal for ourselves. Remember, we will use everything we have learned to help us."* Set the goal as having all four parts, plus more than three ideas. *"Do you think we'll be able to meet this goal? What do we need to remember? We also need to remember that longer essays are often better. Let's set a goal for the number of words we'll use. Let's look back at our graph of your first essay."* Set a goal for number of words based on their baseline essay.

"Remember what we learned about transition or linking words. You can really improve your essay's quality and clarify your position if you use those words. I want us to try to use at least three transition words in the essay."

2. Be sure that all the goals are appropriate based on the student's previous work.

STEP 3: Collaborative practice

1. Explain that at least two essays will be planned and composed together. Get out the essay topics, chart, cue sheet, and brainstorm sheets.

2. Use the first prompt.

SAY, *"What is the first thing you have to say to yourself before you begin planning an essay?"* They should answer with, "Plan my essay," or equivalent.

"Now we start the steps. What is Step 1?" Students should say, "Suspend judgment."
"How do we suspend judgment?" Students should say, "Brainstorm ideas for and against the topic." Get each student to brainstorm one idea. Write ideas on the brainstorm sheet. Direct the students through cue sheet for this step. Make sure the student reads her or his own cue sheet as you go.

Ask, *"What is Step 2?"* Students should say, "Take a side." You lead discussion here, gaining consensus for the side you will take. If a student disagrees, you decide, and tell him or her that he or she will get a chance to write their own essay next time, and can write an essay from the other point of view then.

Ask, *"What is Step 3?"* Students should say, "Organize ideas." Again, lead the discussion, selecting strong ideas for the selected point of view and one or two arguments. Explain WHY they are stronger ideas. Direct the students to use the cue sheet. *"Now that we have ideas, we need to put them in order. What order do you think makes the best sense?"* Let the students tell you an order first. *"Why do you think this would be best?"* Then you select best order, explaining why you are making that choice. Remind them of the map analogy— deciding the order will help lead the reader to agree with your point of view. Also stress the logic behind the order (that is, not jumping back and forth). Give an example.

Ask, *"What is Step 4?"* Students should say, "Plan more as you write." Read the cue sheet with DARE, and tell the students to keep the sheet in front of them as they compose. Refer to the "D" in DARE, then prompt students to create a topic sentence. Provide needed support. Continue generating sentences, referring to DARE and linking words.

STEP 4:   Review essay and chart performance

1. Have each student fill in his or her check sheet. Note that this essay is better than the previously written essay they examined in Lesson One. If needed, discuss whether the student's goal was appropriate. If a student set too high a goal, it should be lowered.

2. Have students graph the essay's number of words, number of included essay elements, and number of transition words, and note the amount of time spent planning.

3. Compare these results to those of the initial baseline essay.

STEP 5:   Verbal rehearsal

 1. SAY, *"We are going to memorize the cue sheet along with the planning steps and essay parts."* To help the students memorize the planning steps and essay parts, teach them an exercise called "rapid fire." This is called rapid fire because the steps are to be named as rapidly as possibly. Tell the students that if they need to look at the chart or cue sheet, they may; however, they shouldn't rely on it too much because it will be put away after several rounds of rapid fire. Allow students to paraphrase but be sure that intended meaning is maintained.

2. Do rapid fire with planning steps (STOP). If responses are correct, make brief positive comments; if they are incorrect, prompt the students by pointing to the information. Correct wrong answers to ensure that students learn the parts correctly.

3. Do rapid fire without cues. If a student does not know a step, you provide it. Have the student repeat it back to you.

4. After rapid fire, explain to students they must be able to name all the steps, cue sheet, and essay parts in an oral quiz. Give students time to rehearse.

5. When a student indicates he or she has learned the steps, ask him or her to list them orally, including information from the cue sheet. Describe information that the student omitted or named out of sequence.

6. Tell students that writing the STOP & DARE prompts at the top of the page can serve as reminders of the parts and steps.

7. Set goals for essay length, number of essay parts, transition words, and planning time for their next independent essay and note the goals on the graphing sheet.

WRAP-UP

Remind students that you will check next time to see if they can remember on their own the essay planning reminder (STOP) and the essay parts reminder (DARE).

Independent Practice

LESSON OVERVIEW

Students will practice writing an essay independently using STOP and DARE. Feedback from teacher is provided as necessary.

STUDENT OBJECTIVES

The students will verbally state the part of the essay-planning strategy STOP and the parts of a good essay as in DARE. The students will independently practice writing an essay using STOP and DARE. Using his or her individual pretest essay, each student will set a goal for writing the essay.

MATERIALS

STOP and DARE mnemonic chart (chart), STOP and DARE cue sheet (directions), STOP and DARE brainstorming sheet (brainstorm), linking/transition word sheet, paper, pencil

SET THE CONTEXT FOR STUDENT LEARNING

Using the rapid fire method, test the students to see if they remember the planning steps and essay parts. Ask each student if he or she has been thinking about what he or she has learned. Have the student tell you about a time he or she used, or thought about using, STOP and DARE.

SUPPORT THE STRATEGY AND SELF-REGULATION

STEP 1:   Criterion setting

Review goals set at the last session. They should be higher than the first goals. Be sure to include all four parts (DARE), three or more ideas, and more words than their previous essay.

STEP 2:   Independent practice with feedback

1.   Give the student two essay topics and a brainstorm sheet.

 SAY, *"I want you to use your cue sheet, list of linking/transition words, and brainstorming sheet to plan for and write this essay. Planning improves your writing. Remember how much better our essay we did together was compared to the one you did first? We planned a lot more, used our strategies, and used transition words. Those things will improve your writing."*

2.   Provide assistance only when the student skips a step or does it incorrectly. You may need to help if the order can lead to an illogical essay. Encourage students to use at least one word from the list of linking words if they fail to do so on their own.

STEP 3: **Review essay and graph**

1. After students finish, review essays in pairs. Have students read their essay out loud; identify the parts, and point out elaborations as well as the topic sentence, reasons, arguments, and conclusion, if there are any.

2. If any parts are missing, peers should discuss how and where they could be added.

3. Have each student fill in the checklist. Note that they reached their goal (if they did).

4. Graph the results (length, essay parts, transition words) on the graphing sheet. Note how the time spent planning helps them to write better essays.

5. Discuss a goal for next time: all four essay parts, a longer essay, and more transition words. Note this goal on the graphing sheet.

WRAP-UP

Remind students that you will check next time to see if they can remember on their own the essay-planning reminder (STOP) and the essay parts reminder (DARE).

Independent Practice

LESSON OVERVIEW

The students will learn to create their own planning sheet in this lesson. By this lesson the students should set goals for writing and composing essays independently.

STUDENT OBJECTIVES

Each student will verbally state the parts of the essay-planning strategy STOP and the parts of a good essay as in DARE. The student will create a planning sheet for writing the essay. The student will independently write an essay using STOP and DARE. The students will set a goal for writing an essay.

MATERIALS

STOP and DARE mnemonic chart (chart), STOP and DARE cue sheet (directions), linking/transition word sheet, essay topics, paper, pencil

SET THE CONTEXT FOR STUDENT LEARNING

Using the rapid-fire method, test the student to see if he or she remembers the planning steps and essay parts. Ask the student if he or she has been thinking about what he or she learned. Have the students tell you about a time they have used or thought about using STOP and DARE. Discuss with the students that today they will learn a way to use the strategy without the brainstorm sheet. Be sure to emphasize that by planning on their own, they can use STOP and DARE anytime they want to write a good essay.

SUPPORT THE STRATEGY AND SELF-REGULATION

STEP 1:   Create a brainstorming plan sheet

1. Show students how to create their own planning brainstorming sheet by taking paper, writing STOP at top, drawing a vertical line down the page, and writing DARE at the bottom. Model how to cross out letters in each word as they complete the steps. Explain that this can help them when they have to write an essay for an exam and they do not have teacher resources. In addition, crossing out the letters helps them to make sure they complete each step.

2. Briefly model a plan for an essay with a topic that students used during collaborative practice or independent practice. Do this quickly, but emphasize the steps that students haven't mastered yet, such as making order of ideas logical. If they have been doing this well, model a different organization than they have been using.

STEP 2:   Goal setting

Review the goals set together at the end of the last meeting. Remind the students that using their strategy will make meeting their goals much easier. Show them their progress in previous graphs if needed.

STEP 3: **Independent practice with feedback**

Give each student two essay topics.

SAY, *"I'm going to ask you write an essay today. After looking at the topic I want you to begin by making your own brainstorming sheet like we just talked about. Once you've gone through all your STOP planning steps, use a new sheet of paper to write your essay. You can use your linking/transition words list if you need it."* Make sure they plan before composing. Be sure to check each student's plan! Provide assistance only when student skips a step or does it incorrectly.

STEP 4: **Review essays and graph**

1. Once the student has completed her or his essay, ask her or him to read it out loud. Ask the student to identify the parts, and to point out elaborations as well as topic sentence, reasons, arguments, and conclusion, if there are any.

2. If any parts are missing, discuss how and where they could be added.

3. Have each student fill in the checklist. Graph essay parts, length, and transition words. Note the amount of time planning. Note that he or she reached the goal (if they did).

WRAP-UP

Each student should repeat this Lesson Five until he or she reaches a criterion performance of all essay parts present and correct.

REFERENCE

De La Paz, S., & Graham, S. (1997). Strategy instruction in planning: Effects on the writing performance and behavior of students with learning difficulties. *Exceptional Children, 63,* 167–181.

Essay Topics

Across the country school systems are beginning to use a year-round school model. Your school district is looking into the idea of having school year round. Your school newspaper asks you to present your view in the paper.

Write an essay answering the following question: *Do you think students should have to go to school in the summer?*

Not all teachers give homework. Your teacher tells the class that she will decide whether or not to give homework based on your suggestion.

Write an essay answering the following question: *Do you think teachers should give homework?*

Many teenagers argue with their parents about keeping their room clean. What do you think?

Write an essay answering the following question: *Do you think kids should be required to clean their room?*

Because of safety concerns, a number of states are considering changing the driving age to 18. The hope is to eliminate many of the teenage driving deaths.

Write an essay answering the following question: *Do you think the driving age should be changed to 18?*

The Parent-Teacher Association is having a meeting about parenting. They would like the views of a high school student represented in their discussion. They have asked you to come to speak on the evening's topic.

Write an essay answering the following question: *Do you think parents should decide who your friends are?*

The nutritional value of school lunches is a big topic these days. As a student of the public schools you have been asked for your opinion.

Write an essay answering the following question: *Should children be allowed to eat whatever they want?*

(continued)

Your younger sister wants a gerbil. Your father says no way. Your mom hasn't made up her mind about it yet.

Write an essay answering the following question: *Should kids be allowed to have their own pets?*

- -

Grades are a big part of school. As a high school student, do you feel parents should give their children money for having good grades on their report card?

Write an essay answering the following question: *Should parents give their children money for having good grades on their report cards?*

- -

When I was in high school my parents made me turn my light off by 10 p.m. on school nights. Many of my friends were allowed to stay up late.

Write an essay answering the following question: *Should teenagers be allowed to choose their own bedtimes on school nights?*

- -

Some people have put an idea before the school board asking to have the school day shortened.

Write an essay answering the following question: *As a student, do you think the school day should be shorter?*

- -

Most of the courses that are taken in high school are required to graduate. There is only time for a few electives.

Write an essay answering the following question: *Should students be able to choose the things they study in school?*

- -

There are many opposing views about punishing kids when they do something wrong.

Write an essay answering the following question: *Do you think kids should be punished when they do something wrong?*

- -

Television is a part of most children's daily life. Many kids watch two or more hours a day.

Write an essay answering the following question: *Should children be allowed to choose the television shows they watch?*

(continued)

A couple you know has one child and is considering having more. They ask for your opinion.

Write an essay answering the following question: *Is it better to be an only child or to have brothers and sisters?*

- -

Your school district is trying to decide if computer classes should be required for students in every grade K through 12. As a member of the student body, they ask you to speak on the subject.

Write an essay answering the following question: *Should kids be required to learn how to use computers?*

- -

Many kids today are involved in sports, many starting at a very young age. Parent involvement in children's sports often is discussed in the news.

Write an essay answering the following question: *Should parents coach their children's teams?*

- -

Many high school students have jobs. Federal law limits students to working no more than three hours on a school day and not after 7 p.m. during the school year.

Write an essay answering the following question: *Should teenagers be allowed to work longer hours during the school year?*

- -

In Chicago and Boston there has been discussion of having some classes that are divided up into only boys and only girls.

Write an essay answering the following question: *Should boys and girls be taught in separate classes in school?*

- -

Many people look to their favorite athletes as heroes. They look to them as models of what and who they want to be as adults.

Write an essay answering the following question: *Should sports stars be treated as heroes?*

- -

As a person under 18, you are not able to participate in the government though voting. Some people think that should change.

Write an essay answering the following question: *Should kids your age should be able to vote?*

(continued)

Essay Topics (continued)

Many schools require students to volunteer for 20 or more hours before they graduate.

Write an essay answering the following question: *Should high school students be required to do volunteer hours to graduate?*

- -

Many public schools on the East Coast require students to wear uniforms. The school board is interested in the idea and has asked you to come give your opinion.

Write an essay answering the following question: *Should students be required to wear uniforms to school?*

Word Count Graph

Words in your essay	Essay 1	Essay 2	Essay 3	Essay 4	Essay 5	Essay 6
250 + !						
240 – 249						
230 – 239						
220 – 229						
210 – 219						
200 – 209						
190 – 199						
180 – 189						
170 – 179						
160 – 169						
150 – 159						
140 – 149						
130 – 139						
120 – 129						
110 – 119						
100 – 109						
90 – 99						
80 – 89						
70 – 79						
60 – 69						
50 – 59						
40 – 49						
30 – 39						
20 – 29						
10 – 19						
0 – 10						

Linking Words

First

Second

Third

Fourth

Fifth

Finally

In sum

In addition

Likewise

Specifically

For example

Another

Besides

Moreover

In fact

In *Building Comprehension in Adolescents: Powerful Strategies for Improving Reading and Writing in Content Areas* by Linda H. Mason, Ph.D., Robert Reid, Ph.D., and Jessica L. Hagaman, Ph.D. (2012, Paul H. Brookes Publishing Co., Inc.)

162

STOP and DARE Directions

1. **S**uspend Judgment

   • Consider each side of your topic before taking a position.

   • Brainstorm ideas for and against the topic.

2. **T**ake a side

   • Read the ideas you brainstormed.

   • Decide which side you believe in or which side will make the strongest argument.

   • Place a star on the side that shows your position.

3. **O**rganize ideas

   • Choose ideas that are strong and decide how to organize them.

4. **P**lan more as you write

   • Continue to plan as you write.

   • Use all 4 essay parts:

     Develop your topic sentence

     Add supporting ideas

     Reject arguments for the other side

     End with a conclusion

From Harris, K.R., Graham, S., Mason, L.H., & Friedlander, B. (2008). *Powerful writing strategies for all students.* Baltimore, MD: Paul H. Brookes Publishing Co., Inc.; adapted by permission.

In *Building Comprehension in Adolescents: Powerful Strategies for Improving Reading and Writing in Content Areas* by Linda H. Mason, Ph.D., Robert Reid, Ph.D., and Jessica L. Hagaman, Ph.D.
(2012, Paul H. Brookes Publishing Co., Inc.)

163

My Goal

	Essay 1	Essay 2	Essay 3	Essay 4	Essay 5	Essay 6
End with a conclusion						
Reject arguments for the other side						
Add supporting ideas	3 2 1	3 2 1	3 2 1	3 2 1	3 2 1	3 2 1
Develop your topic sentence						
	Essay 1	Essay 2	Essay 3	Essay 4	Essay 5	Essay 6
How many minutes did I spend planning?						

Brainstorming

My topic: _____

Suspend judgment.

Brainstorm ideas for and against your topic:

For	Against
1.	1.
2.	2.
3.	3.
4.	4.
5.	5.
6.	6.
7.	7.
8.	8.

Take a side—draw a star at the top of the box that shows which side you will take

Organize ideas—decide which of the above ideas are strong and which ideas you can dispute

Plan more as you write. Remember to use DARE to continue planning!

From Harris, K.R., Graham, S., Mason, L.H., & Friedlander, B. (2008). *Powerful writing strategies for all students.* Baltimore, MD: Paul H. Brookes Publishing Co., Inc.; adapted by permission.

In *Building Comprehension in Adolescents: Powerful Strategies for Improving Reading and Writing in Content Areas* by Linda H. Mason, Ph.D., Robert Reid, Ph.D., and Jessica L. Hagaman, Ph.D. (2012, Paul H. Brookes Publishing Co., Inc.)

165

Chapter 11

TWA and PLANS for Informative Writing

MATERIALS

TWA Outline for Notes

PLANS Mnemonic Chart

PLANS Worksheet

Sample Goals for Informative Essay

Sample Goals for Persuasive Essay

Sentence Combining Worksheet

Sample informative and persuasive writing prompts

This chapter presents lessons for teaching students to use information accumulated, after using TWA, to write an informative or persuasive essay with the PLANS strategy (Graham, MacArthur, Schwartz, & Page-Voth, 1992). A variety of goals for content, vocabulary, and sentence structures are presented for essay writing at levels designed to meet the needs of students and the teacher's curriculum objectives. For example, the teacher may want to evaluate students' writing to learn performance with a simple essay, an essay that contains a main idea statement with supporting details for each text paragraph that includes words from the TWA vocabulary journal. This essay format replicates in writing what students have learned to do in the oral retell. The teacher, however, may choose to ask students to write a persuasive essay, using the information in the text to write a convincing argument.

Prior to starting instruction, the teacher should collect a sample of the students' informative and/or persuasive writing after reading. It is best that this sample be collected as an assessment, without teacher guidance or support. Student writing samples can be used by the teacher to develop goals based on individual students' performance. Students can use their writing sample to evaluate current level of performance and select goals for improving performance. Regardless of the writing task (i.e., informative or persuasive), goals should be developed to ensure students success in meeting the teacher's expectations. Students need to "buy in" and agree to use goals. Providing goal choice is an important component of PLANS instruction, therefore we recommend collaboratively establishing goals as a class, for groups of students, or for students individually.

As with TWA instruction, we recommend using short informative passages below students' instructional reading level for initially teaching the PLANS strategy. In fact, passages used during TWA instruction may be used for initial lessons. We do have one caution, especially for struggling learners; researchers have documented that it is best that students become fluent in using TWA prior to beginning note-taking and essay instruction (Mason, Hickey Snyder, Sukhram, & Kedem, 2006). In addition, students with significant writing difficulties may benefit from additional, supplemental instruction for specific writing strategies as noted in Chapter 9 and Chapter 10. PLANS was developed by Graham, MacArthur, Schwartz, & Page-Voth (1992).

REFERENCES

Graham, S., MacArthur, C., Schwartz, S., & Page-Voth, V. (1992). Improving the compositions of students with learning disabilities using a strategy involving product and process goal setting. *Exceptional Children, 58*, 322–334.

Harris, K.R., Graham, S., Mason, L.H., & Friedlander, B. (2008). *Powerful writing strategies for all students*. Baltimore, MD: Brookes Publishing Co.

Model Writing Notes

LESSON OVERVIEW

The first lesson for TWA and PLANS provides a transition from the activities completed throughout TWA lessons in Chapter 7 to writing lessons. The teacher will model writing notes after using TWA.

STUDENT OBJECTIVES

Students will complete a TWA outline while following the teacher-led modeling lesson.

MATERIALS

Passage sample "Yellowstone," TWA outline overhead or PowerPoint, TWA outline for each student, learning contract, vocabulary journals, self-instruction sheet

SET THE CONTEXT FOR STUDENT LEARNING

Test students' TWA memorization.

DEVELOP THE STRATEGY AND SELF-REGULATION

STEP 1: Model writing notes with TWA

1. Tell the students that you will show them how to write notes with TWA when reading a passage. Tell them that you will first review the steps of TWA with the "Yellowstone" passage. Quickly go through all TWA steps. Ask students to support you in this process.

2. After completing a collaborative oral retell, SAY, *"I really think I know a lot more about Yellowstone now. What do I need to do next? I need to write what I have learned on the TWA notes outline. Well, the first step is the main idea for the first paragraph. The next step is to list the important details for the main idea."* Model how you write notes for the main idea and details in outline format (see *TWA Notes Outline for a Five-Paragraph Passage* on page 178):

Main idea	
Detail	
Detail	
Detail	

SAY, *"Am I finished? Well, there are three more paragraphs in this passage about Yellowstone. I think there were some other main ideas with details in the passage. The next three paragraphs talk about …"* Model writing notes for the main idea and summary with the last three paragraphs. *"Wow! I came up with a lot of main ideas and summaries. I am almost done! I have really learned a lot about Yellowstone. And that is a good thing because the last thing I need to do is to think about what I learned."*

STEP 2: Model a retell

Model how you will use the outline to help you with the oral retell. Ask the students, in pairs, to practice using the outline for an oral retell. Tell the students that in the next lessons they will use the outline for writing a written retell.

WRAP-UP

Ask students to add to their learning contract and self-instructions developed when teaching TWA to help them with writing the outline. **Repeat this lesson with another passage for students having difficulty taking notes.**

Introduce and Discuss Using TWA for Writing with PLANS, Establish Effective Goals

LESSON OVERVIEW

PLANS will be introduced. Class, group, or individual goals will be established collaboratively with the teacher. Methods for meeting goals will be noted.

STUDENT OBJECTIVES

Students will establish personal goals for writing (from those developed in class, groups, or individually with the teacher). Students will record methods for meeting the goals.

MATERIALS

Learning strategy contract, PLANS mnemonic chart, PLANS worksheet, vocabulary journals, self-instruction sheet

SET THE CONTEXT FOR STUDENT LEARNING

Test for student knowledge of steps of TWA. Do this orally and very briefly. Tell the students that they will be learning a new strategy to help them use information gathered by reading with TWA for writing.

DEVELOP THE STRATEGY AND SELF-REGULATION

STEP 1: Introduce PLANS

Ask the students if they know the meaning of the word "plan." Discuss how planning helps improve writing. Give examples, "makes writing more organized," "makes an essay longer." SAY, *"I am going to teach you a strategy for planning and writing a paper. We will learn how to use the steps while writing informative (or persuasive) essays with TWA. The strategy steps, however, can also be used for other types of writing as well. For example, you could use the steps to help you write either stories or reports that you do in class."*

STEP 2: P–Pick Goals

1. Give each student the PLANS mnemonic chart. Tell them that they will need to look at each step on their sheet as you are talking about the steps. Point out the bold letters **P**, **L**, **A**, **N**, and **S**.

2. Cover your paper so only the first step shows. SAY, *"The first thing that you need to do when you write a paper is to figure out what you want to do. Or in other words,* pick goals

171

for what you want your paper to say. The goals that you set for your paper should help you in deciding what to do. For example, if you read a passage about whales, and need to write an informative essay about the passage, the first thing that you should do is set some goals for what you would like your paper to do. For instance, you might write a paper that includes all the main ideas and important details. If you need to write a persuasive essay about the passage, the first thing that you should do here also is set some goals for what you would like your paper to do. For instance, you might write a paper that includes reasons and important supporting details from the passage. Can you think of any other types of goals that I might set?" Note goals for improving vocabulary and sentence development, organization, and so forth.

3. Brainstorm ideas for goals. SAY, *"As you can see, there are many types of goals that I can pick that will help me write my paper. I can set goals for how much I want to say, for the types of things I want to include, for the types of words I use, and so forth. Also, the type of goals that I pick will depend on the type of paper I am writing. Some of my goals for an informative essay will be different from my goals for a persuasive essay."* Collaboratively develop a list of goals for the class, for groups of students, or for individual students. Look at the sample goal sets in chapter materials. Make a chart of these goals for the class, for the group of students, or for individual students.

4. SAY, *"To help you use our (your) goals for your paper we are going to use this chart* (hand each student the PLANS worksheet). *You are to keep this chart and you can use it when you are asked to write a paper in the next lessons."*

5. Review each of the goals on the (class, group, or individual) goal chart. Read each goal to the students and have them repeat it. Briefly discuss each goal and why it is important. For example, why is the main idea (or reason) for each paragraph important? It helps us know what to write about! Why are writing vocabulary words important? They make our paper better and more fun to read.

STEP 3: L—List ways to meet goals

Uncover the second step on the PLANS worksheet. SAY, *"Once I have written down my goals, I need to think about how I will meet or accomplish my goals. In other words, next to each goal I would list one or more things that I can do to meet my goal. For example, if I was writing a paper about what I read about whales* (point to the first goal on the goal chart), *one way I might be able to successfully meet this goal is by looking at the main ideas and details I noted when reading with TWA. I know about how many paragraphs I will need to write by looking at the number of main ideas and details from the passage I read. To add vocabulary words, I can refer to my vocabulary journal."*

STEP 4: A

Point out that the "A" in PLANS doesn't do anything, that it is just a filler letter.

STEP 5: N—Make Notes

SAY, *"Once I have finished picking my goals and listing ways to meet those goals, I would make notes about the kinds of things that I might use in my paper* (uncover N). *Because I will use the notes on my TWA outline, this step is easy. I should also add to the notes to help me meet my goals. For example, if my outline does not include vocabulary words, I can add them to the outline."*

STEP 6: S—and Sequence notes

SAY, *"When I finished making all of my notes, I would think about what I wanted to come first in my paper, then second, third, and so forth (uncover S). Using my TWA outline, I would put a 1 by what I wanted first, a 2 by what I wanted second, a 3 by what would go third, and so forth. This will help me when I write my paper."*

STEP 7: Write and say more

SAY, *"Once I have finished the last step in PLANS, I am ready to write (uncover Step 2). My TWA notes would be my plan and would guide what I was to write. However, as I write I may think of other things to say, and I want to be sure to include them as well. To help me do this, I will remind myself to say more as I write, and to remember my goals."*

STEP 8: Test goals

1. SAY, *"The last thing I need to do is to test to see if I met my goals. To do this I would read my paper again, and check to see if I met each goal that I set. For example, if I set a goal to write a paragraph for each main idea in the passage, I would count the number of paragraphs written and write it next to my goal. If I do not meet one of my goals, I will think about how I might meet that goal on my next writing assignment."*

2. SAY, *"In the next lesson we will write an essay using the goals we have established. It will be easy to come up with ideas to write because we know TWA!"*

WRAP-UP

Ask students to get out their learning contract and self-instruction sheets. Note that students met their goal on the contract by learning TWA. Revise the contract and self-instructions to include PLANS. Remind student that you will check next time to see if they remember TWA and PLANS.

Optional Focus Lesson for Sentence Writing

LESSON OVERVIEW

This optional lesson is for students who need additional practice in using connector words to write combined sentences. The teacher can use the essays, collected prior to instruction, to determine individual students' need for the lesson.

STUDENT OBJECTIVES

Students will practice combining two sentences into one using TWA notes and their vocabulary journals.

MATERIALS

Learning strategy contract, "Yellowstone" passage, TWA notes for "Yellowstone," sentence combining worksheet, vocabulary journals, self-instruction sheet

SET THE CONTEXT FOR STUDENT LEARNING

Test for student knowledge of TWA and PLANS steps.

DEVELOP SENTENCE COMBINING

1. Give each student a copy of "Yellowstone," their previously written TWA outline for "Yellowstone," and a sentence combining worksheet. Discuss the meaning of the term "sentence combining." Sentence combining is when you take two sentences and write one and use words connective words such as "and," "but," and so forth as you have found in the text and written in the vocabulary journal.

2. Model how to find and underline a combined sentence in the "Yellowstone" passage. Let students find and underline combined sentences in the passage. Let each student select an example to add to the sentence combining worksheet. Complete the other sentence combining activities on the sheet.

WRAP-UP

Ask each student to get his or her learning contract and write a goal to write combined sentences, or underline this goal if written in the prior lesson. Have each student list ways to meet the goal. For example, "I will write at least three combined sentences in my essay by using the connecting words in my vocabulary journal." **Repeat this lesson for other passages as needed to support fluency in writing combined sentences.**

LESSON 4
Guided Practice

LESSON OVERVIEW

In order to focus on writing notes and an essay with the PLANS worksheet, a passage previously read with TWA will be used. The teacher will circulate, closely monitoring each student's ability to write in note form and to apply goals in their writing.

STUDENT OBJECTIVES

Students will practice writing an outline and an essay.

MATERIALS

Passage from previous TWA lesson, informative or persuasive prompt, blank TWA outline, PLANS worksheet, learning contract, vocabulary journals, self-instruction sheet

SET THE CONTEXT FOR STUDENT LEARNING

Orally test memorization of TWA and PLANS.

SUPPORT THE STRATEGY AND SELF-REGULATION

STEP 1: Write notes

Give each student a passage that has been previously read and highlighted (or marked) for main ideas and details. Tell students to transfer the information to the TWA outline in note form.

STEP 2: PLANS

1. Tell the students that they will write an (informative or persuasive) essay. Tell students to use their notes and the PLANS worksheet to guide their writing.

2. Remind students to say more as they write, and to remember how to meet their goals.

3. Tell students to test their goals. Verbally reinforce them for working hard to meet the goals and/or for being successful in doing so.

WRAP-UP

Ask students to get out their learning contracts and self-instruction sheets and make revisions if needed. Remind students that you will check next time to see if they remember TWA and PLANS. **Repeat this lesson for students having difficulty writing an essay with PLANS.**

Independent Practice with TWA and PLANS

LESSON OVERVIEW

Students will apply the TWA and PLANS strategies to read and write about a passage. The teacher will circulate, closely monitoring each student's ability to use TWA for reading, to write in note form, and to apply goals in their writing.

STUDENT OBJECTIVES

Students will read with TWA, write notes on an outline, and write an essay using PLANS.

MATERIALS

Passage (select, adapt, or write new passage for this lesson), informative or persuasive writing prompt, blank TWA outline, PLANS worksheet, learning contract, vocabulary journals, self-instruction sheet

SET THE CONTEXT FOR STUDENT LEARNING

Orally test memorization of TWA and PLANS.

SUPPORT THE STRATEGY AND SELF-REGULATION

STEP 1: Read with TWA

Give each student a new passage to read. Tell students to use TWA to read the passage. Tell them to create their own check sheet to monitor all the steps. Students should identify main ideas and details by marking the passage lightly with a pencil.

STEP 2: Write notes

Tell students to transfer the information to the TWA outline in note form.

STEP 3: PLANS

1. Tell the students that they will write an (informative or persuasive) essay based on the prompt that you give them. Tell students to use their notes and the PLANS worksheet to guide their writing.

2. Remind students to say more as they write, and to remember how to meet their goals.

3. Tell students to test their goals. Verbally reinforce them for working hard to meet the goals and/or for being successful in doing so.

WRAP-UP

Ask students to get out their learning contracts and self-instruction sheets and make revisions if needed. Remind students that you will check next time to see if they remember TWA and PLANS. **Repeat this lesson by scaffolding to longer, more difficult passages as students demonstrate mastery in using TWA and PLANS to write an informative and a persuasive essay.**

TWA Notes Outline for a Five-Paragraph Passage

Main idea	
Detail	
Detail	
Detail	

Main idea	
Detail	
Detail	
Detail	

Main idea	
Detail	
Detail	
Detail	

Main idea	
Detail	
Detail	
Detail	

Main idea	
Detail	
Detail	
Detail	

From Harris, K.R., Graham, S., Mason, L.H., & Friedlander, B. (2008). *Powerful writing strategies for all students.* Baltimore, MD: Brookes Publishing Co., Inc.; adapted by permission.

In *Building Comprehension in Adolescents: Powerful Strategies for Improving Reading and Writing in Content Areas* by Linda H. Mason, Ph.D., Robert Reid, Ph.D., and Jessica L. Hagaman, Ph.D.
(2012, Paul H. Brookes Publishing Co., Inc.)

178

PLANS Mnemonic Chart

Three steps for planning and writing with PLANS

1. Do:

P **P**ick Goals

L **L**ist ways to meet Goals

A **a**nd

N Make **N**otes

S and **S**equence Notes

2. Write and say more

3. Test goals

From Harris, K.R., Graham, S., Mason, L.H., & Friedlander, B. (2008). *Powerful writing strategies for all students.* Baltimore, MD: Brookes Publishing Co., Inc.; adapted by permission.

In *Building Comprehension in Adolescents: Powerful Strategies for Improving Reading and Writing in Content Areas* by Linda H. Mason, Ph.D., Robert Reid, Ph.D., and Jessica L. Hagaman, Ph.D. (2012, Paul H. Brookes Publishing Co., Inc.)

179

Worksheet for Completing PLANS

Pick Goals	**L**ist Ways of Meeting Goals

And, make **N**otes

Sequence notes

Ask yourself:

Are you finished with **PLANS**?
If you answer yes, you can write, say more, and test your goals!

From Harris, K.R., Graham, S., Mason, L.H., & Friedlander, B. (2008). *Powerful writing strategies for all students.* Baltimore, MD: Brookes Publishing Co., Inc.; adapted by permission.

#1 Sample PLANS Goals for Informative Paper

_____ Write a paper that has main ideas for each paragraph I read.

_____ Write a paper that has important details for each main idea.

_____ Write a paper that has a paragraph for each paragraph in the passage read.

_____ Write a paper that uses three vocabulary words.

_____ Write a paper that includes three combined sentences with connecting words.

_____ Write a paper that has a good summarizing ending sentence.

#2 Sample PLANS Goals for Informative Paper

1. Goals for starting my paper

   _____ Write a paper that has a paragraph for each main idea in the passage read.

   _____ Write a paper that uses the main idea as a topic sentence in each paragraph.

   _____ Write a paper that has details that support the main idea in each paragraph.

2. Goals for writing my paper

   _____ Write a paper that has at least three adjectives (words that describe).

   _____ Write a paper that has at least three vocabulary words.

   _____ Write a paper that includes three combined sentences with connecting words.

3. Goals for revising my paper

   _____ Check my punctuation and capitalization!

   _____ Check my spelling!

   _____ Read my paper out loud to myself. Does it make sense?

From Harris, K.R., Graham, S., Mason, L.H., & Friedlander, B. (2008). _Powerful writing strategies for all students._
Baltimore, MD: Brookes Publishing Co., Inc.; adapted by permission.

In _Building Comprehension in Adolescents: Powerful Strategies for Improving Reading and Writing
in Content Areas_ by Linda H. Mason, Ph.D., Robert Reid, Ph.D., and Jessica L. Hagaman, Ph.D.
(2012, Paul H. Brookes Publishing Co., Inc.)

181

Sample PLANS Goals for Persuasive Paper

_____ Write a paper that has strong statements about what I believe.

_____ Write a paper that states a reason for each paragraph I read.

_____ Write a paper that has important details/explanation for each reason.

_____ Write a paper that uses three vocabulary words.

_____ Write a paper that includes three combined sentences with connecting words.

_____ Write a paper that has a good summarizing ending sentence about my belief.

From Harris, K.R., Graham, S., Mason, L.H., & Friedlander, B. (2008). *Powerful writing strategies for all students.* Baltimore, MD: Brookes Publishing Co., Inc.; adapted by permission.

In *Building Comprehension in Adolescents: Powerful Strategies for Improving Reading and Writing in Content Areas* by Linda H. Mason, Ph.D., Robert Reid, Ph.D., and Jessica L. Hagaman, Ph.D. (2012, Paul H. Brookes Publishing Co., Inc.)

182

Use Combined Sentences!

Combined sentences are sentences that have two sentences that use connecting words. Look in your vocabulary journal for examples!

The black dog ran home fast.

The black dog ran to the park slowly.

- The black dog ran home fast but ran to the park slowly.

The boy read his favorite book.

The boy lent his favorite book to his best friend.

- The boy read his favorite book and then lent it to his best friend.

The man pounded the nail too hard.

The man hurt his hand.

- The man hurt his hand because he pounded the nail too hard.

Write two combined sentences from the passage:

_____

_____

_____

Write two combined sentences from your TWA outline notes:

_____

_____

_____

Sample Writing Prompts for TWA Passages

Gum

Using the information in the passage, write about the discoveries that led to the development of bubble gum.

Is it better to use chicle or man-made substances to make gum?

Man Walks on the Moon

Using the information in the passage, describe humanity's first walk on the moon.

Would you like to walk on the moon? Why or why not?

Pesticides

Using the information in the passage, write about the effects of pesticides on the environment.

Should people use pesticides? Why or why not?

Yellowstone

Write a retell about everything you read and learned in the passage.

The U.S. government designated two million acres for the Yellowstone National Park. Should they have done this? Why or why not?

Chapter 12

Quick Writes

POW

Pick my idea

Organize my notes

Write and say more

MATERIALS

Sample prompts for narrative, informative, and persuasive Quick Writes

Anchor narrative, informative, and persuasive Quick Writes

POW+TIDE Mnemonic chart

POW+TIDE graphic organizers for informative Quick Writes

POW+TREE Mnemonic chart

POW+TREE graphic organizers for persuasive Quick Writes

POW+C-SPACE Mnemonic chart (see Chapter 9)

POW+C-SPACE graphic organizers for narrative Quick Writes (see Chapter 9)

Graphing chart

Writing self-statements sheet

Learning strategies contract (see TWA, pg. 96)

Transition word list

A Quick Write is a short, informal, timed written response to a specific topic prompt. Quick writes can be used prior to learning, during learning, or after learning to activate students' prior knowledge, to link personal knowledge with content, or to assess understanding (Mason, Benedek-Wood, & Valasa, 2009). Quick Writes are similar to the extended constructed responses used to assess students' learning after reading and are generally one paragraph in length. Although time for writing may vary, 10 minutes is adequate for the majority of students. Many students, however, will need explicit instruction for planning and composing the Quick Write within any set time frame.

QUICK WRITE INSTRUCTION

In the following Quick Write lessons, a three-step general writing strategy, POW (**P**ick my idea, **O**rganize my notes, **W**rite and say more), is first taught to support the writing process from idea generation to composing across writing genres. Students are taught to use a genre-specific strategy for organizing notes: 1) C-SPACE (**C**haracter, **S**etting, **P**urpose, **A**ction, **C**onclusion, **E**nding) for narrative Quick Writes; 2) TIDE (**T**opic sentence, at least three **I**mportant **D**etails, **E**nding) for informative Quick Writes; and 3) TREE (**T**opic sentence, at least three **R**easons including one counter reason with a refute, at least three **E**xplanations, **E**nding) for persuasive Quick Writes.

It is critical that students master one genre before the teacher introduces the second and third genres. Genre selection order can suit the needs of the teacher and the class content; in other words, the choice is yours! After student mastery in a genre, subsequent lessons will generally require less time for establishing strategy acquisition and self-regulation. The students' prior knowledge of Quick Writing and their ability to plan and write in 10 minutes, for example, will be established. Students will be fluent in establishing goals, self-monitoring their performance, using effective self-statements, and self-reinforcing. To support generalization of strategy use and self-regulation, the teacher should consider using instructional materials across the genre-specific lessons. For example, self-statement sheets can be added to, as instruction moves from genre to genre. To foster generalization and maintenance of quick writing across content, teachers should collaborate to support use across classrooms and tasks, and provide distributed practice over time.

Prior to Instruction

An informal assessment of students' ability to construct a timed Quick Write for the selected genre should be conducted prior to instruction. Prompt sets, two prompts which provide students a choice in writing, for this assessment and instruction, should be selected or developed. The assessment serves two purposes: 1) documents student-specific instructional needs and 2) provides each student a preinstruction Quick Write that will be used during the lessons. Anchor Quick Writes, to illustrate the genre, should be selected or written. Be sure to check that the chosen anchor has all genre parts. Teachers will model writing a Quick Write in two lessons: 1) Lesson 2 to illustrate using the strategies and self-regulation procedures for planning and composing the Quick Write, and 2) Lesson 5 for modeling planning and composing the Quick Write in 10 minutes. The ability to model these processes fluently, while talking aloud, are essential for teaching students to write fluently (i.e., quality in a set time). Be sure to practice!

Introduce Quick Writes and Establish Prior Performance

LESSON OVERVIEW

The purpose of this first lesson is to develop the students' background knowledge and discuss the strategies. The teacher will introduce two strategies POW (**P**ick my idea, **O**rganize my notes, **W**rite and Say More) and the genre-specific strategy (e.g., C-SPACE, TIDE, or TREE). It will be important to establish students' understanding of the term "Quick Write" and how it will be applied to the specific genre. The students will find genre-specific parts in an anchor/example Quick Write and in a previously written Quick Write. The correct number of parts will be graphed. It is important for the teacher to discuss that although a student may have a part, that part could be made better. Timing of responses should also be discussed. For example, if the students wrote less than 10 minutes during preinstruction, the teacher and students would discuss how using the total time given can result in better papers. Students should be given the opportunity to share how they would improve quick writing.

STUDENT OBJECTIVES

The students will orally state what makes a good Quick Write. The students will be able to find the genre-specific parts in an anchor/example Quick Write. Students will locate and graph parts in their own previously written Quick Write.

MATERIALS

Mnemonic charts, graphic organizers, Quick Write anchor, students' previously written Quick Write, transition word chart, graphing chart, learning contract, paper, pencil

---

SET THE CONTEXT FOR STUDENT LEARNING

Tell the students that you will be working with them to learn a new strategy. Ask the students to tell you what they know about the word "strategy." Ask them to provide examples for strategies used in school and in other places (e.g., sports). Tell the students that they will be learning a new writing trick—one that will help them write a response in a specific genre. Briefly discuss the genre (narrative, informative, persuasive).

DEVELOP THE STRATEGY AND SELF-REGULATION

STEP 1: Develop background knowledge

1. Review POW. Put out the mnemonic chart so that only POW shows. Tell students that POW gives them POWER when they write because of the three steps: P—Pick my idea, O—Organize my notes, W—Write and say more.

2. Tell the students that POW is more powerful when combined with other writing strategies and that they will be using the selected genre-specific strategy for the "O" in POW—Organize my notes.

3. Describe and discuss what makes a good quick response. Some students may not be at all familiar with this. You will be practicing this with the students later; just be sure they have the idea here. Note that good Quick Writes make sense and have several parts. Tell the students that they will learn a trick for remembering good response parts. Be sure to tell students the following:

    Narrative: A good narrative Quick Write tells a reader about the character(s) and setting, the characters' action(s), detail about actions, a conclusion, and characters' emotion.

    Informative: A good informative Quick Write tells the reader the main idea, gives at least three important details to support the main idea, and concludes with an ending sentence.

    Persuasive: A good persuasive Quick Write tells a reader what I believe, gives a reader at least three reasons why I believe it and an explanation for each reason, and has an ending sentence. The best persuasive Quick Writes include a counter reason and refute too.

STEP 2: Introduce the genre-specific strategy

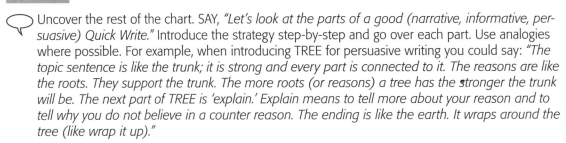

Uncover the rest of the chart. SAY, *"Let's look at the parts of a good (narrative, informative, persuasive) Quick Write."* Introduce the strategy step-by-step and go over each part. Use analogies where possible. For example, when introducing TREE for persuasive writing you could say: *"The topic sentence is like the trunk; it is strong and every part is connected to it. The reasons are like the roots. They support the trunk. The more roots (or reasons) a tree has the stronger the trunk will be. The next part of TREE is 'explain.' Explain means to tell more about your reason and to tell why you do not believe in a counter reason. The ending is like the earth. It wraps around the tree (like wrap it up)."*

STEP 3: Find parts in a Quick Write

1. Tell the students that now they are going to read a Quick Write to find out if the writer used all of the genre-specific parts:

    Narrative: Six C-SPACE parts (**C**haracter, **S**etting, **P**urpose, **A**ction, **C**onclusion, **E**nding)

    Informative: Five TIDE parts (**T**opic sentence, at least three **I**mportant **D**etails, **E**nding)

    Persuasive: Ten TREE parts (**T**opic sentence, at least three **R**easons including one counter reason with a refute, at least three **E**xplanations, **E**nding)

2. Introduce the transition word list. Tell the students that this is a list of words that can be used to help them organize and write their paper.

3. Give each student a graphic organizer. Point out the strategy mnemonic at the top, and review what it stands for. Point to the boxes and tell them that when they find a part, to write the part in the box.

4. Give each student a copy of a genre-specific anchor Quick Write. Ask the students to read along silently while you read the paper out loud. Tell them to raise their hands when they hear a part or if they hear or see a transition word. Together, complete the organizer. It is okay to move around the organizer (i.e., go out of order as the parts are found). In other words, the parts do not have to be found in order. Call on students as they raise their hands. As a part is identified, write each in the appropriate space on the graphic organizer. Do not use full sentences—do this in *note form.* Check to make sure students are writing notes, not sentences!

5. Repeat this for another anchor Quick Write. *Do this only if needed.*

STEP 4: Look at current writing behavior

1. Hand the students their previously written Quick Write, collected prior to instruction.

2. Tell students to read their Quick Write and see which parts they have. Have them write their parts in note form on a graphic organizer.

3. Briefly note, with each student, which parts they have and which they don't. Note transition words. As a group, briefly note common parts missing.

4. Discuss also that even though the Quick Write has a part, that part could be better next time—this makes a Quick Write more fun to write and read. Orally, discuss examples of each part could be improved. ***Do not make additional notes today!***

STEP 5: Graph current level of performance and set goals

1. Give each student a graphing chart. Have each student fill in the graph for the number of parts in their pre-instruction Quick Write. Be very positive by reminding students that they are just now learning the trick of writing good Quick Writes.

2. Explain the goal, to write better Quick Writes with all the strategy parts. Remind students that good Quick Writes have all the parts of the strategy (review the steps of the specific strategy). Also, remind the students that good Quick Writes are fun to write and read, and they make sense.

3. The goal is to have all of the parts, and "better" parts the next time a Quick Write is written.

STEP 6: Learning contract

Introduce the learning contract. Tell the students that you will sign the contract indicating that you will do your best to teach them POW + (strategy). Ask them to commit to learning POW + (strategy). You will add more to this later. For now, get a commitment to just learning the strategy.

WRAP-UP

Tell the students that next time you will ask them to write POW + (strategy) from memory and will "test" (nongraded) what it means. Let each student write POW + (strategy) on a scratch piece of paper. Tell the students they can practice with each other to help with memorizing.

Model Quick Writing

LESSON OVERVIEW

The teacher models, while thinking out loud, how to use POW + (strategy) for writing a Quick Write. The teacher models the use of goal setting, self-monitoring, self-statements, and self-reinforcement during the writing process. Students will write their own list of personal self-statements and then revise their previously-written Quick Write using the graphic organizer created in Lesson 1.

STUDENT OBJECTIVES

The students will orally say the mnemonic for POW+ (strategy) and state what each letter stands for. The students will attend to the teacher's modeling lesson, write self-statements for writing a Quick Write with the strategy, and revise their Quick Write.

MATERIALS

Mnemonic charts, graphic organizers, Quick Write anchor paper, students' previously written Quick Write and organizer, transition word list, graphing chart, self-statement sheet, learning contract, genre-specific prompt, paper, pencil

SET THE CONTEXT FOR STUDENT LEARNING

Test to see if the students remember POW + (strategy). Do this out loud to save time. It is essential that each student memorize the strategy mnemonic and steps. If students are having trouble, spend a few minutes practicing. Tell the students you will test them each day to make sure they have the strategy memorized. Ask the students if they noticed any time POW + (strategy) could be used in other classes.

DEVELOP THE STRATEGY AND SELF-REGULATION

STEP 1: Model the strategy

Note: It is okay to ask students to help you generate ideas, but you do all the writing! Be sure to involve the students as much as needed to keep their attention. You can model on chart paper, the chalkboard, a white board, overhead, or computer.

1. Pick my idea.

 Lay out a copy of the mnemonic chart, graphic organizer, and graphing chart. Then explain: *"Remember that the first letter in POW is 'P'—Pick my idea. Today we are going to practice how to write a good Quick Write. To do this we have to be creative, we have to think free. Today I will show you how to write a Quick Write and then we will practice by revising our Quick Writes."* Read aloud the genre-specific prompt you selected and practiced for modeling.

2. Organize my notes.

The second letter in POW is 'O'—Organize my notes. Tell the students that today you are going to write a Quick Write with their help.

SAY, *"I will use POW + (strategy) to help me. I will use the graphic organizer to make notes and organize my thoughts."* Briefly review—point at—the parts of a good Quick Write on the graphic organizer. Review what should the goal be? To write better Quick Writes with all the strategy parts. Remind them that good Quick Writes have the following elements:

Narrative: In a good narrative Quick Write, the writer describes the character and setting. The writer also includes the character(s) purpose for the actions which will occur in the narrative. Of course, the best narratives have conclusions and emotions!

Informative: A good informative Quick Write first tells the main idea for the content. Next, the writer selects at least three important details to illustrate or support the main idea. A good ending is also including in the Quick Write.

Persuasive: A good persuasive Quick Write response tells a reader what I believe, gives a reader at least three reasons why I believe it, an explanation for each reason, and has an ending sentence. The best persuasive Quick Writes include a counter reason and refute too!

Remind the students that the transition words will help them organize their Quick Writes too. Also, good Quick Writes can be fun to write and for others to read, and make sense. Model the entire process for organizing your notes. Explain that you will be talking out loud all the steps of completing the graphic organizer. Use problem definition, planning, self-evaluation, and self-reinforcement self-statements as you go. Model how to use good word choice. Follow the strategy steps and statements below, filling in ad lib statements where indicated. Ask the students to help you with ideas and the writing, but be sure you are in charge of the process.

SAY, *"What is it I have to do? I have to write a good Quick Write. My Quick Write needs to makes sense and have all the parts. Remember 'P' in POW—Pick my idea—let my mind be free. Pause. Take my time, think about what I believe and good ideas why will come to me."*

SAY, *"Now I can do 'O' in POW—Organize my notes. I can write down ideas for each part. I can write ideas down in different parts of this page as I think of ideas."* Be sure to model moving out of order during your planning. SAY, *"First…,"* then talk out and fill in notes for the first strategy step in the Quick Write. *"Good I like this idea! Now I'd better figure out the remaining parts. Let my mind be free, think of good ideas."* Talk out and briefly write notes for the remaining parts, use coping statements at least twice. Be sure to model writing notes. After generating notes for all Quick Write parts say, *"Now I can look back at my notes and see if I can add more notes for my Quick Write parts."* Actually model this, using coping statements. *"I will remember to use transition words too. I can also look for ideas for good word choice or million-dollar words."*

3. Write and say more

SAY, *"Now I can do 'W' in POW—Write and say more. I can write my Quick Write and think of more good ideas or million-dollar words as I write."* Talk yourself through writing the Quick Write; the students can help. Start by saying, *"How shall I start? I need a first sentence."* Then pause and think, then write out the sentence. Then write the next part, refer to the transition list, and select/use a transition word. Be sure to add one or two more ideas and million-dollar words that are not on your plan as you write. Don't hurry, but don't slow it down unnaturally. Also, at least twice, ask yourself, *"Am I using good parts and, am I using all my parts so far?"* Use a coping statement. Also ask yourself, *"Does my Quick Write make sense? Will the reader like this?"* Model writing the ending sentence. When you have finished the Quick Write, model by counting and graphing your performance. SAY, *"I got ____ parts; I met the goal of (minimum number of parts) or more. Good work, I'm done!"*

STEP 2: Self-statements

1. Ask the students if they can remember: 1) things you said to yourself to get started, 2) things you said while you worked, 3) things you said to yourself when you finished.

2. Ask the students to write some things they could say, in their own words, on the self-statement sheet. Note that we don't always have to think these things out loud; once we learn them we can think in our heads or whisper to ourselves.

    What to say to get started. This must be along same lines as, *"What is it I have to do? I have to write a Quick Write using POW + (strategy)."*

    Things to say while you work: self-evaluation, coping, self-reinforcement.

    Things to say when you're finished: self-reinforcement.

STEP 3: Student revisions

1. Give the students time to make additional notes on their previously written graphic organizer. Be sure to work with the students to get all strategy parts. Encourage them to use transition words. Have the students rewrite the Quick Write to get all the strategy parts.

2. Ask the students to count the parts.

 3. Graph the number of parts in the revised Quick Write on the graphing chart. Ask students, *"Does this Quick Write have the minimum number of strategy parts?"* Then ask the students to fill in the graph. Discuss improvement in performance.

STEP 4: Learning contract

Hand each student their contract. Ask students to add new components to what they can learn: *"Write a Quick Write with all strategy parts." "Work as partners to learn the strategy, and to remember to use the strategy in other classes."*

WRAP-UP

Remind the students again of the strategy test next time and to remember to use the Quick Write strategies in other classes.

LESSON 3

Collaborative Practice

LESSON OVERVIEW

The students and the teacher collaboratively write a Quick Write using the genre-specific strategy.

STUDENT OBJECTIVES

The students will orally state the mnemonic for the strategy and what each letter stands for. The students will collaboratively write a Quick Write with the teacher. The students will identify the parts of the Quick Write that is written.

MATERIALS

Mnemonic charts, graphic organizers, transition word chart, graphing chart, self-statement sheet, learning contract, paper, pencil

SET THE CONTEXT FOR STUDENT LEARNING

Test to see if the students remember the strategy mnemonic and parts; do it out loud to save time. It is essential that each student memorize these. Tell the students you will test them on it each day to make sure they have it. If any student is having trouble with this, provide individual, paired, or group practice time with rapid fire practice.

SUPPORT THE STRATEGY AND SELF-REGULATION

STEP 1: Support collaborative writing

1. Give each student a blank graphic organizer, the transition word list, their self-statement sheet, and a set of practice prompts.

2. Tell the students that during the next couple of lessons they will be writing Quick Writes and that each time, because they have practiced, they will be a little faster and have more added to the Quick Write. Tell them that the goal is to see how many GOOD parts they can write. This practice will help them write more in all their assignments.

3. Ask them to describe times that they have to complete an assignment quickly. If they do not give you ideas, provide some. For example, in a class test, in a sports activity, or in some games you need to think quickly. Tell the students that writing is like all activities; with practice and some tricks you can write a well-written response in a short time.

4. Go through each of the following processes; students can share and use the same ideas, but each student should write a Quick Write using their own notes.

 SAY, *"Remember that the first letter in POW is 'P'—Pick my idea."* Refer students to their self-statements for creativity or thinking free.

SAY, *"The second letter in POW is 'O'—Organize my notes. I will use* (strategy) *to help me. I will use this page to make my notes and organize my notes."* Review: *"What should my goal be, to write a better Quick Write with at least (six, five, ten) parts. Good Quick Writes...."* Note the parts. *"Also, good Quick Writes can be fun to write and for others to read, and they make sense."* After students have generated notes for all parts say, *"I should remember to look back at my notes and see if I can add more notes for my Quick Write."* Help them do this. Remind the students to think about and write more ideas for good word choice or million-dollar words Help them do this.

SAY, *"The last letter in POW is 'W'—Write and say more."* Encourage and remind the students to start by saying, *"What is it I have to do here? I have to write a good Quick Write—a good Quick Write has at least* (the minimum for the genre) *parts and makes sense. I can write my Quick Write and think of more good ideas or million-dollar words as I write."* Help students as much as they need to do this, but try to let them do as much as they can alone. Encourage them to use other self-statements of their choice while they write.

STEP 2: Graph the paper

Have each student count the parts in their Quick Write and determine if their Quick Write has the minimum parts. Let them fill in the graph. Reinforce them for reaching more than the minimum parts.

WRAP-UP

Remind of POW + (strategy) test again next time, and remind them to think about how they can use POW + (strategy) in other classes.

LESSON 4

Guided Practice

LESSON OVERVIEW

In this lesson, the students continue to practice the POW + (strategy) for writing Quick Writes. The focus of this lesson is to wean the students off the graphic organizer and transition word list.

STUDENT OBJECTIVES

The students will write their own organizer and write a Quick Write with the minimum strategy parts.

MATERIALS

Graphing chart, self-statement sheet, paper, pencil

SET THE CONTEXT FOR STUDENT LEARNING

Test to see if the students remember POW + (strategy). They should have it by now! Ask students about times that they could use POW + (strategy) in other classes.

SUPPORT THE STRATEGY AND SELF-REGULATION

STEP 1: Wean off support materials

Explain to the students that they won't usually have a (strategy) mnemonic chart or transition word list with them when they have to write a Quick Write, so they can make their own notes on blank paper. Discuss and model how to write down the reminder at the top of the page, making a space on the paper for notes for each part.

STEP 2: Support Guided Writing

1. Ask each student to get out his or her self-statements sheet. Put out a practice prompt set. Each student can select one to write about. This time, let the students lead as much as possible, but prompt and help as much as needed. Students can make notes on the paper they wrote the reminders on. Go through each of the following processes; students can share ideas, but each student should write their own response using their own notes:

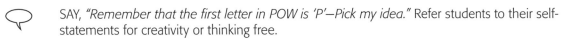 SAY, *"Remember that the first letter in POW is 'P'—Pick my idea."* Refer students to their self-statements for creativity or thinking free.

 SAY, *"The second letter in POW is 'O'—Organize my notes. Use the* (strategy) *reminder you wrote on the blank paper to help you. Also, use the paper to make notes and organize your notes."* Review, *"What should your goal be? To write better Quick Writes with at least (the minimum number) parts. Good Quick Writes have...."* Note the parts. *"Also, good Quick Writes can be fun to write and for others to read, and make sense."* After students have

CHAPTER 12
LESSON 4
Quick
Writes

generated notes for all Quick Write parts say, *"Remember to look back at the notes and see if you can add more notes for your Quick Write parts."* Remind them also to look for more ideas for good word choice or million-dollar words.

2. The last letter in POW is 'W'—Write and say more. Encourage them and remind them to start by saying, *"What is it you have to do here? You have to write a good Quick Write; a good Quick Write has all the parts and makes sense. You can write your Quick Write and think of more good ideas or million-dollar words as you write."* Help students as much as they need to do this, but try to let them do as much as they can alone. If parts can be improved, or better word choice can be used, do make suggestions. Encourage them to use other self-statements of their choice while they write.

3. Have each student count parts and graph his or her paper. Ask each student to determine if his or her paper has the minimum number of parts. Reinforce them for writing more than the minimum.

WRAP-UP

Repeat this lesson if necessary. If you believe they have it, celebrate student learning! Remind them to use POW + (strategy) in other classes.

Timed Writing Practice

LESSON OVERVIEW

The students will use POW + (strategy) for writing a Quick Write. The teacher will model writing a Quick Write in 10 minutes. The focus of this lesson is to establish the students' independence.

STUDENT OBJECTIVES

The students will write their own organizer and a Quick Write with the minimum number of strategy parts in 10 minutes.

MATERIALS

Graphing chart, learning contract, prompt set, paper, pencil, timer

SET THE CONTEXT FOR STUDENT LEARNING

Tell the students that today you will first show them how to write a Quick Write in 10 minutes, and then they will write a Quick Write for you.

SUPPORT THE STRATEGY AND SELF-REGULATION

STEP 1: Model writing in 10 minutes

Before the students attempt to write a 10-minute response, you will model how to do this. This will take practice; you will need to time it so that you have everything planned and written in nine minutes and then show the students how to wrap up and check the work in the final one minute. Model by using all 10 minutes, adding more reasons and explanations before wrapping up in the last minutes.

STEP 2: Student practice

Hand students a practice prompt set. Ask each student to select a prompt to write about. Tell the students you will time their writing. Tell them you want them to try on their own, but you will be watching carefully to help them with timing. Help students as needed to write in the 10 minutes by asking them to write more, check their work, and so forth.

STEP 3: Graph performance

Have students graph their performance. Then spend some time discussing how they performed in the timed writing. Ask them to tell you what they think they did well and what they could do better.

WRAP-UP

1. Repeat this collaborative and supportive lesson two to three times, with or without modeling, if necessary. A minimum of three timed practices support generalizing and maintenance of quick writing.

2. Remind students to help each other with POW+ (strategy) in other classes.

3. In the last lesson or practice, note that they are to remember what they learned with you when another teacher asks them to write. *Get a commitment for this by completing the learning contract.*

REFERENCE

Mason, L.H., Benedek-Wood, E., & Valasa, L. (2009). Quick writing for students who struggle with writing. *Journal of Adolescent and Adult Literacy, 53,* 313–322.

Sample Science, Social Studies, and Health Prompts

Narrative

1. a) Write about a time that you or someone you know has benefited from a new invention. What did you or they do with the new invention?

    b) Write and tell about the life of Marie Curie. Describe what she is best known for.

2. a) Write about a time that you or someone you know faced discrimination. What did you or they do?

    b) Write about the life of Frederick Douglass. Describe what he is best known for.

3. a) Write about a time that you or someone you know had food poisoning. What did you or they do?

    b) Write and tell about the life of Lou Gehrig. Describe what he is best known for.

Informative

1. a) Describe the effects of DDT on the decline of the bald eagle.

    b) Define the "environmental movement," and note subsequent key legislation.

2. a) Describe the effect of The Great Depression on American farm families.

    b) Define "The New Deal," and note resulting programs that are still in effect today.

3. a) Describe the effects of high cholesterol on the body's health.

    b) Define "high blood pressure," and note the potential causes of this condition.

Persuasive

1. a) Should students your age encourage their families to use alternative energy sources? Explain why or why not.

    b) Is it better to use wind, solar, or hydro energy sources? Explain your answer.

2. a) Should students your age enlist in the military if there is a "total war," like World War II? Explain why or why not.

    b) Is it better for the U.S.A. to adopt a policy of isolationism or become involved in world affairs? Explain your answer.

3. a) Should students your age go on a sugar-free diet? Explain why or why not.

    b) Is it better to have a healthy snack or a dessert snack after school? Explain your answer.

Anchor Quick Writes—Narrative

Prompt: Write about a time when you felt like a stranger in another culture.

In summer 2002, my parents and I were fortunate enough to travel to Belgium. Belgium has two cultures, a French-speaking culture and a Flemish-speaking culture. The best part of the trip was driving through the countryside, seeing the small towns and villages in both French and Flemish Belgium. One day, we stopped for lunch at a small café in French-speaking Belgium. Well, neither my parents nor I speak French! We felt so uncomfortable. Only the café owner's dog seemed to understand us. The owner was so excited to have Americans in his café that he was going to give us his most special dish—Steak American. We did not want to disappoint him, so we placed three orders. What a surprise; Steak American was raw ground meat! We ate the food given to us and thanked the owner for being so kind. Of course, we smiled a lot as we certainly did not understand each other. We were worried about getting food poisoning from eating the raw meat, but did not. Obviously, the café owner knew more than we did about making special dishes for foreigners.

Anchor Quick Writes—Informative

Prompt: Describe the three states of matter.

Matter can be a solid, a liquid, or a gas. A solid is one state of matter. Solids have a definite shape and a definite volume. For example wood, nails, pencils, coins, and ice are all solids. A liquid is another state of matter. Water, milk, vinegar, and vegetable oil are liquids; they do not have a definite shape, but do have a definite volume. For example, fifty milliliters of orange juice will take up fifty milliliters of space whether you pour it into a glass or spill it onto the floor. The third state of matter is gas. Oxygen, carbon dioxide, and helium are gases. Think about the shape of balloons. If you take the same gas and blow it into a differently shaped balloon, the gas will take the shape of the new balloon. Like liquids, gases do not have shapes of their own. They take the shapes of their containers.

The volume of a gas can also change. If the gas inside a balloon escapes into the room, it will spread out until it takes up all the space it can. Its volume would then be much greater than its volume in the balloon. A gas always fills its container completely. If you push on a balloon filled with a gas, you may be able to squeeze the gas into a smaller space. A gas has no definite volume and no definite shape.

From Harris, K.R., Graham, S., Mason, L.H., & Friedlander, B. (2008). *Powerful writing strategies for all students.* Baltimore, MD: Brookes Publishing Co., Inc.; adapted by permission.

In *Building Comprehension in Adolescents: Powerful Strategies for Improving Reading and Writing in Content Areas* by Linda H. Mason, Ph.D., Robert Reid, Ph.D., and Jessica L. Hagaman, Ph.D. (2012, Paul H. Brookes Publishing Co., Inc.)

201

Anchor Quick Writes—Persuasive

Prompt: Should people be paid for recycling? Explain why or why not.

I do not believe people should be paid for recycling; after all, everyone should want the earth to be a better place! We all need to think of making the earth better for us now and for people in the future. The Disney movie *WALL•E* showed what could happen if we do not recycle; it was not a pretty picture. Also, if people were paid for recycling, crime could increase. I can just imagine the scams and the things people would do to make money off of others' trash. Then again, you might have other people who do not need money and just throw things in the trash. This could create another whole set of problems—trash diggers. Finally, I do not think our local, state, or national government can afford to pay people for recycling until we are out of the recession. Some people might think that by paying people, more recycling would occur. I agree that this is a good reason for paying people, but I think the problems that would result and the cost to the government would outweigh any benefit. If for no other reason, people should want to recycle for the good of future generations.

POW + TIDE Mnemonic

P **P**ick my idea

O **O**rganize my notes

W **W**rite and say more

T **T**opic sentence
- Tell the reader your main idea.

I **I**mportant
- Will your reader think your idea is important?

D **D**etails
- Be sure to include at least three details.
- Will your reader think your details are important?

E **E**nding sentence

In *Building Comprehension in Adolescents: Powerful Strategies for Improving Reading and Writing in Content Areas* by Linda H. Mason, Ph.D., Robert Reid, Ph.D., and Jessica L. Hagaman, Ph.D. (2012, Paul H. Brookes Publishing Co., Inc.)

POW + TREE Mnemonic

P **P**ick my side

O **O**rganize my notes

W **W**rite and say more

T **T**opic sentence

- Tell what I believe!

R **R**easons—three or more

- Why do I believe this?

- Will my reader believe this?

- Do I have one counter reason?

E **E**xplanations

- Say more about each belief.

- Does the counter reason change my belief?

E **E**nding sentence

From Harris, K.R., Graham, S., Mason, L.H., & Friedlander, B. (2008). *Powerful writing strategies for all students.* Baltimore, MD: Brookes Publishing Co., Inc.; adapted by permission.

In *Building Comprehension in Adolescents: Powerful Strategies for Improving Reading and Writing in Content Areas* by Linda H. Mason, Ph.D., Robert Reid, Ph.D., and Jessica L. Hagaman, Ph.D.
(2012, Paul H. Brookes Publishing Co., Inc.)

Transition Words

Words to start:	First of all, To begin with, To start with
Connecting points:	and, also, as well, because, furthermore, what's more, in addition, moreover, secondly
Opposing side:	however, on the other hand, conversely, but, that said
Examples:	for instance, for example, in fact
To conclude:	thus, in conclusion, in summary

Graphing Chart

Fill in or check a space for every Quick Write part. Write the number of transition words below the column.

Date:						
Transition words =						

POW + TIDE Topic Sentence

Tell the main idea! Will your reader think this idea is important?

Transition words	**ID** Important Details (three or more) Will your reader think each detail is important?	Can you say more about the detail?

Ending

POW + TREE Topic Sentence

Tell what you believe!

Transition words	**R** Reasons (three or more) Why do I believe this? Will my readers believe this?	**E**xplain reasons. Say more about each reason.
	Do I have a counter reason?	Does it change my belief?

Ending

From Harris, K.R., Graham, S., Mason, L.H., & Friedlander, B. (2008). *Powerful writing strategies for all students.* Baltimore, MD: Brookes Publishing Co., Inc.; adapted by permission.

In *Building Comprehension in Adolescents: Powerful Strategies for Improving Reading and Writing in Content Areas* by Linda H. Mason, Ph.D., Robert Reid, Ph.D., and Jessica L. Hagaman, Ph.D. (2012, Paul H. Brookes Publishing Co., Inc.)

Writing Self-Statements Sheet

Before writing

_____

_____

_____

_____

While writing

_____

_____

_____

_____

After writing

_____

_____

_____

_____

From Harris, K.R., Graham, S., Mason, L.H., & Friedlander, B. (2008). *Powerful writing strategies for all students.*
Baltimore, MD: Brookes Publishing Co., Inc.; adapted by permission.

In *Building Comprehension in Adolescents: Powerful Strategies for Improving Reading and Writing
in Content Areas* by Linda H. Mason, Ph.D., Robert Reid, Ph.D., and Jessica L. Hagaman, Ph.D.
(2012, Paul H. Brookes Publishing Co., Inc.)

209

Section IV

Homework

Chapter 13

Homework Strategies

A-WATCH

Assignment notebook—get it out

Write down the assignment and due date

Ask for clarification on the assignment if needed

Task analyze the assignment

Check all work for completeness, accuracy, and neatness

Hand it in

MATERIALS

Self-Monitoring Form

Self-Monitoring Log sheet

A-WATCH Lessons 1–5

A-WATCH prompt sheet

Task Analysis Example Calendar

A-WATCH Self-Monitoring Sheet

Self-Instructions Worksheet

Example assignment

Homework Home Planner

Homework Home Check Sheet

Homework completion can be a chronic problem for some students. Research suggests that problems with homework completion can adversely affect grades and can be a factor in referral for special education services. Homework problems can be difficult to address because they involve both the home and school environments. Problems in either area can result in difficulty with homework completion. In this chapter we address what teachers can do to improve homework performance. First, we discuss what teachers need to understand about homework. Second, we address the home environment—parents are a crucial part of homework completion. Third, we provide examples of self-regulation procedures to enhance classroom preparation skills (e.g., seated when bell rings, eye contact with teacher when instruction begins, pen or pencil on desk, relevant instructional materials open when the lesson begins). Last, we provide lesson plans for the A-WATCH strategy (**A**ssignment notebook—get it out; **W**rite down the assignment and due date; **A**sk for clarification on the assignment if needed; **T**ask analyze the assignment; **C**heck all work for completeness, accuracy, and neatness; **H**and it in). A-WATCH is based on the WATCH strategy (Glomb & West, 1990).

HOMEWORK: THE SCHOOL'S ROLE

Teachers' practices can directly affect the likelihood of homework completion. Teachers' practices are also the only ones that can be directly controlled. Teachers have three major responsibilities in assigning homework: organization, appropriate assignments, and feedback.

Organization

Teachers should develop and follow regular rules and procedures for assigning, collecting, correcting, evaluating, grading, and returning homework assignments so that students know exactly what is expected of them (Epstein, Polloway, Foley, & Patton, 1993). Ideally there should be consistent, school-wide procedures. Students should be taught the rules and procedures for homework at the beginning of the year, and these should be reviewed when students fail to understand or to follow procedures. Organizational supports such as assignment notebooks are critically important. Students with homework problems can benefit from this organizational support structure. However, simply handing a student a homework notebook and telling him or her to use it is unlikely to help. Teachers need to instruct the students in how to use the notebook, remind them to use the notebook, provide practice in how to use the notebook, and reinforce them (e.g., praise them) when they use it (Margolis & McCabe, 1997). Teachers should also keep parents "in the loop" and communicate any special procedures to the parents. For example, some schools require parents to sign students' homework organizers or logs. Teachers should also indicate, to both the students and the parents, roughly how much time should be spent on homework. This can help teachers determine if homework assignments are too lengthy. Given the problems that some students have in returning homework, teachers should help students develop ways to ensure that homework will be returned and handed in (e.g., put completed homework in your backpack). Then, at school, put the homework in the homework box immediately. Teachers should also check students' use of the homework notebook: (e.g., Are assignments written down correctly, are all assignments included).

Appropriate Homework Assignments

Appropriate homework assignments are ones that are of the suitable length (i.e., time needed to complete) and difficulty. Too much homework can actually be counterproductive, resulting in students feeling overwhelmed. Some students, in this case, may not even attempt to complete it. There is no hard and fast rule for how much homework should be assigned. For typically achieving students, a good guideline is the "10–minute rule" (Cooper, 2007); no more that 10 minutes of homework per grade level. For example, a typically achieving eighth grader would receive no more than a total of 80 minutes of homework. Note that this is for typically achieving students. For students with academic difficulties (e.g., learning disabilities), this amount of homework might be too much because it is likely that they will need much more time to complete the assignment. Students should not spend hours doing assignments that other students do in a few minutes (Margolis & McCabe, 1997). Teachers often assign homework that is simply too difficult for many students (Salend & Schliff, 1989). Teachers should be sure to match the difficulty level of the homework to the student's academic abilities. For example, the student should be able to read almost all words in an assignment fluently. One tip for assessing the difficulty level of an assignment is to begin homework assignments in class. If students experience difficulty in class, assignments can modified accordingly. Teachers should be sure the student understands the assignment by discussing any aspects of an assignment that might be confusing (Margolis & McCabe, 1997).

Feedback

Teachers should give students detailed, written feedback on what aspects of their homework they did well (e.g., "You factored the equations perfectly!") and what needs improvement (e.g., "Remember to show all your work."). Feedback on performance over time can also be helpful. For example, a teacher might graph the percent of homework a student completed each day. This gives students valuable, ongoing performance feedback. It also can be highly motivational.

HOMEWORK: THE PARENTS' ROLE

Parents play an important role in homework completion. They can help to establish a home environment that is conducive to successful homework completion. There are a number of important environmental factors that influence students' abilities to complete homework effectively (Margolis & McCabe, 1997; U.S. Department of Education, 2003).

- Establish a homework location. Establish a quiet, well-lit location for homework with minimal distractions. Homework should not be done in front of the television or in places with other distractions (e.g., people coming and going). Note that for some students, background noise (e.g., music or white noise) can be helpful (Zentall, 2006).

- Materials. The homework location should have all normally needed materials (e.g., paper, pencils, or a dictionary) readily available. If special materials will be needed, these should be procured in advance.

- Create a homework routine. Working on homework should become an established part of the student's daily routine. Parents should block out a specific time each day for homework and *stick to it*. Parents should not allow the student to put off homework. For large projects, they should establish times on the weekend in advance, especially if the project involves getting together with classmates. Reinforce the student for following with homework routine.

- Help with time management. Help the student to be sensitive to time management and to develop time management. Work with the student to set times for completion for each assignment (e.g., 15 minutes for algebra problems). A timer can help students become more aware of the time spent on activities as well as the total time remaining.

- Do hard work first. Students should do the most difficult work first when they will be fresh and alert.

- Help. Parents should provide only as much support as needed. Parents should not do homework for the child. This defeats the purpose of homework.

- Frustration and fatigue. If the child becomes frustrated or too fatigued to focus on the task, allow a short break. For long sessions, it may be useful to schedule short breaks at regular intervals (e.g., every 30 minutes, there's a 5 minute break).

- Reinforce homework completion. Parents should demonstrate that they realize the student has worked hard. When the student is able to consistently complete assignments successfully, or after long and difficult assignments, celebrate success (e.g., go out for ice cream or watch a video) to reinforce effort.

ORGANIZATIONAL SKILLS

Organizational skills are critical for success in the classroom (Krishnan, Feller, & Orkin, 2010). Students who come to class without needed materials or who fail to complete or turn in assignments are at high risk for academic problems. They may not master course content or may receive a failing grade in a class because they did not complete assignments. We suggest that teachers consider organizational skills as a part of their curriculum. Teaching organizational skills is useful for most students; for some (e.g., students with LD or ADHD) it can literally be a lifesaver. Even a simple organizational problem can seem insurmountable for some students. This in turn can result in increased frustration and stress. Teachers also should be aware that behavior that seems "careless" or "irresponsible" may actually result from problems with organization. Self-regulation interventions can be very effective in improving organizational skills of students.

The first step in teaching organizational skills is to meet with students and establish that there is a problem. Target one class for the self-regulation intervention. Later, the same intervention can be used with other classes. Discuss the potential consequences of the organizational problems (e.g., low grades, parents upset). Tell the students that there is a trick they can learn that can help them be better organized and prepared for their classes. Get a commitment from the student to learn and use the self-regulation procedures. Stress that it will require some work on their part but that there will be a big payoff. After students agree, discuss the specific problems that they have, and specific activities they need to perform to be prepared for class. Be sure to define the problems in terms of specific behaviors. For example "forgetting stuff" is not a good example of a problem. "Not bringing a pencil" or "forgetting the text" are more appropriate. Make a list of the problems. Note that different students may have different problems so their lists may differ. Talking to the classroom teachers involved beforehand is a good idea. Students may be unaware of or reluctant to bring up some problems. If students omit important behaviors bring them up. Make a list of the important behaviors the students need to perform to be ready for class. Teachers may also wish to add behaviors that students should perform *during* class.

Next introduce the Self-Monitoring Log. Talk with the students about the self-monitoring procedures noted on the checklist. After the class, they are to go through each item on the list and mark the response "yes" or "no." Tell the students that this self-monitoring checklist will help them to see what they are doing well and what they need to improve, and that when they know what they have a problem with, they can work to improve it! Tell the students that they are to set a weekly goal (e.g., get 7 of 11 "yes" check marks). Talk about why goals are important and that when they accomplish their goal they can give themselves a mental "high five." Also discuss that if they do not met their goal, they will need to think about why and how they can improve. Next, introduce the Self-Monitoring Log sheet. This self-questioning sheet will help them evaluate their performance and improve. Work through each of the questions and talk about why each is important.

Tell the students that you will meet with them each day to look at their self-monitoring sheets and their logs. Establish a time for the meeting and tell the students that during the meeting they will complete the log sheet, and you will then discuss performance on the self-monitoring sheet and the logs. The teacher should ask the students where they could do better and where they did well, discussing any ideas for improving. Students should set a new goal each week. Daily meetings should continue for each student until they are able to perform all the behaviors consistently (e.g., 100% of behaviors performed four out of five days).

Individual student performance. When a student has reached the 100% level it is time to begin to fade the daily meetings and change to meeting every other day. Continue this schedule for at least a week. If the student is able to maintain high performance level, reduce the meetings to once weekly. In this phase, the student may be given the option of ceasing the log if he or she chooses. If a student's performance begins to deteriorate, return to the more frequent meeting schedule. Note that the self-monitoring strategy can easily be incorporated into the A-WATCH strategy presented next.

Introduce A-WATCH

LESSON OVERVIEW

The purpose of the first lesson is to discuss the students' current performance and to introduce and discuss the A-WATCH strategy. The teacher describes the steps in the strategy and begins to support students' memorization. A commitment to learn and use the strategy is obtained.

STUDENT OBJECTIVES

The student will commit to learning and using A-WATCH. The student will orally state the steps of A-WATCH.

MATERIALS

Poster with A-WATCH steps, A-WATCH prompt sheet for each student, graph of homework performance (percent homework completed and handed in each day)

SET THE CONTEXT FOR STUDENT LEARNING

Ask the students why it is important for them to complete their homework. Have students generate ideas and write them down (e.g., to learn the material, to get a better grade, so you won't have to worry about it). Then tell the students that you are concerned that they are having problems completing their homework.

DEVELOP THE STRATEGY AND SELF-REGULATION

STEP 1: Obtain commitment

Show the students the graph of their homework performance. Discuss the extent of the problem and the problems that might result (e.g., failing a course). Tell the students that you believe that they can do much better. Tell them that you will teach them a way to help them get their homework completed and handed in. If they learn the strategy, and use it, they will be able to complete their homework and get it handed in. Tell the students that it will take some work on their part, but if they commit to the strategy it will really help. Ask the students if they will agree to learn and use the strategy. For example, you can say:

"Let's take a look at the last few assignments we did. You did pretty well on this algebra assignment, but do you see how you forgot to do the last six problems? It looks like maybe you forgot to do them or wrote down the assignment wrong. Then there's this report you did on volcanoes. You forgot to include a paragraph on the major types of volcanoes, and you did not include anything on where most volcanoes occur. It looks like maybe you didn't understand the assignment? And, look at the appearance. It's really hard to read your writing. It looks like your wrote it really quickly. These little problems all hurt your grade."

"It also looks like you have a problem completing your homework. I've made a graph of how many completed assignments you turned in. It looks like you are only getting your assignments completed and handed in about 50% to 60%. I think that you can do much better than this. You just need a little help with doing your assignments. I have a trick that I learned that can

help you get your assignments done correctly and handed in on time. It is called 'A-WATCH.' If you use it, I believe you will do much better on your assignments. This graph right here (point to assignment graph) *will go up and up, and so will your grade. You won't find yourself trying to race through homework late at night, and your work will be better. Would you like to learn about A-WATCH? It will take some effort on your part but I think that it can help you a lot."*

STEP 2: Introduce the strategy and explain steps

1. Pass out the prompt sheets for A-WATCH. Go through each step of A-WATCH. Make sure to tell students why they do each step.

   SAY, *"The first 'A' stands for Assignment book. This step tells you to get out your assignment book. You need to have the assignment book out so that you will be ready to write down an assignment."*

   SAY, *"'W' stands for Write. The next step is to write it down. When the teacher gives you an assignment you need to have your assignment book ready and write down the assignment immediately. Otherwise you might forget. Write down the details of the assignment, the day it is due, and any other things to remember with your assignment."*

   SAY, *"'A' stands for Ask. After you have written down the assignment the next step is to ask any questions you might have. If something about the assignment isn't clear or you don't understand something, you need to ask the teacher about it."*

   SAY, *"'T' stands for Task Analyze. When you are ready to get started with your assignment you will task analyze it. When you do a task analysis you will look at the whole assignment and break it into parts. This will help you because instead of one huge assignment you make it a series of small ones. You will also learn to make a time line. When you make a time line you estimate out how much time it will take you to do each of those parts. Then you use your calendar to see how long it will take you to finish the assignment. This will help you to make sure all of the parts are done before the due date."*

   SAY, *"'C' stands for Check. This is one of the most important parts of A-WATCH. After you have finished your assignment, you will go back over it. You will look to make sure it is completed, correct, and neat."*

   SAY, *"'H' stands for Hand it in. Doing the homework is only half the battle. You need to remember to hand it in also. If you don't then you won't get credit. You need to remember to bring the homework back to class and to give it to your teacher."*

2. After presenting the steps in the strategy, brainstorm with the students how the strategy can help them. Ask them to think of one or two problems they have with homework. For example:

   • Remembering to hand in my assignment

   • Getting everything finished before handing it in

   • Making sure it is neat

   • Forgetting about an assignment until the last minute

   • Running out of time to do an assignment

STEP 3: Memorizing strategy steps

Tell the students that before they can use the strategy they must memorize the steps. Break the students up into pairs. One student gets the A-WATCH prompt sheet. The other student tries to give as many steps as he or she can remember. When a student can't get a step, the student with the prompt sheet provides the answer and the other student repeats it. Then the students switch places. Allow each student to have at least one turn providing steps.

WRAP-UP

Tell the students that the next lesson will begin with a quiz over A-WATCH. Remind them that they need to know the steps and what to do at each step.

LESSON 2

Model Strategy and Introduce Self-Regulation

LESSON OVERVIEW

The purpose of this lesson is to model the use of the strategy and to introduce the self-regulation components. The teacher will use a think-aloud to show the students how the A-WATCH strategy would be used. Self-regulation techniques will also be modeled and discussed. Students will practice memorizing strategy steps.

STUDENT OBJECTIVES

The students will be able to write the steps of the A-WATCH strategy and what occurs at each step. The students will develop self-statements for use with A-WATCH.

MATERIALS

A-WATCH poster, enlarged planner page or overhead, self-monitoring chart, self-instructions sheet

SET THE CONTEXT FOR STUDENT LEARNING

Ask the students why it is important that they be better organized with their homework. Brainstorm with students on how the strategy can help them. Remind students that they must know the strategy steps.

DEVELOP THE STRATEGY AND SELF-REGULATION

STEP 1: Memorize the strategy

Give the students a sheet with A-WATCH written vertically. Ask them to write out each step and what is done at each step. After they finish, go over the steps with the students. Stress that they must know not only the step, but they must also know what they should do at each step.

STEP 2: Model the strategy

1. Model the strategy for the students.

 SAY, *"Let's pretend that you have a social studies assignment to write a paper on a famous 19th century American. The teacher might say, 'This month you will be doing a report on a famous 19th century American. You may pick any American you wish. The report should be three to five double-spaced typed pages. In your report, you will tell me about the life of WHO you chose. This should include WHAT he or she did to make you pick them. You should also include a detailed reason for why you chose the famous American. The paper should include at least three sources, which should be listed at the end of the paper. This report will be due on April 30th. Part of your grade will be on grammar, spelling, and neatness.'"*

SAY, *"Let's practice our new strategy together. I will show you how you can use the A-WATCH strategy. I will go through each of the steps and show you how you can use them and how they can help you. I will do it as though I am a student using the strategy so you can tell what I am thinking about as I use the strategy."*

SAY, *"Okay. I need to focus and use A-WATCH. If I use my strategy I'll be able to handle this assignment. The first step is 'A'. That means I need to get out my assignment planner. I've already done that step. I decided that I would get out my assignment planner first thing when I get to class. That means when the teacher gives me an assignment I am ready to write it down. If I have to rummage around in my backpack for my planner I might miss something important. So, I decided it's easier just to have it out. Okay, one step down."*

SAY, *"The next step is 'Write down the assignment.' When I write it down I need to make sure that I get all the important information. I will make sure and write down the information immediately, otherwise I might forget. Let's see: I need to write, 'Report due April 30' on today's date."* Model writing the assignment on the board or on a planner page.

SAY, *"Has that got it? No. I don't think so. Let's see, the teacher said it had to be on a famous 19th century American. I also have to tell about the life of WHO I choose; WHAT he or she did to make me pick them. I also have to include a detailed reason for why I picked them. Okay, that's better. Anything else? Oops. I almost forgot to write down how long it is three to five pages, double-spaced, typed." Anything else? Oh yeah. I need to include three sources and list them at the end. I'll write that down too. Good thing I checked or I would have forgotten an important part. If I forget something I need I won't be able to complete the assignment. I am doing great! Boy this is really useful. I have everything important written down so I can include it in my assignment."*

SAY, *"When I hear about an assignment, I need to look for important things to write down like:*

When it is due.

How it needs to be done: (Does it need to be typed or written? How many pages do there need to be?)

What do I need to do in the assignment? (In this assignment, I need to tell about the life of an American and why I picked him or her.)

I don't need to write every single thing the teacher says when I am getting the assignment, but I do need the important parts. Man—this strategy really helps me."

SAY, *"The next step in A-WATCH is 'Ask.' Let's see is there anything I'm not sure about. The teacher said I had to list three resources. I'm not sure what she means by that. When should I ask her? In the middle of a discussion probably isn't a good idea. I need to pick a time when she is free. I will put a question mark by resources on my assignment book to remind me to ask her at the end of class."*

"After class, I will go up to my teacher and ask my question. I need to be sure I am clear. I will say something like: 'Mrs. Harris, I have a question about the report. You said that we needed to list three resources we used. I'm not sure what you mean by resources and how we list them.'"

Once my teacher answers my question, I will repeat back her answer to make sure that I understand her correctly.

"I'll say, 'Thanks, Mrs. Harris. So I need to find three books or magazine articles about the famous American and list them at the end of the paper on a separate page. I can't use Internet sites.' Good thing I asked. Otherwise I would have used the Internet and then I'd have lost points!"

SAY, *"What's my next step? I can't remember. I guess I should check my A-WATCH sheet. Oh yeah, it's 'T' for task analyze. This is where I break down my assignment into smaller steps. If I break it down into smaller steps it won't seem overwhelming. Small steps are a lot little easier to do. I need to remember to list each step in order though. I will write down each step as I break it down."*

"I have to write about a famous 19th century American, so I guess the first thing is to pick who I will write about. I think I will pick Abraham Lincoln. He was a very famous president. Okay, what do I need to do next?"

"I need to have a bunch of information about Lincoln. How will I get it? I think I need to break this step down farther. To get the information I will need to go to the library and find some books or articles about Lincoln. I know how to do that. They have a neat computer."

"I guess then I have to read the parts about Lincoln. Oh yeah. I need to take notes when I read so I will have all the information I need. I'll need to make sure I get a lot of information about his life and also why he was important."

"After I read and take notes I will need to organize my notes so I can put all the information together, like things about his life and why he was important. That will make it easier to write."

"Next I have to write the paper. It has to be three to five pages long. After I do the first draft I probably should go through it and edit it, then do a final draft."

SAY, *"What about resources? I have to list them, but I'm not really sure how. I'll need to ask Mrs. Harris about that. I'll write it down in my planner so I won't forget. Good thing I did this task analysis. It really helps me get organized. Is there anything I should do now? Oh wait. I need to check the paper for spelling and grammar."*

"Am I done with my task analysis yet? No, I remember that I need to make a time line. I need to estimate how long it will take to do each step and block out time on the calendar to do each step. That will tell me how long it will take to do the whole project. That way I won't be late or have to rush. I don't do my best work when that happens."

2. As the teacher goes through the time line write the tasks and time on the blank calendar. A filled out example is shown on page 235.

SAY, *"I'll take my April calendar and write in the things I need to do. Okay. I need to get to the library to find the books. I don't think that will take me very long, but I can't get there till Wednesday so I will mark that on the calendar. Now I have to read and take notes. I'm not a fast reader so I better allow myself plenty of time. I will give myself five days to read and take notes. It's okay if I get done early. That just means I'm ahead of schedule. Next I have to organize my notes and make an outline. That's really important. I'll give myself two days for that so I can be sure and do a good job. Wow. I'm already up to writing the first draft. I think it will take at least one day to write the first draft. I'm going to put down two days for that task just in case I need more time. Now all that's left is to edit the first draft and check for corrections. I will give myself one day for each of those. Wow! If I follow this plan I will be done a week early. I think it's a good idea to try and finish early. That way if anything happens that slows me down I will have extra time. I like that idea. I am really doing great."*

SAY, *"After I have the paper written I can move on to the next step: check for completeness, accuracy, and neatness. This should not be hard. I just need to go through what I had to do for my assignment. First I had to pick out a famous American from the 19th century. Check. I had to write about his life. Let's see, I wrote two-and-a-half pages on Lincoln's life. I think that should be good. Then I had to say why I thought he was important. I wrote a whole page and a half on that and gave a bunch of reasons. It had to be three to five pages type-written double-spaced. Check. I looked at it for grammar and I used the spell checker so I'm pretty sure that's okay. I had to have three sources listed. Oh no! Where are the sources? Oh, yeah, I did those separately. I just need to print it out and put it with the rest. Wow! Good thing I checked. This A-WATCH really helped!"*

"I'm almost done. The last step is hand it in. I need to be sure I get it handed in. That means I need to get it to school and then be sure to give it to my teacher. How can I be sure to get it there? I think I will put it in my assignment planner, and then put it in my backpack. I always remember my backpack. That will get it to school. Since I take out my assignment planner first thing, that will remind me to hand it in because I will see it when I open the planner."

Note: Students may offer comments when the teacher models; try to address them or even incorporate them in the modeling.

STEP 3: Introduce self-statements

1. Ask the students if they noticed some of the things you said to yourself (e.g., about how you were feeling, what to do next, planning) when you modeled the strategy. Make a list of the statements on the board. It's not important if students remember exactly; the gist of the self-statements is what is important. Tell the students that there was a reason for doing this. Talk about how what you say to yourself can influence what you do.

SAY, *"Sometimes we say very negative things to ourselves like, 'I can't do that,' or 'I'm dumb,' or 'I'm never going to get this done.' When we say things like that it hurts us. Instead of saying things that hurt us we need to say positive things that help us like: 'If I use my strategy I can get this. Boy—I'm doing a good job.'"*

2. Describe how famous professional athletes talk to themselves to help themselves do better. For example, when a basketball player is about to shoot a free throw he might imagine the ball going through the hoop and say, "Nothing but net."

3. Tell the students that you want to help them use talk to help themselves. Pass out the self-instruction work sheets. Have the students think about roadblocks they experience with homework. Have them write them in the left column. Then discuss what they could say to themselves that would help them to overcome the roadblock. Help the students to develop meaningful self-statements. Write the self-statements in the right column. Tell the students that when they experience the roadblocks they can use the self-statements to overcome them. Tell the students that when they first start using the statements they should say them aloud to themselves. Later, they can just say them "inside their heads." Stress that when the strategy is practiced in class, they should use the self-statements.

STEP 4: Introduce self-monitoring sheet

Tell the students that A-WATCH can help them, but they have to remember to use all the steps. Tell them that you are going to show them a way to help them remember to use A-WATCH. Pass out the A-WATCH self-monitoring sheet. Tell the students that they will use the sheet when they practice A-WATCH in class and when they use it for assignments. Each time they get an assignment they are to use A-WATCH. When they use the strategy, they are to check off the appropriate box when they do a step. There is space for three different assignments, because they might get more than one assignment in a class. The sheet will help remind them do the steps. They will start with one class. Eventually, they will keep a copy for each class in their assignment notebook.

WRAP UP

Remind the students to practice memorizing the steps. Tell the students that next class you begin with a quiz again. This time they will not get cues to the steps.

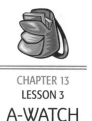

LESSON 3

Collaborative Practice
with A-WATCH

LESSON OVERVIEW

The purpose of this lesson is to practice using the strategy and self-regulation components of the strategy. Students will conduct a practice task analysis. They will continue to practice memorizing strategy steps.

STUDENT OBJECTIVES

The students will be able to complete a task analysis with time lines. Students will be able to schedule different tasks correctly. Students will correctly use the self-monitoring sheet. Students will identify when they would use self-statements and practice their use.

MATERIALS

Filled in self-instruction sheet, self-monitoring sheets, blank monthly calendar, practice assignments, assignment notebook.

SET THE CONTEXT FOR STUDENT LEARNING

Tell students that they will practice using the strategy. They will pretend that they are in class and will practice using the strategy just as they would in a real situation. Remind them that some steps (e.g., task analysis) would be done at home, and they will practice those also.

SUPPORT THE STRATEGY AND SELF-REGULATION

STEP 1: Memorize strategy steps

Begin class with a quiz over the strategy steps. Have the students get out a blank piece of paper and write each of the steps and what is done at each step. When they are finished, go over the steps and have the students check their work. By now the students should be able to get all the parts accurately and understand what is done at each of the steps.

STEP 2: Scaffolded practice with strategy and self-regulation

1. Pass out the self-monitoring sheet. Remind the students that they are to check off each step as they do it. Ask the students to read through their self-instruction sheet that they filled out in the previous lesson. Tell them to think about situations where they would use the self-statements. Ask them to raise their hand when they encounter a situation and share their self-instruction.

 2. SAY, *"Okay. Pretend that class is starting. What is the first thing you should do?"* They should respond by getting out their assignment books. Watch to see if students check off the first step on the self-monitoring sheet. Praise students who do this without a reminder.

3. Tell the students that they have an assignment to build a model rocket. All students will get to demonstrate the rocket that they build. Pass out the "Building a Rocket" instructions. Tell the students that the project is due in two weeks. Pass out the instructions for building the model rocket. Ask students what they should do next. Students should respond, "Write down the assignment." Check to see that the students have written down the information correctly.

4. Ask students to say the next step. They should respond, "Ask any questions." Have the students look at the instructions and develop questions. Ask the students when they should ask their questions (at appropriate times). Ask them to give some examples of appropriate times. Ask them why it's important to ask their questions at appropriate times.

5. Ask the students to say the next step. They should respond, "Task analysis." Ask them what they do in a task analysis (break task down into small steps, make time lines), then ask why they do a task analysis (helps organize the task, keeps you on track). Discuss their responses. Remind the students that they will do the task analysis at home. Have students do a task analysis. Hand out blank calendar pages and have students do a time line for the assignment. After they finish, have students compare their task analyses and time lines they created. Discuss any differences. Note that it often possible to break up tasks differently (e.g., sometimes people combine steps), but that the important thing is to get all the important steps identified and put on paper. Then talk about the time lines. Stress that it's better to be conservative (i.e., overestimate time required). If you overestimate, you get done early.

6. Ask students to say the next step. They should respond, "Check your work." Have students tell you what they would check. Write out their responses and discuss how they would check them and why it is important.

7. Ask the students to say the last step. They should respond, "Hand it in." Ask students what they could do to be sure that they got their rocket and materials to school on the day the assignment was due. Write responses on the board and discuss them.

8. Check to see that the students used the self-monitoring sheet. Ask students for examples of times when they would use their self-statements.

STEP 3: Additional task analysis practice

1. Tell the students that so far you have had them look at one large assignment. Tell them that sometimes they will have two or three shorter assignments to deal with. The short assignments don't need to be broken down, but they will need time lines. Have the students make estimates for some example assignments:

   • reading a chapter in social studies and answering the questions at the end of the chapter

   • doing 10 math problems on a worksheet

   • watching a 15-minute biology video on the web

2. Have the students compare their estimates.

 SAY: *"It's normal if some of you have different estimates for how long it will take to complete the assignments. Some of us are better at one task than another, or we may like one task more than another. The important thing is to know how long it will take to complete the assignment so that you can start early enough to allow plenty of time to complete the assignments."*

3. Tell the students that there is another important step to remember when there are several smaller assignments to deal with. They need to figure out which order to do the assignments in. Have the students rank the assignments by how hard they believe they would be to complete: 1 = hardest, 2 = middle, 3 = easiest. Remind them that their rankings may differ.

Then tell the students that they should always start with the assignment that they rank as the hardest. They should remember, "Worst is first."

SAY: *"The reason we do the hardest first is that we want to do the hard work when we are fresh and at our best. Then we can do the easier work later. When we get the hard assignment out of the way it makes the rest seem easier. It's like going downhill."*

STEP 4: Introduce time management

Tell the students that it's important for them to be aware of the time when they are doing homework. It's important for several reasons. First, they need to know if they are on schedule. They may need to speed up or allow more time. Second, it tells them how long they have been working. Sometimes students feel like they have been working "forever" when they actually have only been working a few minutes. Knowing how long you have worked can make you feel good. You can tell yourself, "Good job. I'm really staying on it." Third, you don't want to work too long at a time without a break. If you get too tired you will not do your best work. You might take a *short* break between assignments or schedule breaks (e.g., 5-minute break every 30 minutes). You can also reward yourself. For example, tell yourself that after you finish your first assignment you get to have a snack. However, you have to make sure that it's a short break. You can't watch a TV show or play video games. That would take too much time away from homework and get you off track. Discuss how students could keep track of the time they have worked. List some good activities for short breaks.

WRAP-UP

Tell the students that next time you will quiz them on A-WATCH memorization. **This lesson should be repeated until the students are able to quickly break down a task and construct realistic time lines.**

Establish Homework Environment

LESSON OVERVIEW

This lesson will provide additional scaffolded practice using the strategy. The students will use the Homework Home Planning Sheet to establish a home environment conducive to homework. The Homework Home Checklist will be introduced. Memorization practice of A-WATCH will continue.

STUDENT OBJECTIVES

Students will gain mastery of the strategy and be able to use the Homework Home Checklist.

MATERIALS

Homework Home Planner Sheet, Homework Home Check Sheet

SET THE CONTEXT FOR STUDENT LEARNING

Orally quiz students on the steps of A-WATCH. By now the students should be quite fluent and be able to supply the steps and the activities at each step quickly and accurately. Tell the students that today they will learn about how to make their house "homework friendly."

SUPPORT THE STRATEGY AND SELF-REGULATION

STEP 1: Establish importance of the home environment

Ask the students, "Where do we do homework?" When they respond, "Home," tell the students that today they are going to talk about the "home" in "homework." It's very important for them to understand that getting their home organized can help or hurt them. They need to think about three main things: 1) where they do homework, 2) when they do homework, and 3) how they do homework.

STEP 2: Help students plan for a supportive home environment

Pass out the Homework Home Planner sheet. Tell the students that they will fill out this sheet to help them plan to make their home "homework friendly." Teachers may wish to share this sheet and the homework checklist with parents beforehand. Tell the students to look over the planner sheet. Note that many of the items have already been discussed. Briefly discuss with students why it is important that the home environment should support their homework.

STEP 3: Physical environment

Have the students write down where they do their homework. Then ask the students if the place they do their homework is:

- quiet

- well lit

- free from distractions (people aren't passing by, instant messaging and e-mail on computer are turned off, cell phone is turned off)

- adequate space (e.g., surface for writing, computer, comfortable chair)

Discuss why each of these is important. Stress that trying to do homework while watching TV or checking e-mail is really a bad idea. **Do not accept the "multitasking" argument.** Stress the doing good homework means focusing on the homework. If a student's physical space does not meet the criteria, work with the student to think of how to improve the environment. **Note that in some instances it may be difficult of impossible for a student to meet all criteria. If this is the case try to work with the student to meet as many as possible, and discuss how to deal with problems.**

STEP 4: Establishing a routine

Ask the students write down when they do their homework. Talk to the students about why it's important to establish a regular routine time to work on homework. They need to establish set times to work on homework. Talk about establishing good habits. If they make doing homework at a set time a habit, it is easier to get started because it's part of a normal routine. Homework is easier when they are "in the groove." Talk about the problems that occur when students put off starting homework (harder to start, don't get finished, have to work too late). Stress that the best time is when they are fresh and rested (e.g. it might be better to do homework before soccer practice than after). Have the students establish daily homework time(s). Stress that the time doesn't have to be the same each day, but there should be a set time each day.

STEP 5: Working smart

Remind the students about working smart. Go through the important tasks in working smart.

- **Worst is first.** Do the hard homework first, save the easy parts for last.

- **Monitor time.** Keep an eye on how long you've worked so you can see if you are on schedule or behind. Have the students brainstorm how they could monitor the time they've spent. Then have each student write out how they could monitor time. Remind students that this is also a good time for self-instructions: (e.g., "Boy I worked for a long time," or, "Great job, I really stuck with it.")

- **Getting help.** If you get stuck or don't understand something it's okay to ask your parents. It's not okay for your parents to do homework for you. You won't learn if you do that. They can't take a test for you. Have the students give examples of things they needed help on and what kind of questions they would ask. Stress that they need to ask the question the right way. Don't say "this is dumb," or "I can't do this." Instead, ask if what you are doing is correct, or if they understand what to do. As soon as you understand, thank your parent and go back to your homework spot.

- **Getting tired or frustrated.** If we go too long without a break we might get tired or frustrated. That's one reason to monitor time. When you get tired or frustrated you need to do something about it. Take a short break (five minutes). Remind the students that if they feel frustrated they should use self-instructions: (e.g., "If I stick with it I can get it. I need to cool down.")

- **Reward yourself.** Schedule short breaks at regular intervals. This keeps you fresh. Talk with students about what "short" means. About 5 to 10 minutes is a good amount of time. Talk about how to make sure they keep the break short (e.g. use timer). Stress that they have to keep the break short or they won't finish. Discuss what they could do on the break (take a short walk, check e-mail). Tell them that when they finish a really long or difficult assignment, they should reward themselves (e.g., ice cream or computer games).

- **Use A-WATCH.** Remember to use all the steps in A-WATCH. You can use your check sheet to help you. That way you won't forget. Remember to tell yourself "Good job!" when you use the strategy.

STEP 6: Introduce the Homework Home Check Sheet

Tell the students that you are going to give them something to help them to make the home a better homework environment and to remind them of good habits. Pass out the Homework Home Check Sheet. Point out to the students that each item on the sheet is something that they should be doing to make their homework easier for them to do. Ask the students how many of the items they already do. Discuss their current habits. Help the students plan how they can do all the items. Help the students to set a goal for how many items they do by the next lesson.

WRAP UP

Tell the students that next time you will quiz them on A-WATCH memorization.

LESSON 5

Start-Up

LESSON OVERVIEW

The purpose of this lesson is to prepare the students to begin using the A-WATCH strategy. The teacher and students will define what classes the A-WATCH strategy will be used in. Students will set homework completion goals. The teacher will establish monitoring sessions.

STUDENT OBJECTIVE

Students will begin to use the A-WATCH strategy.

MATERIALS

Homework planner/organizer, A-WATCH self-monitoring sheet, homework home check sheet

SET THE CONTEXT FOR STUDENT LEARNING

Briefly test for memorization of A-WATCH.

SUPPORT THE STRATEGY AND SELF-REGULATION

STEP 1: Review home environment

Go over the homework home check sheet with students. Discuss how they have addressed each of the items and any potential problem areas. Stress that paying attention to these tasks will pay off. It will be easier to get their homework done and they will do a better job.

STEP 2: Review self-monitoring

Review the A-WATCH self-monitoring sheet. Stress that filling it out each day will help them remember to do all the steps of the strategy. The students can have one sheet for each class or use one sheet for all their classes.

STEP 3: Establish when A-WATCH will be used

Tell the students that they are now ready to start using A-WATCH for real class assignments. Decide in what class or classes the students will start to use A-WATCH. This will depend on the students and the classes they are currently taking. It may be best to start in one class and then, after the students are successful, expand to more classes. *If at all possible, try to involve the teachers who will be assigning homework. Inform the teachers that you are working with the students to help them complete more homework. Provide them with an overview of A-WATCH.*

STEP 4: Establish homework goal

Show students the homework graph from Lesson 1. Ask them to set a goal for how much homework they will finish for the next week. Check students' goals to see if they are appropriate.

STEP 5: Establish monitoring times

Tell the students that you will be checking with their teachers to see how much they have completed. Tell the students that you will look at completion rates each day. We recommend that initially the teacher and students meet daily to discuss progress in homework completion. This will help the teacher to spot any problems early on and address them. It can also serve to motivate students when they see progress toward goals or meet goals. As the students become more capable of completing their homework, the teacher can gradually reduce the frequency of meetings (e.g., every other day, once a week, every 10 days).

REFERENCES

Cooper, H. (2007). *The battle over homework*. Thousand Oaks, CA: Corwin.

Epstein, M.H., Polloway, E.A., Foley, R. M., & Patton, J.R. (1993). Homework: A comparison of teachers' and parents' perceptions of the problems experienced by students identified as having behavioral disorders, learning disabilities, or no disabilities. *Remedial and Special Education, 14*, 40–50.

Glomb, N., & West, R.P. (1990). Teaching behaviorally disordered adolescents to use self-management skills for improving the completeness, accuracy, and neatness for creative writing homework assignments. *Behavioral Disorders, 15*, 233–242.

Krishnan, K., Feller, M., & Orkin, M. (2010). Goal setting, planning, and prioritizing. In L. Meltzer (Ed.), *Promoting executive function in the classroom* (pp. 57–85). New York, NY: Guilford.

Margolis, H., & McCabe, P. (1997). Homework challenges for students with reading and writing problems: Suggestions for effective practice. *Journal of Educational and Psychological Consultation, 8*, 41–74.

Salend, S., & Schliff, J. (1989). An examination of homework practices of teachers of students with learning disabilities. *Journal of Learning Disabilities, 22*, 621–623.

U.S. Department of Education, Office of Intergovernmental and Interagency Affairs, Educational Partnerships and Family Involvement Unit. (2003). *Homework tips for parents*. Washington, DC: Author.

Zentall, S.S. (2006). *ADHD and education*. Columbus, OH: Pearson.

Example Organizational Skills Self-Monitoring Sheet

Name _____   Date _____

Was I prepared today?

Was I on time for class?	Yes	No
Was I in my seat at the bell?	Yes	No
Have I handed in my assignments?	Yes	No

Did I bring my:

Paper/binder	Yes	No
Pen/pencil	Yes	No
Book	Yes	No
Homework assignments	Yes	No
Plan book	Yes	No

During class I:

Sat up in my seat	Yes	No
Wrote down assignments	Yes	No
Asked questions when needed	Yes	No

My goal for today is _____

Example Self-Monitoring Log

Name _____   Date _____

How did I do today?

Did I accomplish my goal?

_____

What did I do to help me achieve my goal?

_____

_____

_____

_____

_____

What did I do that did not help me with my goal?

_____

_____

_____

_____

_____

What can I do tomorrow that would help me achieve my goal?

_____

_____

_____

_____

_____

A-WATCH Prompt Sheet

A   Get out my **A**ssignment book.

W   **W**rite down the assignment.

A   **A**sk for clarification if needed.

T   **T**ask analyze the assignment.

C   **C**heck to see if the assignment is complete, accurate, and neat.

H   **H**and it in. Make sure I bring it to class and hand it in.

Task Analysis Example Calendar

Sunday	Monday	Tuesday	Wednesday	Thursday	Friday	Saturday
1	2	3	4 Get books at library	5 Read & take notes	6 Read & take notes	7
8	9 Read & take notes	10 Read & take notes	11 Read & take notes	12 Read & take notes	13	14
15	16 Make outline	17 Make outline	18 First draft	19 First draft	20	21
22	23 Edit & final draft	24 Check over	25	26	27	28
29	30					

A-WATCH Self-Monitoring Sheet

Assignments

Did I Remember To:	1	2	3
A—Get out my **A**ssignment book.			
W—**W**rite down the assignment.			
A—**A**sk for clarification if needed.			
T—**T**ask analyze the assignment.			
C—**C**heck to see if the assignment is complete, accurate, and neat.			
H—**H**and it in.			

Self-Instructions Worksheet

Homework Helper

When I have this problem:	I can say:

Example Assignment: Building a Rocket

Build your own rocket using paper and fizzing tablets! Watch it lift off. How high does your rocket go? Print this page for the instructions.

Materials:

Regular 8½ by 11-inch paper, such as computer printer paper or even notebook paper.

Plastic 35-mm film canister (see hints below)

Cellophane tape

Scissors

Effervescing (fizzing) antacid tablet (the kind used to settle an upset stomach)

Paper towels

Water

Eye protection (like eye glasses, sun glasses, or safety glasses)

Hints:

The film canister MUST be one with a cap that fits INSIDE the rim instead of over the outside of the rim. Sometimes photography shops have extras of these and will be happy to donate some for such a worthy cause.

Keep in mind:

Just like with real rockets, the less your rocket weighs and the less air resistance (drag) it has, the higher it will go.

Making the Rocket

You must first decide how to cut your paper. You may cut it the short way or the long way to make the body of the rocket. There are many ways to make a paper rocket. Try a long, skinny rocket or a short, fat rocket. Try a sharp nosecone or a blunt nosecone. Try it with fins or without fins. Experiment!

Here's just one idea for how you might cut out your rocket using only one piece of paper:

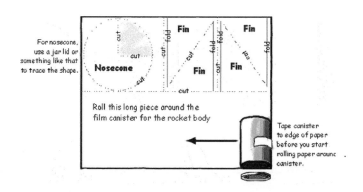

(continued)

Here are the basic steps:

Cut out all the pieces for your rocket.

Wrap and tape a tube of paper around the film canister. Hint: Tape the canister to the end of the paper before you start wrapping.

Important! Place the lid end of the canister *down,* this will be the bottom of your rocket.

Tape fins to your rocket body, if you want.

Roll the circle (with a wedge cut out) into a cone and tape it to the rocket's top.

Blasting Off

Put on your eye protection.

Turn the rocket upside down and remove the film canister's lid.

Fill the canister one-third full of water.

Now work quickly on the next steps!

Drop one-half of an effervescing antacid tablet into the canister.

Snap the lid on tight.

Stand your rocket on a launch platform, such as your sidewalk or driveway.

Stand back and wait. Your rocket will blast off!

239

Homework Home Planner

Where do I do my homework? Is it a good spot?

_____

_____

_____

When do I do my homework? Do I have a routine?

_____

_____

_____

Do I work smart? _____

- Worst is first

- Do I monitor time (how)?

- Getting help

- Getting tired or frustrated

- Be nice to yourself

- Use A-WATCH

Homework Home Check Sheet

I worked in my homework spot	Yes	No
My homework location had all needed materials	Yes	No
I worked at my established time	Yes	No

I monitored time by _____

I did hard work first	Yes	No
I asked for help the right way	Yes	No
Frustration and fatigue	Yes	No

Reward myself

I rewarded myself for completing homework by: _____

_____

_____

I used my A-WATCH strategy	Yes	No

My goal for this week is to do _____ .

241

Appendix

Reading to Learn:
Instructions for Using Retells

Prior to reading the passage, review key familiar vocabulary words, discussing any words that the student might not know. Then, provide the student with directions for reading the passage. The following is an example of instructions for students before a passage:

"Read this passage carefully. Take as much time as you need. I will tell you any word you want to know. When you're done reading the passage, I want you to tell me everything you can remember about it."

After the student finishes reading a passage ask him or her to tell you everything he or she can remember about the passage. Use the score sheets to record students' retells. Check off each main idea or detail as the student provides it. Exact wording is not important. For example, if the student says, "Sutter made a factory" rather than "Sutter built a mill" it should be counted correct.

Sometimes students recall details other than those included on the score sheet. There is a space to write in these details, and they can be counted in scoring. After the student is finished, compute the percent of recall for main ideas and details. Share the score with the student and record it on his her graph.

The retells included in this passage, similar in reading level to passages in content textbooks, will be difficult for many low-achieving adolescents. Teachers should modify passages and scoring sheets, as needed, for informal assessment of a student's reading to learn ability. Flesch-Kincaid grade readability levels have been included at the end of each passage.

The California Gold Rush

John Sutter was a wealthy northern California businessman. In 1848 he needed a new sawmill to make lumber for the flour mill he was planning. He hired John Marshall to build the mill near what is now the modern-day city of Sacramento. After only a few days, Marshall returned from the mill site. He told Sutter that he had some very interesting news for him, but that he must tell him the news privately. Marshall and Sutter went to a private office to meet. Marshall immediately pulled a rag from his pocket. Wrapped in the rag were many lumps of yellow metal. Marshall believed that it was gold. At first Sutter could not believe that it was true. Sutter decided to test the metal and, to his great surprise, discovered that it was a nugget of nearly pure gold! Sutter traveled to the mill site and was shocked to find that the workers found dozens of gold nuggets in the stream used to power the mill. Sutter hoped to keep news of the discovery a secret until he finished his mill. He asked his workers to keep the secret for four to six weeks, but they did not. The news was out—there was gold in California! Stories of huge gold nuggets found there spread rapidly.

When the news of gold in California spread, it caused a flood of prospectors and people who hoped to get rich quick to head for California. Most of the people who went to California to hunt for gold came in 1849. These people were called 49ers. However, for these 49ers, getting to California was not as easy as it is today. In 1849 most of the people in the United States lived in the eastern part of the country. There were no railroads and no rivers that connected the east and west coast. To travel to California meant that the 49ers had to take a three- to four-month dangerous trip by land or travel by sea to South America, which took even longer.

Taking the overland route had several advantages. Traveling overland was less expensive and faster than sea travel. Most 49ers traveled by covered wagon. The typical wagon was 9 feet long and 4 feet wide. The 49ers had to pack everything they would need for the trip to California into this small space. The wagons were usually pulled either by mules or by oxen. Mules could go faster than oxen, but could not pull as heavy a load. Traveling by covered wagon allowed 49ers to bring more gear. They could pack shovels, picks, and other equipment they would need for mining. However, they also needed food and cooking supplies. Deciding how much food to bring was literally a life or death decision. Taking too little food meant the 49ers could starve to death. Taking too much could overload the wagon and wear out the mules or oxen. Many 49ers died along the trail because they were poorly prepared.

Traveling by sea was more popular, even though it took longer and was more expensive. The sea voyage from the east coast to California could be done in two ways. One way was to travel south around the tip of South America and then north to California. This was a 12,000-mile voyage through some of the most dangerous parts of the ocean. Many ships were lost on this route. The second route was to travel by boat to Panama and then travel overland to the west coast. This route was much shorter; however, it meant that travelers had to brave the jungles of Panama. These jungles were disease ridden and many travelers died of malaria or yellow fever. If a traveler was lucky enough to survive the

Building Comprehension in Adolescents: Powerful Strategies for Improving Reading and Writing in Content Areas by Linda H. Mason, Ph.D., Robert Reid, Ph.D., and Jessica L. Hagaman, Ph.D.

(continued)

trip across Panama, there was no guarantee that they could find a ship to California. Many travelers waited for months to find a ship to California. One reason was that many ships were abandoned in California. Sailors would jump ship when they arrived in California and head to the gold field to try to strike it rich.

The 49ers arrived in California with dreams of riches, and some did become rich. For most, however, it was a different story. They found that they needed to find several ounces of gold each day simply to make enough money to feed themselves. The people who benefited the most were those who sold supplies to the 49ers. Because so many people had come to California to seek gold, merchants raised their prices as high as they could. The merchants of California were able to sell equipment, food, and other supplies at five to ten times what they paid for them. As a result, many merchants became rich from selling supplies to miners. These merchants found creative ways to make a profit. In the early days of the Gold Rush, one merchant bought up all the shovels, picks, and food that he could find. Then he filled a glass jar with gold flakes and went through the streets of San Francisco waving the jar and shouting, "Gold! Gold on the American River!" People rushed to his town and he sold his supplies at a huge profit. Another merchant who made a fortune in the Gold Rush was Levi Strauss. He made the first blue jeans for miners who needed pants for the rough job of mining for gold. Some merchants took advantage of the 49ers along the route to California. Many 49ers did not take enough water for the hot and dry deserts of Nevada. Merchants brought barrels of water and sold it by the glass to thirsty 49ers. According to one story, some 49ers paid 100 dollars for a single glass.

The gold did not last for long. After a few years, the gold became more and more difficult to find. The gold fields were taken over by large companies and the miners became their employees. It was no longer possible to strike it rich in the gold fields. Many of the people who came to California for the gold, stayed. As a result, the population of California increased. The huge number of people who came to California changed the character of the state and helped make it what it is today. You might wonder what happened to John Sutter on whose property gold was first discovered. Did he become wealthy? No, just the opposite happened. He lost his businesses and most of his land and wealth. For John Sutter the Gold Rush was a disaster!

Flesch Kincaid grade level: 7.03

The California Gold Rush

_____ **John Sutter discovered gold in California**

_____ Sutter built new mill

_____ Marshall came with yellow lump

_____ Sutter did not believe

_____ Tested and found it was gold

_____ Found gold at his mill site

_____ Tried to keep it a secret

_____ **People headed to California for gold**

_____ Most went in 1849

_____ Called 49ers

_____ Difficult trip to California

_____ No railroad or river routes

_____ Went overland or by sea

_____ Both were long dangerous trips

_____ **Overland had advantages**

_____ Less expensive

_____ Traveled by wagon

_____ Could take supplies

_____ Pulled by mules or oxen

_____ Mules faster, oxen stronger

_____ Had to take just the right amount of supplies

_____ Many died on the trail

_____ **Sea route**

_____ Could go around South America

_____ Very long and dangerous

_____ Could go across Panama

_____ Much shorter

_____ Had to brave dangerous jungle to cross

_____ Could get stuck

_____ Many ships abandoned in California when crew left to hunt for gold.

_____ **Merchants benefited most**

_____ Most 49ers barely got by

_____ Merchants got rich selling supplies to miners

_____ Raised prices

_____ Merchant bought supplies and lured people to his town

_____ Levi Strauss invented blue jeans

_____ Took advantage of poor planning (49ers didn't bring enough water)

_____ Sold water for up to 100 dollars a glass

_____ **The gold rush changed California**

_____ Gold played out; couldn't strike it rich

_____ Big companies took over

_____ People stayed

_____ Population increased dramatically

_____ John Sutter lost business and property

_____ Gold Rush was a disaster for John Sutter.

Other details recalled:

_____

_____

_____

_____

_____

_____

_____

_____

Main idea _____ % / 6 = _____ %

Details _____ % / 39 = _____ %

Total _____ % / 45 = _____ %

Building Comprehension in Adolescents: Powerful Strategies for Improving Reading and Writing in Content Areas by Linda H. Mason, Ph.D., Robert Reid, Ph.D., and Jessica L. Hagaman, Ph.D.

The Battle of Gettysburg

During the summer of 1863, the Confederacy was riding high. They had won a major victory over the Union forces at Chancellorsville and were ready to take the war to northern territory. Previously, much of the fighting in the war had taken place in southern territory. Now Robert E. Lee, the commander of the Confederate forces, was going to change that. Lee was a bold leader, and was feared by the Union generals whom he regularly defeated in battle. He planned to invade the north and hoped to penetrate as far as Philadelphia. If he did this, he believed that it would force the north to end the war. The Union forces were caught by surprise, but the Army of the Potomac, commanded by General George Meade, soon began to pursue Lee's army into Pennsylvania. When the two armies met, the result was the most important battle of the Civil War.

The Battle of Gettysburg took place from July 1 to July 3 near the town of Gettysburg, Pennsylvania. The battle began northwest of the town. The first forces to arrive were small groups of Union cavalry. The main Union force was miles behind them. Their job was to slow down the approaching Confederate forces until help could arrive. They hoped to delay the Confederates long enough for the Union forces to occupy the high ground south of the town. If the Confederates were allowed to seize the high ground south of the town, the situation would be very bad for the Union. The Union cavalrymen took up defensive positions and awaited the Confederate attack. They beat back the Confederate attacks for most of the morning, but in the afternoon they were forced to retreat. Despite the fact that they had been driven back, the Union forces had done their job—the main Union forces had arrived and had taken up strong positions on the high ground. The advantage had now shifted to the Union.

The second day of the battle found the Union army dug in along a line on three important strong points: Culp's Hill on their right flank; Cemetery Ridge on their center, and Little Round Top hill on their left. General Lee knew he had to attack the Union forces quickly. Lee planned to attack both the Union left and right at the same time. He believed that two coordinated attacks would cause the Union army lines to crumble. General Longstreet was to attack the Union left. His attack was delayed because some of his men did not arrive until late in the afternoon. Still, Longstreet believed that he would be able to break through the thinly defended Union left. While Longstreet was marching to attack, a Union general made a serious mistake. He ordered his men to advance without telling his commander. As a result, the entire Union left was now weakened. At four o'clock in the afternoon the Confederate attack slammed into the Union lines. At first the Union line buckled and the Confederates advanced quickly. General Meade realized that the situation was desperate and sent his reserve forces, nearly 20,000 men, to shore up the line. Near the end of the fighting Joshua Chamberlin, a school teacher from Maine, led a charge on Little Round Top that saved the day for the Union left. Next, the Confederates attacked Culp's Hill on the Union right. The Union soldiers on Culp's Hill were well prepared and threw back the Confederates after heavy fighting.

After two days of heavy fighting, both armies were tired and had suffered many dead and wounded. General Lee was sure that one more decisive attack could win the

(continued)

The Battle of Gettysburg *(continued)*

battle. He had attacked both the Union right and left flanks. Now he decided to launch the largest attack yet directly at the Union center. Early in the afternoon, the Confederate cannons began to bombard the Union lines. After two hours, the main Confederate attack began. General Pickett led 12,000 brave Virginia soldiers in what is now called Pickett's Charge. Pickett led his soldiers across nearly a mile of open ground toward the Union lines in the distance. At first, the Confederates believed that they had victory within their grasp because the Union solders did not fire. Soon, however, the Union soldiers began to fire. A hail of bullets and cannon shells began to rain down on the Confederate soldiers. More and more of them were cut down. Despite this, they never faltered and continued to advance toward the Union lines. At one point, the Union line broke, however, reinforcements arrived in time and the Confederate attack was broken. Over half of the soldiers that General Pickett led were killed or wounded. The battle ended after the third day with both sides bloodied and exhausted.

The Battle of Gettysburg is often described as the turning point in the Civil War. It was the bloodiest battle in the Civil War. Over 7,000 men were killed and over 25,000 were wounded. The battle marked the beginning of the end for the Confederacy. The point where Pickett's men made their farthest advance is now called "The High Water Mark of the Confederacy." It marked the closest that the South came to gaining independence. The Southern armies were broken. No longer could they seriously threaten an invasion of Union territory. Their armies were exhausted and many of their finest soldiers had been killed or wounded. As a result, they were now forced to fight on the defensive for the remainder of the war.

Flesch Kincaid grade level: 8.19

The Battle of Gettysburg

_____ **Gettysburg–important battle of Civil War**

    _____ Lee wanted to invade northward

    _____ Would end war

    _____ Lee was feared

    _____ Union caught by surprise

_____ **First day of battle**

    _____ When: July 1–3

    _____ Where: Gettysburg, PA

    _____ Began north of town

    _____ Union cavalry delayed Confederates

    _____ Union cavalry allowed main force to take the high ground

_____ **Second day of battle**

    _____ Three Union strong points (Culp's Hill, Cemetery Ridge, Little Round Top)

    _____ Lee to attack both left and right

    _____ Left-side Union general made a mistake, nearly losing battle

    _____ Reserved troops came just in time

    _____ Right-side Union was well prepared

    _____ Joshua Chamberlin was the hero of Little Round Top

_____ **Third day of battle**

    _____ Lee to attack center

    _____ Early afternoon Confederate cannons

    _____ General Pickett led Pickett's Charge

    _____ Over half of the soldiers were killed or wounded

_____ **Battle was the turning point of the war**

    _____ Bloodiest battle; 7000 killed and over 25,000 wounded

    _____ Beginning of the end of the Confederacy

    _____ "The High Water Mark of the Confederacy"; closest South came to independence

    _____ Southern army exhausted

    _____ Finest soldiers killed or wounded

    _____ Southern armies were now on the defense

Other details recalled:

_____

_____

_____

_____

_____

_____

_____

_____

_____

_____

_____

_____

_____

Main idea _____ % / 5 = _____ %

Details _____ % / 25 = _____ %

Total _____ % / 30 = _____ %

Building Comprehension in Adolescents: Powerful Strategies for Improving Reading and Writing in Content Areas by Linda H. Mason, Ph.D., Robert Reid, Ph.D., and Jessica L. Hagaman, Ph.D.
Copyright © 2012 by Paul H. Brookes Publishing Co., Inc. All rights reserved.

Volcanoes

Volcanoes are examples of the amazing power deep within the Earth. We live on the outer layer of the Earth called the crust. Beneath the Earth's crust is a layer of molten rock. This molten rock is called magma. Volcanoes are places on the Earth's surface where magma and gases can rise to the surface. When the magma erupts from the volcano it is called lava. Volcanoes primarily occur along the edges between tectonic plates. Tectonic plates are massive slabs of rock that make up Earth's crust. There are around 1,900 volcanoes on Earth that are considered "active." An active volcano is one that shows some level of activity and could erupt again. Other volcanoes are dormant, which means that they show no current signs of erupting. However, they will probably become active at some point in the future. Others are considered extinct. Extinct volcanoes are unlikely to ever erupt again.

All volcanoes are the result of red hot magma reaching the surface of the Earth. However, there are three different kinds of volcanoes: shield, cinder cone, and composite. Each type differs in how it is formed. Some lava is thick and moves very slowly. Other lava is thinner and can move quickly and spread for long distances. Shield volcanoes have runny lava that flows quickly for miles. As a result, shield volcanoes are very wide with shallow, smoothly sloping sides. They are among the largest volcanoes on Earth. Cinder cone volcanoes are the simplest type of volcano. They are caused by short eruptions. Cinder cone volcanoes are usually smaller than other volcanoes. They are formed when lava from a single vent is shot into the air and falls to earth. As the lava falls to earth it forms cinders that grow into volcanoes. These volcanoes have a bowl-shaped crater at the top. Composite volcanoes are made up of different types of material such as lava, volcanic ash, and rock.

Volcanoes are extremely dangerous. Volcanic eruption can hurl huge rocks and chunks of red hot lava for miles. Lava can flow from the volcano and burn everything in its path. It can rain down ash that can bury the nearby countryside. When Mount Vesuvius exploded in A.D. 79 it buried two nearby towns, killing 16,000 people. Recently, a volcano in Iceland erupted and threw so much ash into the air that flights across the Atlantic were canceled. It was feared that the ash would clog the jet engines of airliners. Another danger is a pyroclastic flow. A pyroclastic flow is a cloud of super-heated ash, steam, and poisonous gases. The temperature of a pyroclastic flow is over 1,000 degrees. These flows travel down the side of a volcano during an eruption. They can move at speeds of nearly 100 miles per hour and will kill everything in their path. Another danger is mudslides. These occur when hot lava melts the snow pack on the side of a volcano. Mudslides can strip a mountainside bare and knock down any building in their paths. The force of the blast from some eruptions can be deadly. The force of the blast from Krakatoa, which erupted in 1883, was so powerful that the sound was heard over 1,000 miles away. It also created a tidal wave that killed over 30,000 people.

Volcanic eruptions occur fairly frequently. At any given time there are around 20 volcanoes erupting somewhere in the world. In an average year, around 10 to 20 volcanoes will erupt. Geologists estimate that 1,300 volcanoes erupted in the last 10,000 years, and

(continued)

these are those that we are aware of. Most volcanic eruptions happen at the bottom of the ocean. These undersea volcanoes occur at the mid-ocean ridges, which are regions where the Earth's tectonic plates are spreading apart. Geologists have no way of knowing how many undersea eruptions are occurring.

The tallest and largest volcanoes on Earth are both in Hawaii. The tallest volcano in Hawaii is over 13,000 feet high. It's only a little taller than the largest volcano. The height of both these volcanoes is a bit misleading. Both are shield volcanoes that rise up from the bottom of the ocean. The largest volcano we know of isn't on Earth. It's on Mars! It is a giant shield volcano that rises to an elevation of over 16 miles. It also covers a huge area. It is over 300 miles across. It was able to erupt continuously for millions and millions of years. This is what allowed the volcano to grow to such an enormous size.

Flesch Kincaid grade level: 7.13

Volcanoes

____ Volcanoes	**Other details recalled:**

____ Volcanoes

____ Molten rock or magma erupts

____ When magma reaches surface it is lava

____ Active have signs or have the potential to erupt

____ Dormant volcano has no signs of erupting, but could in the future

____ Extinct volcano won't erupt again

____ Three kinds of volcanoes

____ Differ on how formed

____ Shield has runny lava that moves quickly and spreads

____ Among largest on Earth

____ Cinder cones smaller

____ Formed from cinders falling to earth

____ Composites made of different types of materials

____ Very dangerous

____ Rock and hot lava shooting and flowing out

____ Suffocating ash

____ Clog jet engines

____ Pyroclastic flow

____ Mudslides

____ Tidal wave

____ Eruptions occur frequently

____ 10 to 20 per year

____ Most at bottom of the ocean

____ Don't know how many undersea eruptions occur

____ Tallest and largest in Hawaii

____ Rise from the bottom of the ocean so height is deceiving

____ Largest is on Mars

____ Over 300 miles

____ Erupted for millions of years

Other details recalled:

For example:
We live on the outer layer of the earth's crust.

Mount Vesuvius erupted in A.D. 79, and it buried two nearby towns killing 16,000 people.

_____

_____

_____

_____

_____

_____

_____

_____

_____

_____

_____

_____

_____

_____

_____

_____

Main idea _____ % / 5 = _____ %

Details _____ % / 24 = _____ %

Total _____ % / 29 = _____ %

Traffic

Everyone hates to be stuck in traffic. We tend to think of the traffic jam as a modern problem. Actually, it's not. Dealing with traffic has been a problem for centuries. Even during the horse-and-buggy days, there were traffic jams. For example, in 1722 the Lord Mayor of London complained of the inconveniences and problems which happen by the disorderly "driving of cars, carts, coaches, and other carriages over London Bridge." To deal with the problem, the Lord Mayor ordered that three men be appointed as public servants to keep traffic moving.

Today we take it for granted that everyone will drive on the correct side of the road. This was not always the case. For example, while we drive on the right side of the road, the ancient Romans used the left side. Until the 20th century there were no established rules for which side of the road should be used (left or right). Deciding which side of the road to use has been an issue for a long time. Over 3,000 years ago, a Chinese ruler decided that men should use the right side of the road, women should use the left side, and carriages should use the center. Sometimes decisions on which side to use were not related to driving. In the Middle Ages, people drove on the left side of the road. This was because in those days the roads were very dangerous places with many robbers. Driving on the left meant that your sword was handy if you met a dangerous character. In the late 1700s, wagon drivers in America began using wagons to haul very heavy loads of farm products to markets. These wagons required several pairs of horses to haul the load. Because the wagons had no seats, the drivers sat on the left rear horse. This made it easier to use a whip. Because the drivers sat on the left, they drove on the left because it made it easier to ensure that their wagons would not collide with others.

Intersections were also a problem because there was no way to stop traffic in one direction so that vehicles going in the other direction could proceed through the intersection safely. This could be a serious problem even in the horse-and-buggy period. It was especially dangerous for pedestrians. For example, in 1860 in New York City horse-drawn buses actually raced each other to try to get to their destinations before their competitors. In the process, these drivers ran down and killed many pedestrians. New York City's police department was given the task of overseeing and controlling these reckless bus drivers. To help control the traffic, the City Council created a special group of policemen that were nicknamed "Broadway's Finest." The policemen were selected because they were the tallest on the force (all were over six feet tall). Because they were so tall, they could be seen above the tangled mix of carriages and pedestrians. They would point and wave with their hands to direct traffic. They were given special white gloves to make their hands more visible.

Using police officers to control traffic helped a great deal. Police officers could control traffic and help prevent traffic jams. However, there were also problems. It was difficult enough for an officer to coordinate traffic flow on one street in one direction with another officer one block away. It was practically impossible for an officer to coordinate with officers more than one block away. Each of the officers had to coordinate traffic in two directions. In practice this was impossible to do. There was another problem too—it was very costly because the police had to be paid. Can you imagine having police officers at every busy intersection? Today we use traffic signals to control traffic at intersections. These traffic signals use three lights to tell drivers what to do: red for stop, green for go, and yellow to indicate that the green light is about to turn red. It's interesting that while there are differences across countries about which side of the road to drive on, the same traffic light colors are used universally.

Traffic signals have changed dramatically over time, however. The first use of a traffic signal using colored lights occurred in London in 1868. The traffic signal was placed at a busy intersection near the Houses of Parliament. The signal was a revolving lantern with red and green signals. Red meant "stop" and green meant "caution." The red and green lights were lit by a lamp fed by a gas pipe, and there were three red semaphore arms. A semaphore is a tall post with moveable arms. When the arms were down (just as if you were standing with your arms at your sides) it meant "go." When the arms stuck straight out sideways, it meant stop. The red and green lights were used during the night. The semaphore arms were used during the day. To ensure that drivers could see the signal, it was mounted on an octagonal pillar that was about 20 feet tall. Four policemen had been responsible for controlling traffic at the intersection. They were kept on duty in case the experiment was a failure. An additional officer was needed to operate the signals. The officer used a handle to move the arms up and down during the day, and changed the color of the lights at night. This new traffic signal was quite an attraction. Londoners flocked to the intersection to see the new invention. People would place blankets on the grass and watch the traffic signal operate. Merchants came to sell food and drinks to the crowds the signal attracted. People were curious to see if the new signal could actually do the work of the four policemen. Unfortunately, this experiment was not successful. On January 2, 1869, the traffic light exploded, injuring the policeman who was operating it.

Flesch Kincaid grade level: 7.81

Traffic

_____ **Traffic jams not modern problem**
 _____ Traffic jams since horse-and-buggy days
 _____ 1722 London Bridge problem
 _____ Three men kept traffic moving

_____ **Driving on which side of road**
 _____ Romans drove on left
 _____ In China, men on right, women on left, and carriages in the middle
 _____ Middle Ages use left so sword hand was ready
 _____ In 1700s men rode rear left horse so it was easier to use whip and to avoid collision with other wagons

_____ **Intersections were a big problem**
 _____ Intersections dangerous, especially for pedestrians
 _____ New York City buses raced each other endangering others
 _____ "Broadway's Finest"
 _____ The tallest and easiest to be seen policemen
 _____ Given white gloves to make hands more visible

_____ **Need to coordinate multiple intersections**
 _____ Police officers helped prevent traffic jams
 _____ Officers could not coordinate multiple intersections
 _____ Using officers was costly
 _____ Now use traffic signals
 _____ Colors are used universally

_____ **Traffic signals have changed over time**
 _____ First traffic signal in London 1868
 _____ On 20-foot tower
 _____ Needed four officers to operate

_____ London 1868, revolving lantern with red and green lights on moveable arms
 _____ Red meant "stop" and green meant "caution"
 _____ The new traffic signal was a sight to see
 _____ It exploded and injured the officer

Other details recalled:

_____

_____

_____

_____

_____

_____

_____

_____

_____

_____

_____

_____

_____

_____

Main idea _____ % / 5 = _____ %

Details _____ % / 25 = _____ %

Total _____ % / 30 = _____ %

Index

*Tables and figures are indicated by *t* and *f*, respectively.

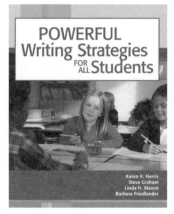